# Praise for
## *Dead Men Don't Leave Tips*

"What's striking about Wilson's books (he's also the author of the IPPY Award winner *Yak Butter Blues*) is that his journeys are not only physical, but highly spiritual as well. His are journeys of body and soul in every sense of the word. The author writes with honesty and a sharp eye for detail, making this an invaluable amalgam of information for readers of adventure travel or anybody who is considering "do-it-yourself" safaris or simply visiting Africa. Interlaced with this honesty and detail are Wilson's beautiful prose, obvious passion for adventure and a deep inquisitiveness about other cultures, making this book a pleasure to read. Highly recommended." (5 stars) ~ Mayra Calvani, *Midwest Book Review*

"It used to be only the British mastered the art of spinning the sweaty traveler's tale. Along comes Brandon Wilson who teaches us that an observant fellow from Hawaii can deal with Africa's grime, dysentery and uncertainty with superior grace and wit. Honest, gritty and insightful. Best of all, it makes the world's most exciting continent read just like that." ~ John Heminway, film producer/author of *No Man's Land: A Personal Journey into Africa*

"Wilson offers great advice for the road...And his concerns about the ecological and social woes of Africa are shared by many who love the continent that Paul Theroux has called the 'Dark Star.'" ~ *Honolulu Advertiser*

"That rare event: a travel book that transcends its genre to become a transformative journey of the soul into a disparate and gorgeously challenging culture, as seen through the eyes of a man determined to experience life as it is, rather than as it's presented to us. This is travel writing at its most sublime, a paean to Africa in all her contradictory beauty, and a tribute to the resiliency of those who travel beyond boundaries not only in search of meaning, but also of understanding." ~ C.W. Gortner, author of *The Secret Lion* and *The Last Queen*

"One of the most engaging travel books we have read... After their 'ship of fools' safari turns into a nightmare, they set off across Africa alone. However, being adventurers and seasoned travelers, they persevered...The trip took over seven months, and they came through it unbelievably intact to tell their fascinating tales. A must read!" ~ Bonnie Neely, RealTravelAdventures.com

# Dead Men Don't Leave Tips

## Adventures X Africa

# Dead Men Don't Leave Tips

## Adventures X Africa

by
## Brandon Wilson
author of Yak Butter Blues

**PILGRIM'S TALES**

## Dead Men Don't Leave Tips

**PILGRIM'S
TALES**

For information:
Pilgrim's Tales, Inc.
P.O. Box 791613, Paia, Hawaii 96779
www.PilgrimsTales.com
pilgrimstales@yahoo.com

LCCN: 2005905467
ISBN-13: 978-0-9770536-4-3
ISBN-10: 0-9770536-4-4

Printed in the United States of America

This story is true.
However, names have been changed to protect the innocent

All photos by Brandon Wilson, unless otherwise noted.

Some fonts by Fonts of Afrika

# Contents

|  | African Route Map |  | iii |
|  | Introduction |  | 1 |
| Chapter I. | Gale Force Getaway |  | 3 |
| Chapter II. | Afffricaaaaa! | *(Morocco)* | 21 |
| Chapter III. | Survival In The Sahara | *(Algeria)* | 39 |
| Chapter IV. | The Cosmic Dance | *(Mali)* | 57 |
| Chapter V. | Voodoo Wakes, Python Snakes | *(Togo/Benin)* | 69 |
| Chapter VI. | Baboon Platoon | *(Nigeria/Cameroon)* | 83 |
| Chapter VII. | Ubangui Anguish | *(C. A. R.)* | 95 |
| Chapter VIII. | Jungle Trance, Pygmy Dance | *(Zaire (Congo))* | 105 |
|  | Photo Gallery |  | 125 |
| Chapter IX. | Gorilla Stalk, Volcano Walk | *(Zaire/Burundi)* | 145 |
| Chapter X. | Whirling Wildebeests | *(Tanzania)* | 163 |
| Chapter XI. | Land of the Masai | *(Kenya)* | 173 |
| Chapter XII. | Challenge of Kilimanjaro | *(The Climb)* | 189 |
| Chapter XIII. | Border Extortion | *(Tanzania)* | 205 |
| Chapter XIV. | Leave Your Pants at the Door | *(Malawi)* | 217 |
| Chapter XV. | Road of Pain, Legacy of Shame | *(Mozambique)* | 229 |
| Chapter XVI. | Zambezi, Sea of Torment | *(Zimbabwe)* | 237 |
| Chapter XVII. | Barking Dogs, Invisible Walls | *(South Africa)* | 253 |
| Chapter XVIII. | Assembling the Mosaic | *(Retrospective)* | 265 |
|  | About the Author |  | 271 |
|  | Other Books by the Author |  | 272 |

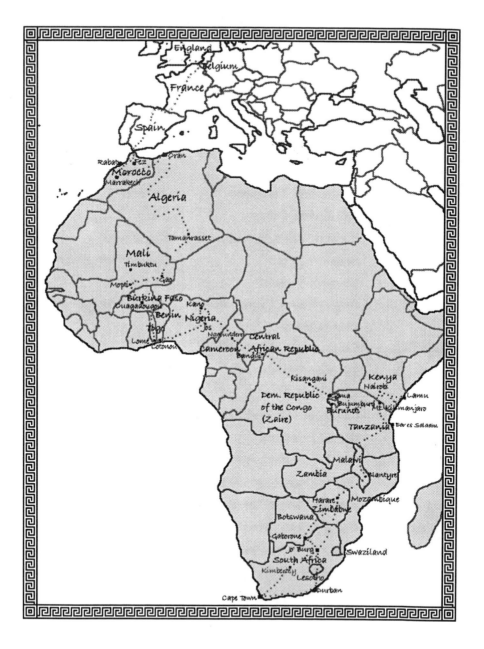

iii

# Introduction

*I*T WAS A TIME WHEN DREAMS WERE SIMPLE. Saturday mornings, long before his family rose from bed, a four-year old boy sat transfixed in front of a new and wonderful box. It swallowed the corner of his parent's living room. It captured his imagination.

There, in the stillness of the country morning, fuzzy images of Tarzan flickered in tones of gray. For hours the boy sat in quiet reverence, a bag of cereal tightly gripped between flanneled knees.

For one brief moment, in that lonely boy's mind, Tarzan was his hero, Jane, his mother, Boy, his buddy. Together they shared adventure in that African jungle. They always did what was right, always won. Life was as simple as black-and-white.

# Chapter I
# Galc Force Getaway

*"A fool will yoke an ox with an elephant."*
~ African proverb

AS THE TRAIN WENDED ITS WAY toward Dover's chalky cliffs, disapproving British eyes shot darts at the eight scruffy travelers. Their overflowing packs, plastic garbage bags and even luggage flooded across twenty seats.

They were a motley collection. On the end of one seat perched a pigtailed earth mother-type in her late 20s dressed in a little girl jumper, beside a tall, strapping New Zealander with a 'guffaw-guffaw' talk show host laugh. He seemed to be a friend of another Kiwi, a scrawny fellow who licked his lips like a lizard in heat. Next to them sat a demure, twenty-something English girl, protectively guarding three stuffed black garbage bags. Chirping non-stop across from her was a birdlike Kiwi dressed in a Granny's house frock. Beside her squatted a chunky girl with an infectious honk, like a goose with emphysema. A young fellow, the wire-rimmed love child of Leon Trotsky, leaned over, hanging on her every word. Literally rounding out the group on two seats, weighing in at nearly three hundred pounds, was a beet-jowled Cockney whose belly cascaded over 'big top' jeans.

They might have passed for ordinary budget travelers—except for those overland company stickers garishly plastered all over their bags. The same company as ours'. Yes, these were our companions for the next seven months. This weird gaggle of psychedelic characters, in some bizarre cosmic twist of fate, had intruded into that small boy's black and white dream—my dream.

Africa's always had her claws in me, but it wasn't until years later that my dream approached some warped semblance of reality. My adventurous partner, Cheryl, and I circled-the-world for a year on our own in a test of our traveling compatibility, a quest to explore the hidden gems and uncommon jewels of life abroad–the parts that guidebooks didn't reveal.

As independent travelers, we moved spontaneously and shifted cultures on a whim, seeking a world beyond the usual 'E-ticket' ride. In fact, the more bizarre the better: from Chinese temples wriggling with pythons to crypts of mummified monks. We quickly learned (much to our relief) that you don't have to be wealthy to see the world. In fact, 'traveling light' is a blessing. It removes artificial barriers. So, steering clear of tour buses and hotels with a synthetic sameness, we haunted intimate guest houses, locals' homes, hostels, pensiones and one star or falling star hotels; the places where thrifty locals stayed. At night, we joined them, sitting shoulder to shoulder in cozy restaurants, while trying not to end up with a plate of sautéed sea slug or tripe paprikás.

And remarkably, taking this 'path less traveled' did make all the difference.

Now, I already found myself missing life on that adventurous trail. It was my sweet addiction. At home, life resumed as if we'd never escaped. Suddenly, the next forty years were predictably mapped out. The world was out there–and we were stuck in a suburbia infected with consumption-itis. One night, while watching an old jungle film on television, the frustrated voice mumbling in the back of my mind blurted out, "Cheryl, I know you think I'm crazy."

She simply nodded.

"But this island's getting smaller all the time. Life's too normal. Too routine." Testing the waters, I added, "Maybe we should get away for awhile?"

Flags went up. She'd heard my pitch before. It meant more than just a trip. It meant dropping everything, putting our lives into boxes and starting all over.

"Again?" she wondered. "We were just getting settled."

"But settled into what? Are you enjoying what you're doing?"

"No, but then again who does?"

"Travelers?"

We'd learned the difference between 'travelers' and 'tourists' on our last trip. The stereotypical 'tourist' was happy with just a superficial taste of local culture. We'd see them frantically running through villages, waving their credit cards at merchants, hurrying to buy some expensive trinket before their ship left for the next port. Others, in shorts, white socks and wing-tips held out the equivalent of a monthly wage to the local fruit seller, saying, "Well, I don't know how much that is in this here funny money. Take what ya want!" And they were happy to oblige.

It's fine, I suppose, if that's all you want out of travel, although it certainly helps reinforce that image of the 'Ugly American'.

However, a 'traveler' goes farther. He chews the fat, breaks bread, practices mangled sign-language, learns customs, talks politics, shares hopes and dreams. It's much more intense and involves giving, as well as taking. But you can depend on one thing. Travelers have more than tacky souvenirs to take home. They learn a little more about the world–and themselves.

"Look," I explained to my curious companion, "you know I've always wanted to take a safari across Africa."

"Sure, I have too," she confided. Even then, her glistening hazel eyes hinted she might be susceptible to my contagious wanderlust.

"Well...maybe *this* is the time," I said, flicking off the TV.

"Now?" She wasn't expecting that. "Crossing Africa's not as easy as hopping a train through Europe or Asia."

"I know, but life's more important than counting calories and office politics."

I was certain that if I could ease her mind she'd probably start packing immediately.

"Look, I'm sure there's a way we can do it–if not by ourselves, maybe with one of those safari outfits. Let them handle the problems."

Obviously, there are two ways across anyplace: alone or with a group. Instinctively, I was certain that we'd prefer the former. Still, after a futile search for recent solo trips, I wondered if it was more than even we could handle? So I explored the two distinct styles of African expeditions.

One, a luxurious safari, was reminiscent of old Hollywood films.

"After viewing the wildebeest migration and friendly Masai from the safety of our Land Rover," their brochure read, "you'll return to camp where our staff has pitched your tent, prepared drinks and has zebra steaks sizzling on the grill."

My intuition told me that high-priced group travel, with all its comfort, might only insulate us from the real Africa; make it too easy to miss the reality of the destination.

For all the comforts of the first, the second promised real adventure.

"After trading with the Masai and shopping for provisions in the market-place, you'll continue across the savanna, keeping an eye out for lions and other wild game. Afterward, you'll pitch your tent by moonlight, cook dinner and share stories around a roaring fire."

There wasn't any doubt which one was closer to my dream. I expected to feel Africa, to eat it, to smell it, to sleep it.

"Cheryl, I've found this overland outfit that supplies trucks, drivers and guides. Otherwise, it's a do-it-yourself safari."

"Do you think it's better than traveling on our own?"

"Look, they know the territory and, best of all, handle all the paperwork. Plus," I said, pulling out the map, "they offer a seven month trip out of England, over the Med, across the Sahara, through Zaire and then down through the Serengeti all the way to Zimbabwe. If we travel with them, we can finish the Harare to Cape Town segment on our own."

"That'd be exciting," she said, the fire sparkling in her eyes. It was good to see that glow again. "Exactly *how* far is that?"

"According to the map," I said, tracing the miniscule red lines, "I'd guess it's more than ten thousand miles."

"Do you really think we can make it?"

"There's no better time to try. We'll never be in this shape again and get-ting away gets harder all the time. Since it's such a long trip, we'll meet peo-ple like us–folks who believe there's more to life than trudging back and forth to work, day after day."

She smiled, adding, "That's for sure."

"Look, we've both dreamed of Africa for so long. Don't you want to see the gorillas and elephants before they become extinct?"

"You know I do. And I've always wanted to see Mount Kilimanjaro."

"Well, maybe we can climb it while we're there. Plus, we'll be able to trek in to see the mountain gorillas in Zaire."

"And the Zambezi? Can we raft the Zambeeezzzzi?"

"Sure. And we'll even go hunting with Pygmies!"

"I think I'll get fitted for lip plates with the Ubanguis."

"Sure. And I'll shoot hoops with Watutsis!" I said, dunking an imaginary ball and hugging her on the rebound.

The following day we phoned that London-based overland company, who instructed us to send our deposit and meet them at the Dover docks in late January. Before our departure, we'd receive packets filling us in on all the details. Meanwhile, there was so much to do.

Now, there's something therapeutic when you consciously turn a chapter in your life. You choose to move on without waiting for the winds of change to do it for you. In our own minds, we made that choice and there was no turning back. As a declaration to the rest of the world, we got married, sold our house and cars, quit our jobs and hung out a sign that read, 'Out to Life'.

Our days were spent learning all we could about the eighteen exotic countries along our route. Surprisingly, as we dug deeper into their cultures, we discovered nations as different as any others randomly picked throughout the world. About the only thing they had in common was that teardrop shaped land called 'Africa'.

One of the more mind-numbing parts of planning any journey is the deluge of paperwork. It didn't make matters any easier when visa requirements changed as quickly as overthrown dictators. Since visas typically expire after only thirty to ninety days, we decided to get most of them at embassies in neighboring countries. We assumed that if they were issued in Africa, they'd probably be less expensive, plus we'd avoid paying excessive visa service charges, which often exceeded the cost of the visas themselves.

It was easy enough to buy a plane ticket. But what if we ended up trekking for miles across some distant border? An overstuffed pack sticks to you like a Parisian Gypsy. Yet how could we prepare for the huge temperature differences between the Sahara and the top of Mount Kilimanjaro–probably eighty degrees? Layering was the only viable option, and since everyone pictured in the overland brochure was covered with mud, 'casual' was definitely in order.

"Really," teased Cheryl with her infectious laugh, "where are we gonna go in the bush that we'd have to dress up?" So we each included only one better outfit to convince border guards of our respectability.

*Besides, the less we take, the less we have to pound to shreds on rocks.*

The next major hump was health. You never worry about illness–until you come down with a 103-degree fever in the boondocks, as I had in the Himalayas. Only then do you discover that hospitals are few, doctors are scarce, dentists are unheard of, English speakers are rare, medical supplies are marginal and transportation is primitive. So we had complete exams, then began the month long process of playing human pincushion.

At the hospital's tropical medicine department, the World Health Organization map's yellow zones indicated the areas we were traveling through were infected with almost everything of any consequence.

"Well, if you're visiting all those countries," the serious young doctor pronounced, "first, I recommend you receive a cholera booster."

*Not bad, I can deal with that.*

"Then," he continued, "you'll want vaccinations for typhoid, tetanus, diphtheria, and don't forget spinal meningitis," he said, running out of fingers on his rubber-gloved hand.

Cheryl and I immediately shot each other a little-disguised look of pain. Then with a maniacal little smirk, he added, "A painful gamma globulin would just about round it out."

As we sat there getting pricked and prodded, we spotted another map showing the wildfire path of Africa's malaria epidemic. Nearly all the countries we were visiting were rife with the mosquito-transmitted disease. In fact, every twelve seconds a child dies of the illness. The doctor spotted us staring vacantly at the map.

"Oh, yes. Almost forgot malaria." A grin crossed his lips. "Now, you'll need to start your medication two weeks prior to entering the infected zone. Of course, there may be side effects."

*Damn. Last trip the side effects were nearly as bad as the disease.*

"Before," Cheryl explained, "when we traveled to Asia, doctors prescribed Fansidar and it always made us nauseous."

"Oh, we don't recommend that any more. Now, it's suspected of causing kidney damage in some people after prolonged use."

"Great. We were on it for over six months."

"Oh, dear. Now, we prescribe Mefloquine and Chloroquine. One you'll take daily, the other weekly. You should begin taking them two weeks prior to entering the infected area and continue them for a month after leaving Africa."

"That means we should start them in Europe, because Algeria's the first country where we'll be in any danger," I quickly figured.

Eventually, the poking and probing were complete. All we had to show for the pain was a trophy-sized set of bruises and the canary yellow WHO

International Certificate of Vaccination booklet required for entry into most African countries. There was one final surprise.

At the last minute, in order to get our marriage license, Cheryl was forced to get a rubella shot. As luck would have it, the night before we flew into London's Heathrow Airport, she broke out in a mysterious red rash. What else? The German measles.

We were thrilled to land in London, figuring we'd have a few days to mentally prepare, pick up trip insurance and drop in to our favorite pub for a pint. However, an awaiting message from the overlanders shattered those plans.

"You must obtain Algerian visas before leaving your native country," it read.

*Well, it's a little too late for that.*

There was no use in leaving without that crucial stamp. So early the next morning, we visited their diplomatic mission ready to plead for mercy. Climbing the granite steps to its massive door, I pushed the buzzer beneath the shining brass plaque scrolled in Arabic.

"Oui, what do you want?" a voice squawked from the tiny speaker.

Feeling like Oz's scarecrow looking for a brain, I replied, "We'd like to talk with someone about our visas."

The door buzzed. Pushing it open, we gingerly advanced down a silent passage toward a larger-than-life portrait of the Algerian president. Dwarfed below sat a no-nonsense receptionist, who looked more at home in a souk.

Approaching, I cleared my voice and mumbled, "Excuse me."

The slight, dark man glanced up, obviously perturbed.

"We're joining an expedition here and it's supposed to leave in a few days to cross Algeria."

The castle hound cocked his head to one side, like a lap dog listening to a high-pitched whine.

"At first, we were told to apply for our Algerian visas in London. Now, they say we need to get them before leaving our country. But as you can see, we're already here."

*Is now the time to offer a bribe?*

"Ah, *oui*. Moment…" he huffed, exasperated by our stupidity. Grabbing our passports, he vanished behind an unmarked door. For several tense minutes we waited until he returned smiling, his pencil-thin mustache stretched to a breaking point. "There ees no prob-lem in applying for your visas here. They weel be read-ee een doo days. Returnez ici."

Even then, as we filled out the paperwork, I couldn't help wondering if this wasn't some early warning sign about our African 'experts'. Still, it was too late to back out now.

Later, we stopped by the International Youth Hostel office to renew our cards. In the past, membership had been a real bargain because it allowed us to stay in some of the world's most beautiful and remote spots and compare 'finds' with fellow travelers. Contrary to their name, they're not just for 'youths'. In Berlin, we met one youth that was an active ninety years old.

However, there was one problem. The YHA secretary with the green spiked hair, steel-tipped brogans and pearl stud in her nose insisted in a thick brogue, "Ya haffta apply in yere own country. Ya canna do it herrrre."

"What's the difference? Sometimes member-ships expire while people are on holiday. Some hostels even renew cards themselves," I countered. "So, why the difficulty in doing it here?"

"Ya jest canna. It's na'policy," she whined. "Ya haffta doo it a'hoome."

It took another fifteen minutes of arguing, pleading and hopping up and down before she finally agreed to accept our hotel address as our permanent home.

"It's all training for Africa," I reminded my partner.

One problem remained. How to safely carry cash through the African wilds for seven months? In the bush there are no ATMs, few phones for money wires. Other travelers recommended leaving home *without* traveler's checks, because they're virtually useless. One national bank had refused a check because 'SPECIMEN' wasn't printed across it like on their sample. Credit cards only had one purpose, proving 'financial responsibility' to border officials. No, I figured it was best to stick with dollars and pounds in the east and south and French francs in the north and west.

"It's amazing how far a few dollars can take you," travelers confided. "Plus, if you're very discreet, there's a bustling blackmarket."

*Still, where do we keep our stash of cash?*

The solution surfaced in a Chelsea storefront. There, amid the clutter sat a stack of phony deodorant cans identical to the real thing except for false screw-off bottoms.

*They're inconspicuous, yet look like they actually belong in our bag.*

At long last we were ready to relax, believing the worst was over. Without warning, my body was racked with a 102-degree fever and chills, as the Asian flu swept through London like the Black Plague. In the darkened cell of our room, I was barely able to move.

"Sorry, Babe. These last two weeks just haven't gone as smoothly as planned," I admitted, shivering under the sheets in the darkness.

"Well, everything will turn out all right," she sweetly reassured me, her warm, soft body cuddling close to mine.

Eventually, with her patience, and heaps of hot Indian curry, I recovered just in time for the race to Victoria Station. As a final farewell surprise, the metros suddenly stopped running and we ended up jogging with full packs down soggy streets to narrowly meet our train bound for Dover.

It was a relief to leave London. We were ready for places more predictable in their unpredictability.

Pulling into Dover with our new overlander companions from that train, we were met by our driver, his assistant and eleven other members of our bizarre band. Nigel, our driver from Cornwall, looked like a World War I cartoon. All that was missing was his doughboy helmet. He wore bright, shiny, red leather boots. Dirty olive socks fell down over his skinny, hairy ankles. A torn, green t-shirt hung over his baggy, khaki shorts with the seat blown out. His boxers peeked through, enjoying the scenery. Nigel seemed pleasant enough. Yet on first impression, you wouldn't mistake him as the 'leader' of anything. He beamed with enthusiasm, but spoke in a whisper, as he welcomed us and introduced his assistant, Henry.

Sneering through hawk-like eyes, Henry had a tough, chiseled look that said, "Don't screw with me." Greasy long brown hair swept over a five-day growth of beard. He was wrapped in an Aussie swagman's leather coat and faded, weathered cowboy hat tilted far over his brow, even though it was ten at night. Walking with an exaggerated swagger in beat up cowboy boots, Henry looked more at home in pubs than jungles. If body language counted for anything, he already saw himself as commander of our cadre. Even then, you could sense an inexplicable tension between them, stretching like an invisible bungee cord.

Digging in the dirt with the toe of his boot, Nigel hemmed and hawed, "We're catchin' this ferry…then headin' to a camp outside Brussels."

*Is he making all this up as he goes along?*

"We'll stay there a couple days to pick up a few visas. Then…" his quivering voice trailed off.

*He is winging it. Has he ever led this trip before? Has he ever been to Africa? Damn. What have we gotten ourselves into?*

"All right," he added, with a vacant flourish. "Grab your stuff and hop aboard."

We boarded the gray overland lorry and quickly left the fog-laden docks aboard the ferry to Belgium. She was a massive rolling refrigerator of a truck with rear seats that popped up through the roof.

"You can take yer turns ridin' up top," Henry explained.

*What, like baby baboons clutching the back of their mother?*

"She's superior to the competition," he bragged. "Her 'diff-lock' system makes it better than four-wheelers when we hit the desert sand and mud of Zaire."

*I hoped this was the voice of experience talking.*

"Yea, our seating is also far better than the ex-Army Bedfords used by other expeditions. Ours face forward, while theirs face center."

*I can't imagine staring at the same people month after month.*

He continued, "Our cab is open, so you can talk to us durin' the day. Yer lucky. Bedford drivers never speak to their overlanders. They only talk by knockin'."

*Maybe a single knock meant, "Stop." Two meant, "Go." Three meant, "Look at that." Four meant, "We just lost another one off the back."*

Our truck was fringed with six sliding glass windows down each side. Two tables were built-in on both sides in the back, where you could write letters or nap without falling out of your seats. For the hedonistic, there was a small fridge for cold beers and stereo with eight, count 'em, eight speakers.

*Great. Everyone will have a little personal music to soothe the savage beasts.*

That short ferry ride allowed us to meet the only other American on our safari. Sprout was a dark, outgoing, pintsized Southerner with an irreverent wit.

Enroute to Brussels, the danger signs continued and Nigel became hopelessly lost.

*How can anyone get too confused in a country the size of New Jersey?*

The machine gun ferocity of the pounding rains began. Seeping through poorly sealed windows, water drizzled down inside our unheated walk-in freezer. Eventually, after an all-night drive, we limped into Camping Beersal on the outskirts of Brussels, Belgium. Any relief, however, soon became a letdown. Hours of downpour had already turned that rural campsite into a soggy bog.

"You're overlanders, damn it!" Henry yelled with sadistic glee. "Get used to 'er."

So, shouting above the thundering din and driving wind, we stoically hunkered down. After introducing ourselves, we chose tentmates or 'tenties' and jobs or 'wallahships' for the long haul ahead.

The first to speak up was the frail, pigtailed, tie-dyed type with the nearly incomprehensible English accent from the train—Pooky. She reluctantly volunteered to be a fire-wallah, one of the keepers of our flame. Her 'tenty' and our truck cleaner was Fluffy, the attractive, twenty-something with poofy hair, who was escorting three 25-gallon black plastic garbage bags stuffed with a cot, inflatable mattress, wardrobe, (and perhaps even a miniature Sherpa).

*Something tells me that it's her first trip away from home, too. Think she brought curlers to Africa to keep her 'big' hair big?*

Another tent would be set up by Slim. As bartender, the tall, gaunt, gregarious Kiwi with the short-cropped hair and beard would try to keep us well lubricated for the next 10,000 miles—a challenging job for sure. His tentmate, Zippy, a shy, curly-haired Canadian computer geek, decided to be a roof-wallah, responsible for tossing our tents from the truck-top each night.

Then we were introduced to Trotsky, the Russian revolutionary clone from the Dover train. That wanna-be accountant, out for his first and possibly last fling, would work as roof-wallah. With his wire-rimmed glasses, wispy beard and frizzy blond hair, he hardly looked the part of a future CPA. Nevertheless, he already boasted, "I really want to grow dreadlocks on this trip."

*So far, they just look like a bad perm.*

His tenty was Flinty, a modern-day Errol Flynn. If you were casting an overland buccaneer, this Brit was your man, complete with large gold earring and thick, black, curly hair. He volunteered to be a fire-wallah in charge of wielding the ax.

*I've read "The Shining" and am a little wary of his strong, silent type.*

The train's lip-licking lizard, Willie, was Clark Kent's virginal brother. Clean-cut, almost to the point of being featureless, he had a great future as a CIA operative, since he could melt into any crowd.

*Why, if he laid motionless on a rock, you'd never see him.*

As our assistant bartender, he shared a tent with Bongo, a gangly, head-banging, Canadian rock-and-roll mutant in his early twenties. His job was to collect firewood; his personal quest was to collect native drums across Africa.

*Already, he tags after Nigel like Sancho after Quixote–or Beavis after Butthead.*

Then, we met that granny-garbed, sparrow-like woman from our train–Dropsy. A self-admitted klutz, she (of all people) volunteered to be in charge of our security. Prudence was her 'tintee', as she'd say, in her nasal twang. At a hulking six foot-two, with dark hair severely drawn back off her bony face, the formidable Aussie was in charge of our food.

*I've never met a person whose face is so permanently etched in a scowl.*

Chester, the rotund Goliath from the train, already reeked like he'd last showered when British Prime Minister Thatcher was in office. The Cockney was a beer swillin', lorry drivin' man with a Moe Howard haircut and bushy mustache. A back locker-wallah with Sprout and me, we'd unload sixty bags and packs twice a day.

*For obvious reasons, he's sleeping alone.*

Then, we had the pleasure to meet the others, not on the train. It was hard to miss the tough, chain-smoking Maxie. The bleached-blonde, Aussie ex-bar-maid eagerly volunteered with a sly grin to control all our food and game park money–our 'kitty'.

*Am I the only one who feels odd about handing the group's $16,000 in cash over to this complete stranger?*

Her tenty, Duchess, our group's youngest, was a nubile eighteen-year old English Lolita with wraparound lips. High-maintenance and bred to have her own way, she'd tally passengers, money, and, if the bug bit, malarial cases.

It was going to be a long journey, so we were fortunate to have a real, live nurse on board. Clara and her husband Bear shared another tent. Our Kiwi medical-wallah seemed endowed with all the right qualifications–iodine, infinite patience and an easy smile. In contrast, Bear, an affable giant and top mechanic, was water-wallah. He'd refill and purify our water several times a day.

*Here's a guy you'd like to have with you in a breakdown or fight.*

The only other married couple was the soft-spoken, inseparable English Siamese twins nicknamed The Perfect Couple. They had that peculiar habit, when asked a question, of answering the same thing at the same time. They were meek, but I suspected a conservative fury simmered close to the surface of their pale skins. He was a roof-wallah; she was truck cleaner and seemed like a more than fastidious person. She already cautioned everyone, "We don't eat any vegetables–except potatoes."

Southern Sprout and Peggy, the sweet Canadian honker, were left after our quick game of Beersal pick-up, and reluctantly decided to tent together for the time being. Although Peggy was off for seven months in the wild African bush, this was her first trip abroad. Plus, she bragged, "You know, I've never even camped before. I have traveled to Hawai'i. But after this trip," she beamed, "I'll be able to do anything–even drive to California."

*Ah, now there's life on the edge.*

Peggy would be a truck cleaner and Sprout would serve as locker-wallah with Chester and me.

Finally, Cheryl took on an awesome responsibility–keeping green things from growing in our petri dish of a refrigerator.

"What a strange group," I whispered to my partner.

"Yea, I hate to rely on first impressions, but I didn't know you could find twenty-three people so different…or so individually bizarre."

As the rain slowed for a second, all of us poured from the truck and splashed down into the muddy quagmire. At first, it seemed that no one, including our two 'experts', knew a thing about setting up the orange neon two-person tents–and tackling it in the rain wasn't the ideal way to learn. But after much splashing and swearing, eleven bright pyramids eventually popped up like pimples on prom night. Henry and Bear, the mammoth Kiwi mechanic with arms the girth of my thighs, hastily tied a bright blue plastic cook tarp to the truck, pegging out the corners with sharp metal stakes. Suddenly, fierce winds struck, whipping the sheet's corners back and forth like a cat-o-nine tails. The stakes slipped from the wet ground, spraying like buckshot. To make matters worse, within minutes after it was finally secured the flat tarp filled with about a hundred gallons of cold rainwater. It grew fatter and fatter like a water balloon with a thyroid problem. Finally, it exploded with a "Kaaaaaahhhh-Poooosssshhh!" scoring a direct hit atop Peggy and Sprout's puny tent.

Once inside our own tiny, day-glow orange tent, as we shivered in our sleeping bags, I whispered to Cheryl, "Yea, it's going to be some trip."

"Do you still think that we'll make it to Harare?"

"Without murdering each other first?"

The harsh reality of overland life dawned the next morning. No one had slept all night. Fragile tents snapped back and forth, popping like gunfire until we thought we'd be tossed into the air. Not surprisingly, Nigel and Henry were far from experienced campers. As we 'overlanders' shivered in gale force winds, those wimps already huddled in the warmth of the truck.

Still, we organized the details of our mutual survival, forming cook groups of three. Once a week, we'd each take turns working miracles in our rustic chuckwagon. 'Kitchen' consisted of heavy metal folding tables and folding cloth stools that slid into the truck's belly. We carried two gas cook stoves to help prepare an assortment of tinned fish and meat, tea and crackers, Marmite and custards, pastas and rice, and special dehydrated meals, which Prudence instructed us to save for the desert.

*Wait. Why save dehyds for the desert where there's no water? Save them in case of a shipwreck, instead. That way, they'd come pre-salted.*

Mornings began with the same ritual. At 6 a.m., a befuddled cook crew fixed breakfast with as much clanging as possible. Within ten minutes, the rest of us struggled to pull on pants in nearly freezing temperatures and a tent just four feet high. Unfortunately, breakfast was hardly a good reason to leave our marginally warm sleeping bags. It was already sadly predictable with overripe fruit, tea, corn flakes or a shredded wheaty biscuit. Those wood-like scouring pads promised regularity, "By Royal Appointment to the Queen Mother."

We were duly impressed.

"Henry," I asked, "do we have any 'real' coffee on board?"

He snapped back, "'Real' overlanders don't drink coffee!"

*Oh, another part of the 'real' overlander myth. Hey, what about all those movies of real he-men on safari, cowboys on the range, or Aussies in the outback?*

The only coffee Henry bought for seven months was a few jars of cheap, English instant with the aftertaste of burnt prune juice. Quickly, Cheryl and I realized we'd have to redefine his image of 'real' overlanders. When we travel, we enjoy the rich smell and bracing strength of a 'real' cuppa made in our own personal one-cup strainer. It was our one secret luxury and we knew we'd have to buy a personal cache of Dutch beans before leaving Belgium.

After breakfast, while the cleanup crew did the dishes and put the food and bins away, everyone else headed back to their cozy sleeping bags or braved the showers. Here in our soggy Beersal kingdom, twenty-three of us shared three shower stalls with timers as unpredictable as our departure. We bought a token, jumped in, soaped up and hopped out before our five minutes ran out. Unfortunately, if we timed it wrong, the water would trickle to a stop, just as we finished lathering. Worst of all, you had to buy a token from the original Mr. and Mrs. Hospitality–a couple as frigid as the weather.

Their prized pigeons were their real concern, not the campers. Hutches were stacked everywhere inside their garage. When the weather finally turned so bad that we couldn't bring our spoon to our mouths any longer without violently shaking, we moved in, right next to their cooing, puffing feathered friends in our Guantanamo of guano.

Meanwhile, those downpours became Europe's 'storm of the century'. Trees fell. Limbs littered the village. Power poles crashed, sending a shower of sparks. As we hunkered in our tents or huddled near pigeon hutches, the temperature hovered near freezing. Still, there was no end in sight to our visa delay. Three were quickly issued. However, the Central African Republic embassy official's wife was having a baby. All we could do was pray for an easy birth. Those soggy days set an ominous tone for the rest of our trip. To help pass the time, Henry devised a scavenger hunt, deviously pitting five from one country against five from another. England was against Australia and New Zealand. And everybody was against the Americans.

*So much for establishing a sense of team work.*

The days dragged on, as frustrations simmered just below the surface. Cheryl and I did whatever possible to avoid the frigid campsite and the growing group hostility. Fortunately, one day as we rode the bus into Brussels, we sat across from a stocky Belgian in his late forties decked out in black leathers. Spotting my Maui baseball cap, he blurted in perfect English, "Excuse me. You are Americans, yes?"

We nodded, surprised at the approach of a normally reserved Belgian.

"Where are you from?"

Cheryl and I looked him up and down a little suspiciously, before answering, "Hawai'i." You never knew what the reaction might be.

"Ahhh, Hawai'i," the man exclaimed in a booming Pavarotti voice. He pulled his long, sleek ponytail out from under his leather jacket. "You see, when I was a merchant marine, I often went to America. Hawai'i, Baltimore, New York, Miami and San Diego, too." With that, Jean-Claude introduced himself like an old friend, shaking our hands with gusto.

Fate was kind. Our new friend was a generous Moto-Guzzi cop and one of few Amerophiles who lived in Beersal. After our chance meeting, we were invited back to his warm and cozy century old cottage near our flooded bog. That evening, his wife Lydie even prepared a spread of crepes and homemade wine in our honor.

Over the following days, we spent more and more time together. He was the finest ambassador Beersal, or perhaps Belgium, could hope for. It's always a pleasure to have people show you their favorite spots, and Jean-Claude drove us to Gran-Sur-Loo where the Battle of Waterloo was fought. A Napoleonic War buff, he knew every troop movement, every skirmish, every shot fired during the battle. Then, returning to their cottage, he and his son Mattieu modeled their replica Napoleonic uniforms that they wore for battle re-enactments. They were magnificent, as they stood at attention with glistening hatchets, white leather aprons and matching ostrich feathered stovepipe hats.

Cheryl and Lydie, Jean-Claude and I chatted into the wee hours. They were as curious about life in America as we were about that piece of earth called Belgium. As the blazing fire turned to embers, mutual misconceptions melted away. Again, travel renewed our faith in the simpler pleasures in life.

Still, sometimes life is stranger than fiction–and that helped us cope. One afternoon, back at the campsite, we were visited by a circus poodle troupe. Ten little Fifis, Yvettes and Pierres, wearing blue and pink tutus, hopped through hoops and pranced on tiny hind legs amid cages of pecking pigeons. Their Hungarian trainer cooed, "Igen, igen," encouraging them, as they tap, tap, tapped their way across the concrete floor while spinning balls on their noses. But you couldn't fool me. From the sound of their tiny smacking lips and the gleam in those sinister eyes, we just knew they'd rather eat those plump little pigeon canapés. Then curl up on their tutus for a long night's sleep.

Nights were spent in a toasty Belgian bar. Hours of drinking kreik, a tasty fruit flavored beer, revealed that many of our companions, just out of high school or university, envisioned this journey as an African love tryst, some *Zambezi Love Boat.*

*Traveling, like politics, makes strange bedfellows.*

Fourteen wet, wasted days passed. Group frustrations and our hopelessness at feeling stuck simmered just below the surface. Then, at last, our visas were approved and we could begin our mad dash across Europe.

The next fifty-two hours and twenty minutes (Cheryl won the "Guess What Time We'll Arrive" contest) were spent racing through Belgium, France and Spain, barely pausing long enough for gasoline and restroom stops. Funny, no matter how tight our schedule, we'd still manage to pause every four hours for 'tea'. There, among the dung, condoms and dirty tampons of the back roads, in pelting rain or pitch dark, gas stoves were lit and cups and saucers set. Far from 'high tea,' this was best described as 'low tea'.

*How very proper. How very strange.*

Originally we'd planned to visit Seville, Grenada and Gibraltar, but those options were tossed by the wayside like used tea bags. There was a schedule to keep. Finally, without fanfare, we dragged into Algeciras, Spain, more than a week late and immediately ferried off toward the land of our dreams.

Steaming past the rocky crag of Gibraltar toward the wild African shore, we savored one last, lingering glimpse of the Western world. Little did we know that her serene silhouette would have to sustain us far longer than we ever imagined.

BRANDON WILSON

# Chapter II
# Afffricaaaaa!

*"Fire and gunpowder do not sleep together."*
~ African proverb

*W*ITHIN AN HOUR, the golden crest of the African coast loomed on the horizon. In celebration, our scowling, Amazonian food-miser Prudence opened a few tins of pilchard fish and offered tiny hunks of French baguette to dip in the oily tomato sauce. As you might expect, stale loaves and tinned fishes did little to feed our famished multitude.

No sooner had we docked in Ceuta, a duty-free Spanish North African enclave, than Slim, Willie, Zippy, Trotsky and I set off on a mission in search of cheap booze. We all knew in the coming months those precious bottles would prove indispensable as border bribes and perhaps an ultimate means of preserving our sanity.

*After all, 'real' overlanders don't live on tinned fish alone. We're headed into Muslim countries where beer is as scarce as a baked ham.*

As we set about our task, I fondly flashed back to the photo in the company's brochure. Secretly, I was that happy overlander pulling a cold brew from the small refrigerator in the truck's belly. Out there, in the midst of the parched desert, a frosty drink was an alluring reward at the end of a thirsty day. Not only that, but toting ice to the Sahara had to rank as a major accomplishment of Western civilization. It was our duty. We owed it to history.

We easily found the liquor store run by a merchant sporting a hairbrush of a mustache and porcupine quill eyebrows. After much haggling, we hauled our precious beverage booty back and set off for camp.

The Ceuta campsite was Shangri-la after our Beersal bog. Bathed in the warm glow of an African afternoon, we pitched tents on a grassy knoll over-

21

looking the cobalt Med. Cold showers sprayed without a token and there were two barbecue pits. Best of all, there was a noticeable lack of pecking pigeons and prancing pooches. As swashbuckling Flinty was quick to point out, it was pure "Luxxxurrry."

The sun radiated crimson streams and set the sea afire. All the frustrating gyrations of the past two weeks left with the tide.

Morning arose with unabashed brilliance. After a predictably Spartan breakfast, the cleanup crew began their usual scouring chores. Meanwhile, the rest of us resumed our daily routine of re-packing.

The human psyche constantly amazes me. Even on the tip of Africa, people have an uncanny knack of creating boring routine from blessed unpredictability. Immediately after breakfast each morning, everyone packed their sleeping bags, as the back locker-wallahs unloaded all sixty bags and packs from the truck. Then, everybody re-stuffed backpacks, refolded tents, tossed them up on the roof for storage, refilled canteens, brushed teeth and searched for the nearest 'loo' or discrete bush. Prepared at last, we loaded into our English camel and set off for hours of bumpy roads ahead.

Ceuta quickly vanished in the distance as we snaked toward Asilah for our first taste of the 'real' Africa. Fortunately, the road's horrendous condition was easily surpassed by Africa's remarkable 'separate reality'.

Moroccan women stooped in manual labor, as they struggled to grow food in parched yards. Legions of grizzled men led dwarfish gray burros down a nerve-shaking, bone-quaking highway, as stubborn as their asses. Others, in elfin hooded robes and pointed slippers, chatted in fields, chatted outside tidy, whitewashed cottages, chatted on street corners, chatted outside latticed mosque doors, or chatted as they walked hand-in-hand down a labyrinth of streets. Obviously, Moroccans were used to seeing Western travelers–but they weren't ready for us. Our rolling gray beast and outlandish entourage always made them stop and shake their heads in disbelief as we drove past.

The coastal road from Ceuta to Asilah took nearly five hours as we inched our way through the hills. However, a good part of the delay was due to frequent photo opportunities.

"Photo stop!" someone would scream and Nigel brought us skidding to a halt. Then twenty eager overlanders squeezed past tons of personal baggage crowding the aisles, climbed down and lined up for one more shot of a mountain, burro, or mud hut, looking just like the last ten.

Of course, we were still saddled with the compulsory English tea parties, except now our 'soirées' were held in some poor, confused Moroccan's front yard.

Diversions aside, by late afternoon we pulled into Asilah Campground, a spacious grassy tract just steps from the ocean. After a quick setup, we eagerly stormed into town to enjoy our first restaurant meal. Already, it came as a welcome relief after two weeks of buttered bread, jammed bread, fried bread, pudding-ed bread, milk-soaked bread, croutoned bread, stale bread and spread bread.

Of course, Maxie our 'banker' continuously justified our miserly menu by saying, "Think of all the money we're saving," and Prudence, her tightfisted alter ego, nodded in stern agreement.

*What's the sense in buying food at the local market, if we're just going to prepare it the same way as we do at home?*

At moments like that, I considered the advantage of traveling with the French next time around–if there ever was a next time.

Early the next morning, Cheryl and I ambled downtown. Heat already radiated off the whitewashed houses. Except for the pungent smell of roast goat, we had the abandoned village to ourselves. Tiptoeing past ancient towering ramparts, we wondered where everyone was hiding. We expected to be mobbed by overeager storeowners. Finally, spying open shops in the coolness of a canopied alleyway, we ducked inside, eager to escape the relentless heat.

"Maybe what we've heard about Morocco just isn't true anymore?" Cheryl whispered.

Suddenly, as if on cue, hawkers popped out of nowhere into the sun-streaked lane. "Come, have tea," cried one pudgy merchant, a barracuda's twinkle in his eyes. *Ah, newcomers. They're actually listening to my pitch.*

Admittedly, there was much less pressure than we'd expected. So, we took advantage of the moment to finger handcrafted leather jackets, hats and purses, boots and sandals, rugs and robes and silver with detached interest. Besides, it was cool inside and the fresh mint tea they offered was refreshing relief. Still, it wasn't the day to buy. Not yet. We were honing our skills for Marrakech.

That night as we slept, Asilah's waves soothed our spirits, tempting us with rhythms of things to come. Meanwhile, Flinty, our ax-swinging pirate, garbed in freshly purchased peasant's robes, wandered up and down the deserted beach, crying a mantra of, "Afffricaaaaa! Afffricaaaaa!" in starry wonder.

The next day, we were packed and en route to Rabat by 5 a.m. Since the Canadians needed to pick up Algerian visas there, we quickly dropped them at the Embassy and pitched camp at another seaside refuge. The glow of a full moon at midday eerily spotlit a sandy swatch of soil next to a Muslim graveyard. Like a faded picture, a latent Dorian Gray, you could tell it once had vigor. That was long before it was reduced to another barren plot, penned in by a concrete wall, topped with shards of broken green and opaque glass.
*Is that to keep the world out? Or us in?*

Rabat was a typical government town and the perfect place to discover the inner dealings of a market without the teeming frenzy of Marrakech, our next destination. Although a troop of guides aggressively offered grand tours of the Andalusian Gardens and local Casbah, I decided to scout it out myself. For just 1/2 dirham, I caught a pilchard-packed tin can of a ferry across the Bou Regreg River with the locals and wandered for hours alone up and down fetid back alleys. Several times, I stepped into the swarming souk or marketplace.

Immediately, my senses were serenaded with a symphony of rich, alien scents. Every turn, each new shop brought a unique thrill. The flowery fragrance of patchouli wafted from perfume shops along with the pungent odor of leather from the tanners. Sweet pies and pastries drew me to the bakeries. The aroma of exotic cloves drifted from conical piles in tiny, open spice carts. Butcheries bombarded me with reeking smells of quickly rotting flesh. Then merchants in embroidered robes and colorful fezzes adroitly leaned out of their closet-sized shops into the alleyway.

"Bonjour. Want to see some rugs? No? Some leather? No? What you want to see?" they cajoled. "Come have mint tea. We talk."

I'd shake my head and walk on, until the hustle and hassle would begin again all too soon, mere paces from the last.

Then I spotted Rabat's most colorful duo, the water sellers. Two men in red velvet smocks with hats like Mexican banditos wove and swaggered toward me. Bandoleers with shiny cups were strung over their shoulders. If someone on the street flashed a secret signal, the fellow lugging the large brass pitcher stopped and poured shimmering water into a shining cup held by the other. In that heat, they did a brisk business, strolling from one stall to the next.

At daybreak, we set off for fabled Marrakech that lay at the edge of the snow-dolloped Atlas Mountains, several hundred miles to the south. But in no way was our truck ever to be confused with The Marrakech Express, because it was nearly four in the afternoon by the time we arrived.

Funny. It all started to sink in. We began to understand what people meant by 'African time' or "polepole!" (pronounced "Poli! Poli!") or "Slowly! Slowly!" in Swahili. Nothing, absolutely nothing, happened quickly, which was both a blessing and a curse.

The relief of arriving in our fantasy village of mosques and minarets was tempered by the shock of discovering ourselves swept up in the craziness of a *Mad Max* Barter Town. Everyone was a salesman. Everyone had a deal or scam.

"Gimme, gimme misstah! Buy dees, buy dees!" cried hustlers and waifs.

After thirty minutes of haggling over prices, Nigel secured rooms for everyone just off the Djemaa el Fna (Assembly of the Dead), and we settled in for the next few days.

*Does "Assembly of the Dead" refer to our hotel?*

A single twenty-watt bulb dangled precariously from an ancient wire in the center of each moldy room. Waffle-sized chips of paint peeled from the walls. Scores of spiders inhabited insect condos under springless beds. Still, even with those slight imperfections, the tiny cells provided a moment of privacy after days of communal urban bivouacking.

Unlike its name, the Djemaa was in the center of all the action. It thronged with snake charmers and cobras, acrobats and tumblers, water sellers and fortune tellers, food carts, hustlers and pickpockets, Muslim 'evangelists' screaming into microphones, would-be guides, and men and their trained monkeys. There were also a few hard-to-miss travelers swept up in its magic.

Night came quickly. As a shroud covered the land, the market burst into new life like a phoenix. The air was vibrant with exotic aromas. Wooden stands boasted barbecued goat. Their hairy heads hung for all to see and marvel at their freshness. Food stalls cooked spicy morsels for locals out for a stroll in the cool of the evening. Bashful girls squeezed fresh orange juice.

Gnarled women dished amber couscous from iron pots and roasted lamb kebabs on sizzling coals. Wizened men huddled over bowls of mud-colored bean soup.

Despite the helter-skelter activity, despite the hype, there was the sense that this was everyday Moroccan life–not some special nightly tourist show.

After curiously making our rounds through the Djemaa, we headed to the rooftops above the square to savor the special coolness of the night air. There, we became magically transfixed by the distant muezzin's call to prayer, "Allahhhhaaaaa…."

At first light we set off, eager to explore the fabled city's famous palaces, pools and Saadian Tombs, modeled after Spain's Alhambra. However, our late afternoon was set aside for a venture into the heart of the medina, the main marketplace, that writhing den of buyers and sellers. Upon entry, a young eager guide quickly adopted us. Since we never hire guides, we initially tried to shake him off, but he was insistent.

"Well, at least," Cheryl figured, "we won't get too lost in this endless maze."

Darkened alleyways were canopied with bamboo sticks and brightly colored material. Sunlight filtered down, casting ribbons of amber across piles of bright kaleidoscopic fabrics. Streets were crammed chock-a-block with shops selling goods of every sort: leather sandals and bags, plated silver and brass plates, mountains of rugs and blankets, herbs and aphrodisiacs, meats and spices, grains and fresh produce.

As we wound our way through mysterious and darkly shrouded streets, merchants bounded out in front of us. Some blocked our way. Others grabbed at our arms. All yelled from their stoops.

"Hey, Barbie. Hey, lookie, lookie. Hey, Fish & Chips. Hey, Ali Baba," they cried, with a dogged persistence that would make the stereotypical used car salesman look downright timid.

Pricing remained an enigma. The cost of everything, whether it was a room, food, a newspaper, a haircut or sandals, was whatever we personally believed it was worth. The worst part was knowing that no matter how much we'd bargain, speak to them in French, or play their game, we'd never pay a 'local' price. Never. In fact, it was difficult to gauge what the 'real' price was.

Maybe there simply wasn't one. There was just 'his' final, rock-bottom price–and what 'you' were willing to pay. It wasn't unusual for merchants to start haggling at eight times the final price. So, when you reached 1/4 the initial price, you felt great and he made more than he would have done selling to a local. That was the Moroccan 'win-win'.

We haggled with a cobbler for forty minutes over a price, before we finally bought some handcrafted camel leather sandals. But even that small bargain was tempered by our guide's demand for his added 'cadeau'.

Giving a 'cadeau' or gift is a time-honored part of the African culture. It entails much more than our concept of the gift. It's the idea of sharing wealth and good fortune. And because all Westerners are thought to be rich, they're expected to be generous and, after awhile, cadeau-ridden.

Finally tired of the frenzied medina, we relented and gave our guide a small 'cadeau' in payment for leading us out of the maze and into the dying light of the Djemaa. Although hundreds of locals milled from stall to stall in search of their evening meal, we immediately spotted Bear the giant mechanic and our nurse Clara, rising heads above the rest.

"Hey, let's join them for a dinner of lamb kebabs and fried eggplant," I suggested.

"Ooh, lamb. My favorite," my attractive partner sarcastically reminded me, since it was undoubtedly her least favorite food.

Before we knew it, two ragtag Fagin's boys, about eight and ten, assailed us.

"Hey, Misstuh, wanna buy a drum?" one chirped.

"Very cheap," the other one chimed in.

"No, thanks."

"For you, a special price, my friend."

I'd heard this all before, from Greece to Thailand.

"How much?"

"Only five dirhams!"

"Not bad," I thought. However, with my bargaining appetite whet at the souk, I countered, "Four."

"Ah, but at five, I only make one dirham profit," the younger boy sighed.

Bear added, "At four and a half, I'll buy one too. Ta."

They eagerly nodded and I carefully gave the kid four and a half dirhams. Exactly.

He looked at it. Then, suddenly shoving it back, he shouted, "No, five!"

"Okay, okay, five dirhams, but that's all," I relented, weary of haggling. I reached for the coin in my pocket.

"Here, hold onto this," Cheryl said, as she handed the drum to Bear.

Quickly, the waifs shot each other a furtive glance. Then, they started tugging at my sweatshirt, pulling at my watch, and dragging on my partner's scarf. As they did everything possible to distract us, I felt a tiny hand slip into my pocket. I quickly spun out of his range and grabbed the drums. The smaller thief hugged them, too. For a moment, we tugged back and forth. But soon he realized his strength was no match. He let loose a bloodcurdling scream.

I suppose he figured that I'd be shocked. I'd let go of the drum and lose that and the five dirhams, as he and his partner disappeared into the crowd.

He was right. It was embarrassing, but I held on tight.

The older boy spat out, "I'll get the Police."

"We'll go with you!" Cheryl shot back.

Since Plan 'A' had miserably failed, the kid pointed to my side pocket where his fingers had been.

"You never gave me any money!" he shrieked, at the top of his lungs. Hearing that, his friend turned and ran away.

I knew I'd paid him, and knew I never carried money in that pocket anyway. Besides, I wasn't so stupid as to empty my pockets in the crowded marketplace.

"So, let's get the Police," I calmly suggested.

Then, just as suddenly as it began, the fight was over. His accomplice abruptly returned and dragged the younger swindler away.

A little sheepishly, we returned to our room with the drums, feeling lucky the scam had failed. But something still didn't fit.

*What exactly was the con?*

As I undressed for bed, I found an Italian one hundred-lira coin in the pocket to which the boy had pointed. In a flash, all the pieces fell into place.

"Look, I've got it! I finally know how it was supposed to work."

"Oh, really?" she wearily asked.

"Well, first we'd hand him the five dirham piece. Then, he'd scream for more. Right? Well, we'd refuse and demand our money back."

"So?"

"So, he'd take the drums, like this," I demonstrated, "and give us back an Italian one hundred-lira coin instead of the five dirhams. In the dark, we wouldn't know the difference, since they're about the same size. Then, they'd disappear with the drums and the dirhams. And we'd be none the wiser."

"And one hundred liras are worth about thirteen cents."

"Exactly."

Still, it was a bittersweet victory. As I lay awake, I was saddened by the thought that they had to earn a living that way, and just a little saddened for the unwary travelers who'd fall for their scam.

The next morning was crisp and fresh like a late autumn in New England. Snow cloaked the mountains and magically transformed the seedy city into a Moorish sundae. As we hopped into the truck and climbed up higher and higher into the frosted Atlas Mountains, I was relieved to leave Marrakech's market madness.

Our truck carefully inched its way past squat adobe villages filled with waving children in brightly colored dresses. It was a world so far removed from the one below. Shepherds and their flocks lined our route along the meandering dirt road. Deep canyons and vast crevasses were etched in earthen hues of rusts and reds, grays and greens. Neatly terraced gardens lined steep hillsides. Craggy trees fought for space amid whole mountains of cactus and pink-blossomed cherry trees.

Hours and several villages later, we pulled off the road to enjoy a leisurely lunch and short stroll through the serene surrounding hills. Those unaffected, simple villagers must have thought we were an odd bunch, setting up tables, chairs and stoves alongside their pasture. Our queer mix of reggae and Reeboks clashed with a lifestyle and landscape little changed over the past millennium.

As Cheryl and I wandered off down the road toward a small village, for a moment, underneath those monumental, white-capped peaks, it was easy to forget you were in Africa. Tree-lined streams led past verdant terraces. Scrawny sheep nibbled at sparse patches of life-sustaining grass. The piercing whistle of the shepherd echoed through the canyon, as he herded his flock to higher ground.

The pastoral solitude was refreshing, only briefly interrupted by the occasional stare and approach of local children garbed in brilliant crimson dresses and scarves. An old, wrinkled, toothless woman, with a face the hue of the earth, spun hand-threaded yarn by the side of the murky river. She smiled as broadly as a jack-o-lantern as we walked past. Weary mothers herded flocks of laughing children and passive cows, sheep and goats back from the fields, as teenaged girls dreamily lounged in the grass and sang what we guessed were love songs.

By the time we reached the cluster of four two-story adobe houses, we led a virtual parade of lumbering animals, grizzled shepherds and curious children. *How lucky these people are to have such roots and continuity in their lives.*

Then, suddenly feeling very intrusive, we quickly said our good-byes, passed out a little hard candy to the squealing children and headed back.

During our spontaneous trek, the rest had finished their tea. So, we quickly loaded back into the truck and started backing up the long hill. Abruptly, the angle and precarious pitch brought us screaming to a halt. We were stuck! Tipping at a thirty-degree angle, Henry drove forward and back, again and again, sinking us deeper and deeper into the oozing mire. It was an accident, soon to become a disaster.

Nigel yelled, "Quick, let's get outta here!" and everyone flew out the door. Grabbing shovels, we started our tiring and feeble attempt at digging out, but were getting nowhere fast. After thirty minutes, we looked like mudwoggies and the truck, thanks to Henry, was deeper than ever.

At just that moment, I spotted a Moroccan Army convoy creeping over the hill. Soldiers leaned over the sides of a troop carrier and pointed at us, waving their rifles. A wave of terror briefly shot through our minds.

"Is dis some kinda restricted area?" Chester, our fleshy companion, wondered with a deep snort.

*Maybe we look more like insurgents than I thought.*

No, again we were in luck. The Moroccan Army Engineering Corps had just finished some highway construction and still had an immense earthmover in tow. After just ten minutes of tugging, pulling and digging, our truck emerged from the mire. Much to their surprise, the Moroccans' kindness was richly rewarded with several beers. Our gratitude was matched only by the huge hole we left in the soggy pasture.

The lone shepherd must have breathed a sigh of relief, too. His worst fears were almost realized. We'd almost become neighbors. Yet for us, this was just another bitter taste of what lay ahead.

The next day, we rose with the sun, climbing over six thousand feet into the mountains en route to Totra Gorge. One sharp turn led to another, then hundreds more. The wind whistled through the truck, unleashing our papers like bats. Then suddenly, we skidded to a stop at the base of a vast, endless canyon–the Gorge. Sheer red and umber cliffs towered up from the streambed. There, neatly tucked into one corner, was a contemporary looking adobe style hotel. Festively colored, flag-flying tents fringed the grounds. Cushions were perfectly arranged for relaxing in the coolness of the canyon. Inside were unexpected treats too–Western (not Turkish squat) toilets and hot showers. It had been weeks since we'd enjoyed such luxuries.

The afternoon quickly passed, as each of us set off to explore the canyon in our own way. Sprout, the brash Southerner, climbed to a rock ledge over the stream and, screaming madly, dove into the icy water below. Other overlanders, like mountain goats, scrambled up the sheer rock face of the canyon wall.

Meanwhile, Cheryl and I explored the vast recesses of the canyon, hiking about three miles farther west into the sun. A gentle wind blew, sending miniature twisters sailing through the valley. It was an ancient area, and as we walked along, I imagined what treasures might be hidden on those craggy, ochre shelves.

As dusk fell, a brilliant harvest moon illuminated the twin peaks guarding the rugged canyon. The chirping of prehistoric insects eerily echoed through the gorge, and I don't know whether it was the day or the place, but there was magic in the air.

We were the only guests of the hotel that night. We royally gorged ourselves on a feast of spicy beef kebabs, juicy tomatoes, beets, Chinese parsley and green peppers, cheese omelets and a steamed lamb and vegetable dish served in peculiar dishes resembling giant clay tops turned upside down. But that was just the beginning.

Rakish local musicians appeared out of nowhere toting several types of drums. One, similar to the flat, Irish drum, was beat with bones. Another was filled with pebbles, giving it a snare drum-like quality. Two other musicians improvised with a banjo-like instrument and the early wooden ancestor of a

31

clarinet. The drumming pounded hypnotically and the overlanders shed their inhibitions and joined in hedonistic frenzy.

The straight-laced Perfect Couple beat bongos in their best imitation of a Cuban bandleader. Bongo, a six-year old at heart, was in seventh heaven, traipsing around with his new toy, a talking drum. "Boinng...Bowoong...Boinng," it echoed, as he changed the tone by squeezing the drum's leather laced sides.

The musicians joined in the festivity, too. They'd play for awhile then leap up and whirl clumsy overlanders across the terra cotta dance floor.

At some point, late in the raucous evening Sprout and Cheryl mysteriously disappeared. I wondered if it had anything to do with Sprout's latest scheme. Both she and Pooky had had their eyes on Nigel the 'leader' from the very start. Pooky was too shy to make the first move on anything, but Sprout was a different story.

"Tonight, I'm makin' my move on Nigel," she'd earlier drawled. "I've been eyein' his skinny little body and scrawny legs for weeks," she confided, wetting her full lips. "And tonight, he's becomin' my boy-toy."

Suddenly, the music stopped. In the dimness of the candlelit room, a dark figure slithered across the floor. The vision was wrapped round and round in tight fitting gauze, like Salome's mummy.

As the rhythm started again, pagan drums beat a slow and sultry rhythm. The clarinet flew into a whining, syrupy solo. In the muted light of the smoke-filled den, the temptress sensuously writhed to the rhythms. She slid across the floor and seductively shimmied to an enchanting melody, slowly unwrapping her flimsy fabric one...layer...at...a...time.

That drove the Moroccan musicians absolutely wild! Their music became more mesmerizing and erotic as they each jumped up and danced with the siren. Then, without warning, the dancer enticingly unwrapped her shroud, reached down, pulled two large oranges from inside an oversized bra and hurled them across the room at Nigel hugging the wall.

He just sat there completely transfixed as the orbs bounced off his head.

With wild abandon, she ripped off her bra and whipped it into the audience. Her breasts assumed a perky life all their own. The entire room erupted into a sexual frenzy. One of the drummers wrapped the bra, cups pointing up, around his head and wildly danced around the room like a horned Bacchus. Two other musicians did a bump and grind in front and behind her, sandwiching her in undulating waves. Then, climbing up onto a heavy wooden table, the dancer shimmied and shook to the pulsating music.

Nigel hadn't budged in ten minutes.

Just as the music reached its grand crescendo, the dancer clad only in boxer shorts jumped down and bounded off into the night.

As the candles turned to puddles on the tables, everyone turned in. Some retired to the tents outside, others to the roof, and Sprout to Nigel's bed.

Early the next morning, amid knowing glances, we packed and left for Fez. Seems there was more than one romantic rendezvous after Sprout's 'Dance of the Seven Veils'.

*Was it the Spanish fly hors d'oeuvres? Or, just the horniness of the highway?*

Later that afternoon, we arrived in Fez where eager Azziz, a greasy son of a Casbah, quickly redirected our energies toward his special marketplace. Ah, there was the sweet smell of travelers in the air and money to be made.

The local olive market buzzed with commerce. Burros, their knees wobbly and shaking, patiently suffered in the sweltering sun. Their bellies hung low from heavy burlap sacks seeping black, oily ooze down their sides. Flies hovered like vultures around their saddened eyes, eager to land on moist flesh.

We explored the medina maze, an ageless montage of life in an ancient Moroccan town. Old men lay under cool shade trees behind latticed doors, gossiping in muted voices. Skeletal women hawked overripe melons at the marketplace. Alleyways were festooned with garlands of brightly dyed cloth and the leather tannery offered a kaleidoscope of richly colored hues.

Teenaged boys toiled in those huge multicolored vats of flesh, stirring and beating animal skins up and down in a perpetual, rhythmic motion. Their sinewy arms and legs were already stained by years of working with those vegetable dyes. Hundreds of skins, some tinted, others waiting their turn, blanketed rooftops. Pelts and hundreds of horns lay stacked in heaps, baking in the hot sun. It was equally fascinating and repulsive. The overpowering stench of decay and death seeped into our clothes and saturated our skins.

As respite, we climbed up a narrow, creaking staircase to a tiny shop where three women, a mother and her daughters, worked at looms in the corner.

Humming as they worked, they threw a wooden bobbin gliding through the web of beige camelhair yarn, brought it back again, then pulled a large wooden arm forward to compact new rows. There was a rhythm, a gentle "shu-shu-ponk, shu-shu-ponk," to their work, but we represented twenty-three potential sales. There was more important work to be done.

The weary weaver proudly pulled out each blanket, gushing, "See the fine workmanship. Notice the colors. What designs."

Then began the mock-serious haggling over a camelhair blanket with his overeager son. We trod a fine line between blasé indifference and blue-light special zeal. Still, after twenty minutes, his price and ours were more than $15 apart. Neither of us was budging. So, disappointed and convinced we'd never agree, we escaped to the harsh glare of the street.

However, Azziz followed us, still struggling to make that sale. "It is a beautiful blanket. One of a kind, yes? Please sir, offer him just $5 more. He is sure to take that."

That sounded reasonable. So we returned with a second offer, but the merchant still stubbornly refused. Frustrated, we left again.

"Wait, wait!" Azziz cried, scrambling into the truck after us. "Sir, I know this man will sell for just $5 more."

"Oh, so that's the routine. You're going to work us back up to $15. No, I don't think so."

"But this man is a very good friend. I know he wants to sell you the blanket," he gushed. "And you want it too, yes?" he added with a wink.

"Okay, tell him just $5 more," I said. "If he wants to sell, have him send it with you to the restaurant tonight."

Azziz flew out of the truck.

That evening, as part of our Fez tour, we were herded to a local tourist-trap of a restaurant, featuring an overweight belly dancer and budget-busting beers at 12 dirhams each. It instantly confirmed two of our foolproof rules for budget travel: "Never eat in places that cater to tour groups," and "Avoid places with credit card stickers plastered everywhere."

From past experience, we knew those restaurants assume: (1) travelers don't know the value of the local money, or (2) travelers are on unlimited expense accounts. They habitually miscalculate bills, charge for items never ordered, or substitute more expensive selections and advise you later. We'd seen that old trick from Prague to Paris and Bombay to Bangkok. At 90 dirhams a head, our dinner, similar to the one in the Gorge, cost nearly as much as a local worker's daily wages.

*And personally, I enjoyed Sprout's gyrations more.*

Finally, at nearly 9:00, Azziz arrived with the blanket and discretely waved us into the back room. I felt like Ali Baba. As we sat among the Persian rugs, I inspected the prized blanket and secretively paid the weasel off. Azziz thanked us profusely and smiled a brown tobacco-stained grin. Allah had truly smiled on him. Not only would he receive his touring fee, but he'd also collect a cadeau from the blanket shop, plus a kickback from the restaurant. Indeed. Good fortune traveled in the guise of gullible overlanders.

The next few days, we continued our headlong collision into an unavoidable logistical problem. Nearly half our group, the English, whom the Aussies and Kiwis unaffectionately had dubbed the 'POMs' (short for "Property of Her Majesty"), couldn't enter Algeria across the Moroccan land border. Because of recent political chaos, they had to fly directly into Oran. The rest of us were forced to drive two full days out of our way to drop them off, then rendezvous near the Algerian coast. Even Nigel and Henry had to fly across.

So, after a rushed tour of Volubulous, the farthest southern outpost of the Roman Empire, they bought plane tickets and returned to our campsite where we met Anton, our temporary Kiwi driver. Relief came early the next day–and not a moment too soon.

For weeks, everyone had done their best to ignore the young, spoiled 'POMs'' constant 'whingeing'. Now, I've known my share of Englishmen before and have had some great times trekking or sharing a pint or three with them. Plus, I make it a point to judge people on their own merits–not their nationality. But these folks, well, they were 'different'. Nothing was ever quite 'proper' enough. In the past weeks, the Aussies, Kiwis, Canadians and, yes, even the Americans bit their tongues and bided their time. However, the tension was thinly veiled and built with each passing day.

Reaching the airport, the POMs gathered up their ton of tea and personal gear and traipsed off to their waiting plane.

"No more POMs! No more POMs!" the remaining overlanders shouted.

The English merely shook their heads and laughed at what they thought was a joke.

*So much for their legendary sense of humor.*

In fact, as soon as they left, everyone instantly relaxed. We smiled and kidded. Finally, there were no more national rivalries, no leader rivalry, no tensions, and none of the constant whining. At last, at least temporarily, we were a team. It felt great. And as for Sprout and her boy-toy, well, it was only for a few days and Nigel just might return a better man.

By 5 o'clock that afternoon, we arrived at the Algerian border, our first 'real' African border experience. The Moroccan border had been too simple, like crossing from Mexico to the US. In contrast, the Algerian concrete cubicle was starkly serious and darkly sinister. Shadowy characters, faces hidden by ragged robes, haunted the stoop outside the Customs room. Furrowed old men rolled cigarettes, coughed and spit phlegm, forming green craters in the red dust. Goats nibbled fermenting trash and the putrid stench from Algeria's nastiest toilet enveloped our truck in a haze.

It all began simply enough. We each filled out multiple forms and had our passports stamped. Then we waited, paced and waited some more. As luck would have it, the Customs hut's electricity suddenly shut off just after the last of our group finished their mandatory one-thousand dinar exchange and we were plunged into darkness. Still, we waited and whispered in hushed tones for another two hours.

"Wonder what the POMs are doin' neeoww?" Dropsy, our head of "Securrriteee," (as she would often shriek), asked.

Mild-mannered Willie snorted, "They're sippin' gin & tonics poolside, I reckon."

"More'n likely," barman Slim ventured, "they've had tea and found a 'proper' steak."

A customs official, dripping with Saharan sweat, popped his head inside the truck.

"Can we leave?" Anton our substitute driver asked, eager to end our sadistic reststop.

"Perhaps," the official replied, in a voice that suggested there were ways to hasten the process.

Anton quickly caught his drift and grabbed five beers from behind his front seat.

The official smiled broadly, whispering, "Do yoo have eeny hasheesh?"

*Is this a trick question?*

"No sirrrr," we sang out, like a group of wayward school kids.

And we were on our way, headed for a blissful night camped under a luminous canopy of a billion stars.

Breakfast and breakdown of the camp the next morning was unusually efficient. We hummed with unheard-of teamwork. Everyone pitched in and we set off in record time.

For the next several hours we snaked along winding roads toward Oran, until finally turning a blind corner, we emerged at the Mediterranean. We knew it was the last we'd see her shimmering waters (or any other) for months. So, like kids on summer holiday, we reveled in the afternoon sun, picnicked on a golden beach and played pickup soccer.

How many realized then that this was the last time we'd ever act like a real team?

Continuing all afternoon into Oran, we arrived at the hotel and instantly locked horns with the anxious POMs. Showered, shaved, sipped and stuffed, they were ready to move on.

"So where are our rooms?" Cheryl asked, eager to relax under cool sheets.

"Oh, you don't want to stay here," Trotsky cautioned, shaking his blond wanna-be dreadlocks.

"This place is just filthy," Fluffy whined, as she stomped her foot on the cool-tiled floor.

"Hey, we've just spent two long days drivin' here to pick you up," Clara added.

"Yes, but there are no hot showers here," Pooky whimpered.

I wiped my forehead, admitting, "Look, we're beat and could use a night in a real bed."

"Disgusting loos. Disgusting!" Duchess added, hydraulically raising her full lips to a pucker.

"Why's this have to be such a problem?" Bear argued.

"We jest wanna scrape the crud off!" reasoned Willie.

"Yea, it's been more 'an a week," Slim added, "since we've slept inside."

"And days since our last bath," Maxie squawked.

To that, Perfect Wife harrumphed, "Well, *we* don't want to spend another night here."

Nigel, in Solomon's wisdom, suggested a vote. It was our first and last of the trip, but we narrowly won. The only concession was that we'd have to share showers.

*Now that, that I can handle.*

# Chapter III
# Survival in the Sahara

*"Blind belief is dangerous."*
~ African proverb

*I*F TRAVEL HAD TAUGHT US ANYTHING in the past it was to approach life with an exuberant skepticism. Trust was never given lightly. With us, it had to be earned. Still, we remained determined to enjoy ourselves, take things in stride and remember that we were in this for a long time, ("not necessarily a good time," as Cheryl cautioned). So we tried to file all the petty irritations, insults and bad choices of the past few weeks away and concentrate on the future–since that's where we were headed.

We left early the next morning, wending southwest toward the oasis town of Taghit. As we reached the Hauts Plateau, the terrain changed dramatically as it flattened out into an endless, chalky expanse. Gnarled, misshapen trees appeared like emaciated scarecrows guarding a field of void. Heat waves rose off cracked, parched earth. Monolithic mountains lay like sleeping giants on saffron sand. There were few people; just the occasional hollow-faced ghost of the desert. No more smiling children. No cries of "Cadeau, cadeau," echoed across the wasteland. It was the most desolate stretch of nothingness ever imagined. And what worried me most was that we weren't even in what was formally known as 'the desert'. Not yet.

Unfortunately, the Sahara is growing in Africa at an alarming rate, due to local human activities and the 'Greenhouse' effect. So, official distinctions often don't keep up with the stark reality.

Throughout the day we continued our weary trek over miles of bleak terrain until just before nightfall when we drove back to the base of a small, crumbling mountain set well off the main dirt road. At first glance, nothing set it apart from dozens of similar craggy slopes passed earlier. But carefully scaling the mountainside, we detected a sight both eerie and awesome. There, in the middle of nowhere, incredible Neolithic sandstone carvings were intricately etched into the mountain wall. There were hauntingly beautiful plumed ostriches, elephants and bounding wildebeests. Primeval hunters tossed timeless spears, while people danced and celebrated life.

It fired my imagination. I'd seen mysterious petroglyphs in the lava beds of Hawai'i and in the Arizona desert, plus we'd studied intriguing Neanderthal cave paintings of Dordogne, France. Yet the Saharan etchings were important for a different reason. They were left as silent testament by ancient travelers, like us, who passed through long ago in search of creatures that no longer exist on that arid plateau. They were our forefathers on that ultimate journey called 'life'.

With nightfall, the sun cast shadows into the etched crevices. Then, as their artists had done, the petroglyphs disappeared with time.

Sometime in the darkness of the middle of the hushed night, we heard an explosive noise. It grew closer and closer, louder and more frightening each second. Rushing from our tents in dazed consciousness, we appeared just in time to see a miniature small-gauge steam locomotive chug by just yards from our fragile neon tent pyramids.

The next morning, we continued our drive along vanishing highways. Miles of fields of rocks and pathetic looking scrub melded into golden shifting sands. Perhaps once an hour, small desert villages of mud and wood-hewn houses appeared, interrupting an otherwise foreboding landscape.

"Wait a second!" Prudence shrieked.

"What's that?" Dropsy chirped.

No, it couldn't be... A tiny shop with a sign dangling by a single chain promised our most erotic fantasy, our most coveted desire of the past few days.

*Is it a mirage? Or is the ninety-degree heat slowly baking our brains?*

Nigel slammed on the brakes. Twenty-three of us leaped down from the truck like kids rushing to a swimming hole in the summer's first heat. We crowded inside the small, darkened, mud walled shop.

"Ice cream?" Dropsy screeched, as Prudence craned over the counter.

The bearded mouse of a man behind the counter looked a little intimidated by all of us pressed so near his vintage icebox in the corner.

"Maybe he doesn't speak English," I offered.

"Glace du chocolat?" Duchess asked in her best Essex French.

"Ah, non," he answered.

"Pourquoi?"

"Parce-que il est l'hiver," he declared, matter of fact.

Duchess snorted, "Because it's winter? It's bloody ninety degrees!"

"Winter? How can that be?" Prudence moaned. "We're in the Sahara!"

"Has he been outside?" Pooky grumbled, at which Bongo chimed in, "In the last century?" Still, no amount of complaining could make that frozen treat magically appear.

"Ya git that on the long trips!" Chester huffed, as we all reluctantly climbed back into our truck, which by then doubled as a Dutch oven. Sensuous, deliciously imagined tastes sat temptingly for a moment on our parched tongues. Then, they too melted away, reclaimed by the desert heat.

*Sometimes life's pleasures are just a mirage.*

As our long drive to the Taghit desert oasis continued, towns became as sparse as cooling breezes. The air itself seemed thrust from a gigantic furnace aimed at every inch of our bodies for sixteen hours and there was no relief.

Nearing the eastern Moroccan border, the road became rife with roadblocks made of empty oil drums. Platoons of bored and greedy soldiers stopped our truck every few miles. Depending solely on their mood, they could ignore us, search us, delay us for hours or send us on a deadly detour into sandy oblivion.

"You have 'cadeau', monsieur?" the rust-colored, mustachioed soldier in rubber sandals demanded. "Une stylo? Une cassette ees good."

For just such occasions, Nigel kept stacks of 'special' cassettes in a separate bag. "Oh, let me see," he said digging deep into Santa's sack. "Ah, this is very popular in England now," he promised, handing the grateful guard an audio cassette. It was all tit-for-tat. We played our own version of the game. Although they looked new, Nigel's 'special' tapes were either empty or broken. By the time the officials discovered it, we were miles across shifting sands.

The soldier beamed a brown-stained smile, glad to win another little round of desert extortion. "Ah, merci!" he laughed. Then, with a tip of his hat, he waved us down the road.

The desert, contrary to popular belief, is far from flat. It's a patchwork of bronze, top-hatted mesas, craggy mountains, far-reaching dunes and small barren hills. As we crested one such rise in the road, an entire ocean of sand soared in front of us, golden with the last rays of the setting sun. Directly below, in its shadow, lay the small adobe town of Taghit: one hotel and two restaurants at the base of enormous dunes of shining undulating sand. It was truly an oasis fringed by tiny bubbling streams and lone date palms. And this time, it was no mirage.

We quickly moved into the Moorish-style hotel, eager to scrub days of desert sand off our encrusted bodies and feast on 'proper steaks'. It was sheer 'luxxxurry' and a haven of relief after days in that inferno.

Early the next morning, while the truck's tires were being changed into Goliath desert sand paws, Cheryl and I hiked to the top of the highest dune we could find. Only when we reached the summit were we struck with just how expansive that moving sea of sand really was. Hundreds of feet above the Lilliputian village, impressive dunes stretched miles behind us, as far as the eye could see. Down below, clusters of palms looked like tiny drink umbrellas poked into a sandbox. Adobe huts, the size of toy train houses, were mere mud splotches. Ancient village walls became thin lines etched on a tapestry of gold. Traces of animal and reptile tracks surrounded us, reminding us that even in the desert you were never alone.

Although you look at them for hours, you never realize how 'great' the great ergs of the Sahara are until you start to cross them. We quickly discovered that, as caressing dunes quickly melted away into another flat, treeless expanse. The next several days became one monotonous stretch of endless wasteland. The simple pleasures of tiny Taghit quickly became phantasms to occupy our restless, sun-stewed minds.

A crust of fine powder shrouded everyone's hair and eyes, coating our tongues and ears. My lips were parched and cracking. Water was rationed. Although our tanks carried over three hundred gallons, we had to conserve it in case of a real emergency–like becoming stranded. It wasn't as if you could just call AAA.

"It's hot," Chester, the three hundred-pound overlander moaned, "damned hot," as he swam in a pool of his own sweat in the back of the truck. Although the rest of us changed seats daily, red-faced Chester stayed sequestered in the back seats, often by himself. Maybe it was best, because his hygiene could seriously ruin our appetites for days. Nurse Clara, at everyone's urging, even tried coaxing him into a bath for everyone's sake, but he remained unfazed, a lump in the backseat.

For the rest of us, much of each day was spent seeking sleep. It was our only respite from an oppressive heat. Still, while we were moving, we were surviving. Each minute brought us closer to In Salah, another oasis with life-sustaining water.

Another day passed. The oppressive heat continued to drain our energy, as one dune led to another. We were too tired to argue. Even the '21' card games, a constant with this overlanding gang, ceased. The seats were filled with twenty-two heaps of searing flesh. Even Henry, our fearless co-leader, lay sprawled out face down out in the aisle.

Meanwhile, the desert played tricks with our minds. The road would be enticingly flawless for ten miles or so. Then, it'd cruelly fade into nothing but unmarked sand.

*I've never had such a feeling of being so totally alone, even with these others. We haven't spotted another vehicle for days, or seen the road for hours. Are we even headed in the right direction? It's anyone's guess.*

The truck's compass fluid had evaporated days earlier. Only the tall, white posts, poking from the sand every five kilometers or so, reassured us that we weren't hopelessly lost.

Still, as bad as things seemed, they could and did turn worse. Driving became more hazardous as we entered the 'piste' or deep, soft sand. It could bury a truck up to its sides in seconds if you didn't know how to drive in it. As soon as Henry took over driving from Nigel, we knew we were in deep trouble. He'd never driven in sand before. In fact, we discovered the only part of Africa he'd ever driven before was the road between Nairobi, Kenya and Harare, Zimbabwe. There was no piste, only hardtop. It only took a few moments with him at the wheel to confirm our worst fears. We were stuck–and stuck deep. We all piled out into the wintry ninety-degree blast furnace.

*There's nothing like a hot slap in the face to make you feel alive. And there's nothing like having sand blanket your tires up to the top of the wheel wells to make you feel dead.*

It began a process we'd repeat far too often over the next few laborious months: Sandmatting 101. It made me appreciate camels.

Sandmats are twelve-foot metal tracks carried on the truck's sides. In theory, they're supposed to give you enough solid, artificial ground to get moving again. In practice, they allow you to plow through the desert for twelve feet at a time.

As a few of us dug the endless stream of soft sand from around the tires, the others shoved the long metal sandmats under the massive front or rear tires, or both. Then we all got behind the truck, dug in and "pushhhhhed!"

Henry gunned the engine like a bull charging at a rodeo gate and hurled our straining truck another fifty feet until he lost momentum and was quickly stuck again. Of course, Henry should have taken it slow and steady, like he was driving in snow. But his driving matched his personality. We repeated the futile exercise again and again until it became obvious we were literally pushing the truck through the Sahara. Finally, even Nigel's infinite patience wore thin and he took the wheel.

Our luck immediately improved. We were moving again, slowly but continuously. We passed the occasional date palm. Impressive buttes and mesas rose off the barren desert sands. And then, just as suddenly, there was nothingness again–or worse. Rising from out of nowhere, like a swarming desert hurricane, sand encapsulated the truck. There was no north or south. No up or down–only sand.

*Where are we? Where's our kilometer marker? We should have seen several by now.*

But we kept on inching through the sandstorm. Finally, another stretch of piste jarred us to a sudden stop. Taking advantage of the pause, I wrapped my red kerchief across my face, climbed to the roof, and with binoculars scanned the horizon for a marker in any direction.

"Hey, there it is!" I shouted to Nigel. As near as I could guess, the post sat about five miles to our east. Within minutes, we'd driven that far off-course.

Hours later, dusty but relieved, we finally staggered into the one-camel village of In Salah on the edge of the Sebkra Mekerrhane oasis. A village never looked so welcome, a hotel so inviting. It was Cheryl's birthday and we celebrated by ordering lamb, the only item in the kitchen, and something capable of making my partner nauseous even on a good day. Still, the sheets lent coolness to the serenity of our own private oasis and we reveled in its romantic seclusion.

Early the next day, we loaded our desert caravan and headed south across the Mouydi to Tamanrasset. I was looking forward to reaching 'Tam'. It was notorious as an ancient desert outpost offering more than one hotel and market, an eatery and a few scrawny mules or camels. However again, our simple fantasies were soon dashed. About five hours outside In Salah, there was a sudden, loud "Kaabouughhhh-pppaaaadon-nnkkkkk, donnnk, donnk." We'd blown out one of our two hundred pound sand tires.

*"Polepole!" indeed.*

As the guys struggled to replace it over the next two hours, the daily cook crew, shirtless and wiping sweat from their grimy faces with our dishcloth, whipped up a typical lunch of salad and fried bread. For some insane reason, we had salad and bread, bread and salad for days. Some days, the bread was fried. On others, it would be sliced in petite pieces and served with tea. Consequently, all the men were rapidly losing weight on the 'Sahara Weight Loss Plan'. I was already down ten pounds and Chester was melting before our eyes.

Finally, tire replaced and fully breaded-up, we visited one of the more mysterious places in the Sahara, a Muslim holy man's house. Tradition had it that you must circle his house three times in respect, or something terrible will happen. We'd heard about an American couple in a VW van who'd scoffed at the story and just drove by. Right down the road, their gasoline can exploded, turning their van into a rolling barbecue.

We circled the house.

It must have worked, because sixteen hours later, completely exhausted but with no major fires, we limped into the last major town in the southern Sahara. Tamanrasset is home to the fabled and ferocious 'Blue Men' (no relation to the Las Vegas troupe of the same name). 'Tam' sits at the base of the Hoggar Mountains. Technically volcanic plugs, the red, craggy monoliths resemble the mesas of Arizona's Monument Valley. However, from its location on a map, you could easily call it one of the most remote spots on earth.

Entering the village's one and only official campsite, we were thrust into the company of every other equally scruffy modern Western nomad who'd made the recent crossing. There was a French couple in an old Citroen, Germans in a VW bug, a motorcycling Dutchman and Japanese camped in ultra-lite tents. There was even another overland beast full of more whiners demanding en masse, "Where's the loo? When's the water come on? Where can we get a beer 'round here?"

Cheryl and I wasted no time in leaving the motley pack and wandering into town. After the past few weeks spent with our odd companions, we desperately needed time alone since our fantasy journey was not going as expected. This warped concept of group overland travel grated against our personal style and very reason for traveling. We were segregated from the exotic life and people we'd traveled a world and lifetime to embrace. Oh, how we craved to meet the locals. We wanted to taste local food, stay in local places, get by on our own wits and feel some well-earned satisfaction at the end of the day.

*Maybe Tam will be our chance.*

As we made the short, dusty walk into that village of mud adobe huts, fierce looking men, decked out in deep blue robes, turbans and daggers, galloped by on camels. These were the nomadic Tuareg Blue Men, so called because the dye of their clothing rubbed off and permanently stained their skin a deep indigo. Legendary for bitterly fighting the French Foreign Legion during occupation, they still considered themselves citizens of the Sahara, not Algeria.

Roaming through that windswept village, its extreme isolation kept slapping us in the face like the grains of sand itself. Stores were fewer than expected and prices higher than in Morocco.

As one wizened, robed merchant explained, "Zat ees because all zee prices are based on zee black market rate of twenty-four dinar to zee dollaire–not zee official rate of eight to zee dollaire."

Still, what treasures the stores did offer up and down that Wild West main street were beautifully crafted. There were brilliant amber filigreed jewelry, silver Agadez crosses, jeweled daggers, black, red and white goat hair tapestries, Tuareg indigo robes, blankets, and intricately woven grass mats.

Tam was undeniably unique. It was an East meets West, 20th century collides with the 16th century sort of place. Tuaregs camped in tents not far from a luxurious air-conditioned hotel. Local women's faces were shrouded behind dark robes and veils. However young men, in their best sense of desert cool, hung out in cafés and ogled Western women in their skintight t-shirts–or less.

We were supposed to continue that same day to a monastery deep in the Hoggars. But arriving back at camp, rival overlanders told us it took them over five hours and 1,000 dinars each to go back into those hills. Even then, they weren't allowed to drive back to the site. Under different circumstances, it could have been exciting. However, sensing it was an accident waiting to happen, Cheryl, Sprout and I decided to stay in town. We opted to learn more about that unusual slice of the desert life, instead of traipsing another ten hours into the mountains.

"Besides," I reminded Cheryl, "it'll be a relief to finally have some time to ourselves away from the others."

So, while Nigel, Henry and the rest departed for what they promised would be a peaceful day in the mountains, we checked into a cozy local hotel. Then we contentedly roamed the village, bargained in the marketplace, satiated our appetites with local cuisine and washed down sand-flecked baguettes with harsh Algerian red wine.

Within two days, instead of one, the other overlanders limped back into camp. Not surprisingly, their trip hadn't gone as planned.

"Yea, the mountains were great," Bear the mechanic confided, "but no luck gettin' to the monastery."

"Henry ground truck gears over mountains and across valleys for two days, non-stop," nurse Clara added, shaking her head.

Still, with everyone now totally exhausted and dispirited, water cans were methodically refilled, the truck was hurriedly repacked and we immediately set off limping south toward Mali.

"Too bad they'll never get to see Tam," I whispered, as we bounced and jostled out of town. For once, Cheryl and I were rested and ready to go. We had no regrets. The peace and serenity we'd discovered in those two short days was worth staying behind.

The tarmac quickly ended just outside Tam, turning into another dusty, rutted sand path running in all directions to the horizon. With Henry at the wheel, we were soon back to sandmatting, as our truck careened from one soft patch of sand right into the next. At one point, we went through this futile exercise four times in an hour. Henry just didn't get it!

"Can't this idiot see where ee's goin'?" Chester, the Cockney truck driver on holiday demanded, as we moaned in unison.

Even Maxie, the tough cocktail waitress and Henry's new overlandin' girlfriend, rolled her blue eyes in exasperation every time he'd get us stuck again.

At some point, I don't know if was delirium from the heat, but it just did not matter anymore. Sandmatting gave us plenty of time for sunbathing, lunch and to search for rare firewood. Meanwhile, it gave the Sahara time to find its way into every cranny and crevice of our bodies–with no water in sight for four or five days.

*Not too long ago, this very area must have been an oasis of green, a respite from the relentless sands. Now, it just another stretch of pitifully parched plains.*

Even in the midst of the Sahara, we were seldom alone. We passed Tuareg encampments with a few scrawny goats, placid, slobbering camels and the ever-smiling, waving children. I suspect they must have found it great fun to see us dig-dig-digging our truck out of their village.

However eventually, we became so desperately stuck that it became our campsite for the night. Then came the bad news.

"I hate to tell you this," Nigel started in his best stiff-upper-lipped tone, "but it seems we have a small gearbox problem."

*It couldn't have anything to do with Henry's continuous gear-grinding, could it?*

"So, it means we either have to return to Tam–or risk a serious breakdown in the desert at any time."

Crestfallen, in the morning we headed back, convinced a few days in Tam were better than a lifetime spent in one of those skeletons of a car protruding from a graveyard of sand we'd passed all too often.

Returning to the campsite at Tam, Bear, Nigel and Chester worked on the truck all afternoon, tearing out the gearbox. It was fortunate we'd stopped when we did. Both lower gears and bearings were shot. We were even luckier to have a real mechanic like Bear on board. Nigel, ever the bureaucrat, fired off a telex to London requesting a new gearbox. He didn't even bother to look for one in town or in Algiers because he was "a little low on personal cash."

"Maybe luck's on our side," Cheryl naively suggested. "Maybe London will have the part, ship it here and they'll install it right away," she added wistfully. "It might only take us five days."

*Right. If wishes were camels, overlanders would ride.*

Five days passed with still no sign of our gearbox. Tam's novelty had turned to tragedy. Having only the illusion of comfort was sometimes worse than doing without completely. At our desert 'campsite,' there was cold running water for an hour each morning and sometimes an hour at night. About seventy overlanders patiently stood in long lines waiting for their spin of the shower wheel, hoping for a chance to cool off, a chance to break up the monotony. Instead, they found a farce in waiting. Some days we'd wait an hour in queue. Finally get soaped up–then the water would drizzle to a stop. However, that was just the beginning.

The camp's squat Turkish toilets overflowed with fresh, steaming sludge by ten each morning and there was no water to wash the waste down. So it sat fermenting through the heat of the day.

Dogs began their barking serenade at 3 a.m., just early enough to wake the roosters. Then the reggae music began as an old stretched Bob Marley tape wailed.

At this point, Prudence, our food policewoman, took the opportunity to further tighten breakfast rations. "Only two wheat biscuits per person," she scowled, then actually hovered near the tables keeping a watchful eye out for breakfast deviants.

Our other haute d'cuisine didn't fare much better. Lunch for twenty-three consisted of four small loaves of gritty, goat-flavored bread with dysentery-laden lettuce leaves and fermenting, squashed tomatoes. Predictably, the bread only lasted through the first twelve campers. Dinner featured succulent half-cooked carrot and zucchini slices with three meager, emaciated chickens split twenty-three ways.

Cheryl and I became increasingly dispirited. Nigel's lack of action was puzzling.

*How can he be so inept? Why doesn't he do something more? Actually look for the part here? Or, in Algiers?*

"He said the London office is sure the part's on its way," Cheryl assured me with a certain tentativeness.

"I guess that satisfies him. He'd done his job. Meanwhile, he's conveniently rented a room at the only air-conditioned luxury hotel in town."

Henry, the 'real' overlander (as he often reminded us), was now bedded down with Maxie and she was reportedly supporting him until the trip ended, then he was headed for Australia.

I secretly hoped there were mounds of sand 'down-under'. Heaps. Already, Henry's never-ending, condescending carping about 'Americans' made me wonder how long it would be before I hauled off and decked him. At first, I tried not to take his insults too personally. I actually felt sorry for close-minded people like Henry, who automatically lump everyone of the same nationality, race or religion together in neat little boxes. Still, I resented the way that those folks assumed that our personal beliefs, priorities and politics, whether Americans, Brits, Muslims or Tuaregs, were identical to our governments'.

Funny. For days, our delegation deviously plotted to mix dried camel dung with oregano then sprinkle it onto Henry's spaghetti dinner, as one sure-fire way to end his constant Yank insults. Oh, how close we'd come. Lucky for him, imagining it was nearly as satisfying as actually doing it.

Meanwhile, each day became a contest of physical and mental survival. Which was the greater challenge? The ferocious biting flies? Or our fight with boredom?

True to form, we handled stress in different ways. Fluffy, our young student friend with the big hair, spent her days reclining, oiled up in a lounge chair where she worked on the ultimate Saharan tan. Duchess, the comely English débutante, eagerly tried to rev the engine of a Dutch motorcyclist. Henry and Maxie, and Nigel and Sprout were holed up at the luxury hotel. Bongo, the head-banging drummer and Flinty, identical in their Algerian robes and high-topped tennies, took off for a night in the desert with our one and only bottle of tequila. Cheryl and I passed hours reading in the 'fly-free zone' of our sweltering tent. The rest of the overlanders promised they'd be fine—"at least till the beer ran out."

Their total passivity was totally inconceivable to me. No one said anything about our dilemma, except Trotsky, that skinny bean-counter.

"Ahheoo, there's sand in my bag," he cried one evening, shaking his dreadlocks in a tizzy.

*Well, what did he expect to find in the middle of the Sahara?*

Even Sprout, relaxing in the luxury of Tam's finest, had her days. A would-be Algerian suitor, whom we unaffectionately nicknamed the Worm Man, worked at her hotel. For days they'd meet at the front desk and exchange "Hellos." Finally, one day he brazenly followed her to her room. Cornering her in the dark shadows of the hall, he grabbed her tightly and growled, "I will have you!"

She slapped him hard across his squirming face.

This only made him more determined. He threw her up against the wall, wrenching her arm behind her, shouting, "I am your boyfriend. And I will have you before I leave for my village!" With that threat, he left.

She was terrified and came running to me with the news. Since the start of our safari Cheryl and I had taken Sprout under our wings. She was like an uninhibited, little Louisiana sister to me. So, I was absolutely livid when I heard.

*Why do they think Western women are such easy prey? They'd never try that with an Arab woman.*

The next day, I cornered Worm Man in the busy hotel restaurant. Grabbing him hard by his lapels, I pulled his face so close to mine that I could smell his stench.

"If you ever speak to my friend again," I snarled, "If you ever touch her, if you ever even look at her again, you will never have children! Do you understand?"

All the color left his face. He gasped for air, nodded a spineless head and disappeared into the kitchen. Sprout never had any more problems.

*Sometimes quiet diplomacy is no substitution for downright intimidation.*

Meanwhile, back at camp, the overlanders started to drop like flies–or because of them. Poor Cheryl spent most of the day in our tent amid loud heaves and diarrhea. Plus, some crawly thing in the night (I know it wasn't me) had bitten her, giving her lips a lopsided swelling like a collagen injection gone bad. Clara, Bongo, Fluffy and Nigel were so ill that they camped out in the loo. Perfect Wife convulsed, then 'perfectly' passed out from heat exhaustion and had to be carried into our truck that was set up as a first aid station. Meanwhile, Perfect Husband's finger swelled to the size of a cucumber after it was bitten one night.

Every day, I questioned what kept us there.

*It's far from what we had in mind–less than our ideal way to see Africa. We're ready to set off on our own. It has to be safer. But no, we're financially forced to suffer through this African boot camp, since I'm sure they won't refund our money.*

It disgusted me to have no other option, and infuriated me that everyone else was so content with playing cards all day and drinking and cranking up the music at night. I could only imagine all the Africa we'd miss because we were stranded–and ultimately had a schedule to keep.

We were tired of their incompetence. Henry's inflated ego and taunting attitude became as tiring as the relentless heat and blowing sands. His lack of experience in Africa was only exceeded by his lack of mechanical skills or leadership.

Oh, he was the master of leading competitions, as if that might make us like each other better or create esprit de corps. One night, after organizing arm-wrestling competitions for the group, including the ladies, he whispered aloud to Fluffy, "As a favor, will you please go over there and kick Brandon in the groin, so I can beat him tonight?"

That pretty much said it all.

*I miss my island home and feel so alone at times. I'm deeply sad that this experience is slowly strangling one of the few real loves in my life–travel.*

Finally, after seven days of scorching in that barren wasteland waiting for the gearbox, Nigel called a group meeting.

"I know you've all been wondering about our part. All I know is that it's supposed to be here any day now."

"Yea, that's what they've been sayin' for seven days now," Sprout drawled.

"I know. I will personally fly to Algiers tomorrow to pick up a gearbox if the London shipment doesn't come in on the morning flight.

*Have a good trip.*

'Tomorrow' came and went, and there was no sign of Nigel. He went into hiding, but hapless Henry finally appeared and said that he was trying to get a ticket to Algiers to pick up the part but, "These things take time."

*Time? What's he want? It's already been eight days.*

In utter frustration, and yet another two days later, Nigel finally called London to have them trace the whereabouts of the missing part. Our gearbox was still sitting in Heathrow Airport. For ten days it had been bumped-off flights and no one bothered to check.

*These past ten days in the desert, the sickness and the boredom have been for nothing. Nada.*

Sprout was furious. Suddenly bounding up, she started digging through the heap of bags in the back locker and threw hers out into the sand. Curiously, no one said anything.

Finally, I walked over and innocently asked, "Can I help?"

"I've had it. I'm leavin'."

"Think about where you are. We're in the middle of the Sahara."

"I don't care!"

"Well, I don't want to run across a bleached skeleton toting a designer bag in a few days."

"Yea, well, I don't know how much more I can take."

"Neither do I. Neither do I."

Sprout slung her bags over her shoulder and slowly trudged the two miles back to town where she spent the next two hours crying on the hotel rooftop.

We'd had enough. Tam had become our prison. During lunch we could set our watches by the relentless storms that blew across the desert. We'd see them swirling off in the distance like brown twisters. They'd spin closer and closer, sweeping up everything in their path, until finally they'd engulf the campsite and our meager meals. We were helpless in their path. We'd just pull kerchiefs up over our faces, cover our bread, duck and hope for the best.

At last, Perfect Husband, Bear and I pored over the maps for several days and decided to continue on our own. Nigel's organization was bad enough. But now, the company's inaction made the trip more dangerous than ever.

The next day, I broke the news to Nigel. "We want out. Cheryl, Sprout, Perfect Couple, Bear, Clara and I have talked. We've had it. We've wasted eleven days in this hellhole."

"Well, I'm s-sorry," he stammered. "Henry's on his way to Algiers now to get the part."

I'd heard that before. "Good luck to him–and you. We'll finish Africa on our own."

A shocked look went over his face. If Bear and Clara left, he'd lose his mechanic and nurse. Would the others leave too, now that the beers were gone?

"I'll telex my boss," he promised, "but I don't think you'll get your f-fares or kitty money back if you leave."

"Well, let us know," I said, disgusted with the whole ordeal.

Our threat was worth a try. Seven of us had made plans, but when push came to shove I knew that only Sprout, Cheryl and I were totally resolute. As we were busy planning the ins-and-outs of finishing the trip ourselves, Henry breezed into camp.

*He's supposed to be on his way to Algiers. Something's strange. What is it? Look at his face.*

The night before, he drank gin with the other overland group until he passed out. As a little surprise, they shaved off his left eyebrow to mail to his boss in London. So, there he was looking strangely lopsided like the cartoon dog with the black ring around his eye–and he was scheduled to go through a strict Muslim customs office the next morning.

Henry finally left (with a bandage above his eye) and eventually returned with our part. Cheers greeted his arrival, as if he'd found the Holy Grail. That afternoon, Bear and pathetic Nigel performed the successful operation in the shade of one of the camp's scrawny trees. Meanwhile, Nigel and I reached an understanding. Cheryl, Sprout and I would continue with the group only to Nairobi and they'd refund our fare from there to Harare. They had such a seat-of-the-pants operation that they couldn't afford to set a precedent by refunding all our money so early.

So, although we'd have preferred to leave right away, we'd hold out till Kenya. That would take us at least halfway through Africa, perhaps the most difficult part.

Later that afternoon, we suggested to the group that we treat Bear and Clara to a free night at the local hotel. He was ultimately responsible for replacing the gearbox (for free) and she'd tended the walking wounded for nearly two weeks. Well, the group was quick to nix that idea and instead decided to give them a cake made from a loaf of bread.

*How pathetic. How true to form.*

As everyone struck their sand-filled tents, packed sand-filled bags with sandy clothes and stuffed sand-filled boxes with sandy food, Cheryl and I took one last nostalgic trek down the familiar windswept streets of Tam. It was a day like all the rest had been. Goats bleated a greeting in the distance. Proud Tuaregs rode past in a whirlwind of flowing robes. Women, with full baskets balanced on their heads, shuffled across the dusty street. Young men checked us out from their corner cafe, and merchants tried to lure us into shops from shadowed doorways.

Every day during our unexpected two-week visit people had asked when we were leaving. Finally, I could reply, "Today, thank Allah, today."

# Chapter IV
# The Cosmic Dance

*"A fool and water will go the way they are diverted."*
~ African proverb

*O*VER THE NEXT SEVERAL DAYS, we wended our way south
through the Sahara until we painlessly entered Mali, the largest country
in west Africa and twice the size of France. Because of the two weeks lost in
Tam, we were uncertain whether it was still wise to veer west across one of
the world's most desolate stretches to the ancient salt caravan town of
Timbuktu. Or simply continue directly south to the larger cities of Gao and
Mopti. Opinions differed about the current condition of the legendary village.
Many said it was virtually in a state of ruin and its famous camel caravans
passed through only once a year. All the same, Timbuktu conjured up such
exotic images of timeless intrigue. How could we travel Saharan Africa without at least attempting a visit?

In a remote village of simple mud huts, where goats roamed freely from
open door to open door, we found and hired a guide. Lute was a tall, lanky
man, the shade of café au lait. Athletic in his white flowing robe, he looked as
though he might be able to run to Timbuktu. With his experience and assistance, we hoped it couldn't take more than two days of slow but steady driving to cross the two hundred miles of unmarked, shifting piste to the desolate
desert outpost. In our naiveté, we vowed to make it no matter how much grit
and determination it would take.

The road to Timbuktu is paved with good intentions. The relentless desert
quickly tested our threshold for disappointment and pain on the first day. As
Henry buried our truck in one piste after another, we groaned in unison then
climbed down to sandmat again and again. Still, we were mere novices
compared to our guide.

Lute was a sandmatting ace, only slowed by our awkward attempts. He sprinted off with the heavy steel mats through the drifting sands, laying one down and then running back for another, before the truck was on sand again. He was a perfectly honed desert machine, while we were as graceful as slugs on a Saharan salt lick.

For awhile, we kept up as best we could, trying to match his smooth pace. One by one, we'd fall back for a moment's rest between long sessions of digging, pushing and matting. In the sweltering winter heat of that unforgiving land, it was easy to become dehydrated. Unlike Lute, our Saharan tri-athlete, we were forced to chug down gallons of fluids from sunup to sundown.

The desert was constant, as relentless as ever. Sandstorms rose out of nowhere. One set of clear tracks would suddenly split into a confusing ten, then disappear completely. As the day wore on, we hoped Lute knew as much about the sandy abyss as he'd promised–because it was evident our drivers didn't.

Then, like an island out in the middle of the vast sea of nothingness, there appeared a single tent, one green canvas dome with not another tent, house or tree to be seen for sixty miles in any direction. It was a Malian truck stop. A lone Tuareg family wrapped in traditional indigo robes sold gasoline from a barrel. Women with faces the texture of dried earth stood nursing tiny brown babies. Boys with Mohawk haircuts offered us cool colas from a guerba skin bag, and one grizzled fellow even offered us an emaciated goat for supper.

In that lonesome desert, firewood was harder to find than ice cream. A living tree wasn't fair game, because they were so precious and rare, and felled trees were scarce. We spent insufferable time on the rooftop gazing through binoculars, as if searching for some great white whale. Spotting a distant log, Nigel would slam on the brakes, nearly sending us careening off our perch.

That afternoon Bongo, Perfect Husband and I trudged off across the thick, golden sand to retrieve our latest fallen booty. As they grabbed the log, I reminded them, "Let 'er drop a couple times." It was one of the first rules of the desert we'd learned.

"Why?" Bongo asked, with a glance similar to his name.

"To knock the scorpions out."

Reluctantly, they hoisted the log and let it drop twice. On the third 'crunchhh', a prehistoric-looking scorpion angrily shot out, its tail dangerously waving in the air. It raced toward Bongo, then Perfect Husband, then me, upset at its rude awakening. Though it was swift, we were marginally more clever. Bongo distracted it long enough for Perfect Husband and me to grab the wood, toss it into a net suspended from the back of the truck and drive on.

Our futile sandmatting continued for two long days. Two more sand tires returned to the earth. We were getting nowhere fast.

Finally in exasperation, Lute cried, "Ni-gel, at dees pace, eet take you seex to ten daze doo Timbookdoo...eef you make eet at all." It was only one hundred fifty miles. As if to punctuate the seriousness of his prediction, Lute announced he was leaving us to our own stupidity. We could drop him off at the ragged desert village that rose miniscule on the horizon.

"Do not go Timbookdoo," he implored us one last time. "You never make eet without zee tires."

His words were absolute. He'd witnessed our fumbling. Our tires were shot and without them it would be suicide to continue across that most unforgiving stretch of piste in the desert.

Pulling into Lute's village on the track-crossed junction, we knew it was a straight shot to Gao. With any luck, we'd be there in a day. Our choice was disappointing, but easily made. We chose life over death in a dune.

The sands quickly faded behind us, as we neared the bustling city of Gao on the banks of the murky, receding Niger River. It was a relief to see humans again, a shock after the quiet solitude of the vast desert. The city abounded in life. There, huddled between buildings in two square blocks, sat row after row of rickety wooden stands selling tons of tomatoes, piles of peppers, stacks of squash, bushels of baguettes, heaps of herbs, mounds of melons, pounds of peanuts. There were tins of fish: dried, salted and fresh. The aromas were powerfully pungent, sensually exhilarating. In the theater of the sprawling open-air market, a potpourri of people surrounded us from vastly different regions that'd come like centuries of Africans before them, sometimes hundreds of miles to trade. Under the improvised canopies and colorful umbrellas of the produce stands, bronze, sharp-featured Tuaregs bought desert supplies. Grinning ebony women with tattooed faces deftly balanced plastic pails of produce on their heads. Jet-black Nigerians, cheeks scarred with catlike whiskers, hustled chickens from woven baskets.

A microcosm of everyday life, this was the first time since landing on Africa's shores that we'd seen black Africans in any number. Arabic facial characteristics had gently morphed into the rounder features of the black Africans, as desert robes blossomed into brilliant kaftans.

Pooky the Pommie artiste, mild-mannered Willie and I searched for food in the market, while Nigel struggled with officialdom. To everyone's shock we were levied a trumped-up tourist fee, photo permit fee, tourist tax, and guide fees amounting to nearly 250 French francs each. That was over $40 U.S. each in a country where the average annual per capita income was just $180.

*Nigel obviously didn't 'cadeau' the right people.*

Licking our wounds, we drove over to the Tizzie Marie Campground that offered the ultimate luxury: showers from a bucket of water behind an adobe wall. Still, after days of strict desert rationing, no one dared grouse. Funny, because just weeks before a dirty loo had caused such an outrage.

A gaggle of twenty ragtag boys followed us. Some quietly purred, "Cadeau? Cadeau?" as we set up camp. Others aggressively tried to peddle every locally made craft and hand-tailored piece of clothing they could set their hands on. Although the rest of us generally ignored their pitches, Zippy, the good-natured Canadian programmer foolishly sent a kid off with $20 to get change. He quickly vanished into the shadows–never to be seen again.

Inside our overland womb, it was alarmingly easy to forget how fortunate we were. Though we traveled with very little and often hadn't bathed for a week or more, locals with next to nothing saw us as rich targets. The mere fact that we were in their village, traveling in a truck, or that we lived in America or Europe, made us blessed in their eyes.

Still, it was hard to convince myself of that, as I stood heaving all night into the stench-filled hole that doubled as our toilet. Seems I'd eaten a rancid meat-filled doughball earlier.

*When traveling, choose your street food wisely, because it might just be the last meal you ever eat.*

Outside Gao, the beauty became electric. Neon red mesas rose as stony monoliths. Baobab trees appeared to grow upside down, roots beckoning to the sky for rain. Nomads tended herds of bleating midget goats, scrawny Brahma-like bulls and bellicose camels. Local huts were shaped like African igloos with sheets of burlap from old feed sacks stretched and sewn over bent stick frames. Some were built of thick mud bricks that were simply pressed, shaped and molded in the field, then repaired after the infrequent heavy rains. Others were round with extravagantly pointed thatched straw roofs–one less meal for slender livestock. In each village, children gleefully darted from their houses and rushed down to the dirt road, greeting us with enthusiastic waves and smiles. Once, a large caravan of rickety mule carts driven by dusty men even spontaneously staged a mock race, and we hammed it up for them as much as they did for us.

Of course, there were more police stops, about every hour along that road. Show your passport. Answer more questions. "Cadeau pour moi, mes amis?" they'd finally croon with an outstretched hand.

That evening we pulled into Mopti, a metropolis of about 40,000 on the banks of the Niger River. It was such perfect timing, because our arrival coincided with their president's. The town gates were adorned with welcome banners and festooned with psychedelic colored ribbons. The local citizenry was decked out in their finest. Women pranced in skirts printed with the president's portrait repeated again and again across ample buttocks. Men stood in small cliques and smoked, laughed and hugged old friends. Little kids, in their Friday best, waved flags and slurped on dripping ice cream cones.

There was no grandstand, but we just happened to be standing in an ideal location. His Excellency arrived at the gate with his huge entourage and stepped out of his new Land Cruiser to the cheering throngs. He was dapper; the perfect Hollywood image of a national hero in neatly pressed camouflage gear, reflector aviator glasses and jauntily cocked beret. His special military detachment all carried submachine guns and did a high step march alongside his rolling car.

We went for our cameras, wanting to capture that contrived display of pomp and circumstance, but were sternly warned by an onlooker.

"No photos! Ze Army ees verree dan-ger-ous," one old fellow whispered. Not wanting to include a Malian prison in our itinerary, we took his advice.

After the president received his welcoming kerchief, his procession passed into the cheering crowd until gunshots rang out! We thought the worst had happened. With throngs of others, we spun for cover. What a relief it was to spot the source of the gunfire. It was a troupe we called The Monkey Men, because of their furry-skinned outfits.

Shrill whistles blew. Drums beat and muskets fired as a brigade of men dressed like a cross between Daniel Boone and *Star Wars* Ewoks strutted down the street. Cheryl and I broke through the swarming crowd and rushed in for a better look. Those crusty old timers were decked out in buckskins, leathers, pointed or three-horned hats, and carried rusty flintlocks. Dancing in a large circle, they shuffled to a hypnotic beat.

At just that moment, a wizened old guy with stubby white beard pranced forward and shook a hairy monkey paw at us. Another gnarled baobab of a fellow suddenly stepped forward and thrust his rifle at my surprised partner, dragging Cheryl into their rowdy rumba line. Rifles were fired again and again. Black smoke poured into the air. You could smell the acrid odor of the burned powder and feel the blast of air as it shot past your face.

For one fleeting, exhilarating moment, a cherished instant, we were finally part of Africa.

As we danced, the overlanders moved their gear onto a huge ship that doubled as a decrepit inn and floating whorehouse. At the opaque river's edge, hundreds of smiling women, babies, children and grandmothers bathed with little fanfare. Heavily muscled women slapped laundry on rocks. Offshore, reed-thin men peddled fish from lean, brightly painted cigar-shaped boats or 'pirogues.' Everyone else mingled and hustled sodas, laundry or guide services, boat trips, food, or crafts. All right there.

After the Monkey Men shuffled on, we joined our group and moved into our dank cabin. The musky smell of lover's sweat mingled with the fishy perfume of the river. Illuminated by a single twenty-watt bulb dangling over the sink, it must have been 120-degrees inside.

"Maybe we'll be more comfortable sleeping on deck?" Cheryl suggested, already dripping in sweat.

As some of the overland ladies (and Rasta Trotsky) had their hair plaited or 'corn-rowed' by nubile natives on deck, Cheryl and I headed off to the ship's air-conditioned bar to help melt the mugginess. Returning an hour later, we met the others back at Mopti's mobile 'Cut 'n Curl'. Some fashion statements were obviously best left to the locals. Six-foot Prudence now sported tight cornrows–with bangs–as did Peggy, the pudgy novice traveler. Even Trotsky got polite snickers from the local men, who'd never seen a man with plaits before.

A little exploring was long overdue. So, fourteen of us caught two pirogues downstream to discover two neighboring, yet unique villages–one Bozo and one Songhai.

The Niger was so low that two men easily propelled our boat with poles at the front and rear, similar to a gondola. Gliding downstream in a peaceful rhythm, we passed boat after boat of stunning young women garbed in colorful wraparound cloths, boubous, and brilliant Fulani gold earrings. Much of their family fortune, we learned, rests in those fortune cookie-sized, crescent-shaped baubles.

As we floated into the Bozo fishing village, eagerly smiling naked children, practically toddlers, met us onshore. Grabbing our hands, they quickly led us to their squat adobe town overshadowed by a small mud mosque. Sepia dirt huts opened onto intimate courtyards where grandmothers slept or tended chickens. Women mended fishing nets, and young bare-breasted girls pounded rice with huge clubs. They'd throw their tree trunk sized rods into the air, clap their hands and sing songs to a steady 'pong-pa-pong' beat. Brass rings glistened in their noses and multiple brass rings shone in their ears. Some sported small decorative scars under their eyes or on hollow cheeks, and intricate tattoos graced their elders' darkened chins.

It was a rushed visit, as the pace of the children hurried us along. Still, it all appeared authentic, not a staged 'This is an African village' production. We literally wandered through their living room, kitchen and bedroom. Life was as it ever was.

As we headed back to the pirogue, we still grasped the tiny hands of the Bozo children. A few of the more precocious ones had already crawled into our arms, while the rest scampered close behind. Reaching our small boats, they started crying their ever-present refrain, "Cadeau, cadeau?"

Fluffy and Bongo tugged a bag of brightly colored hard candy from their daypack. Before they could even open the plastic, they were blinded by a tempest of tiny, flying brown arms. Bonbons flew into the air and onto the shore as the children swooped down to wrestle over the sweets.

"Hey let's get outta here!" Trotsky yelled in a moment of irrational terror.

So, taking advantage of the diversion, we quickly shoved off. Those kids waved and ran along shore until we skimmed out of sight.

Their Songhai neighbors just upstream led a totally different life. They remained aloof, although our pilot was a fellow Songhai. Landing, we gingerly walked through their small village. There was a real sense that we were intruding. No one rushed to greet us. In fact, seeing us, many ducked inside huts of thatched straw they shared with scruffy chickens. Even with their few goats and camels, we could sense those Songhai refugees led a meager hand-to-mouth existence. As poor as the Bozo had appeared, they seemed infinitely better off than those destitute souls.

As night fell, Nigel, Duchess, Sprout, Cheryl and I set off down Mopti's darkened alleyways in search of the dances we'd heard would celebrate the president's visit.

*If only we can find the right house.*

Still, in that dense darkness, it was difficult to see more than a few feet in front of us. Mopti was suffering a blackout. All the electricity was channeled to light His Excellency's compound. As we ricocheted off walls lining the narrow corridors, candles dimly flickered in the squat doorways of shops still open. People brushed past on their way from one outdoor food stall to the next. Pungent, spicy smells of barbecued beef and pork cooking in empty fifty-gallon oil drums filled the air. Strains of Zairois jazz or rhythmic 'soucous' music blared from radios. Locals laughed.

We stumbled through that dark for close to an hour asking shadows whether they knew where the dances were held. No one seemed to know—or admit they knew. At last, finally, another slim passage led to a hidden, weather-beaten gray doorway. A frail, old black woman answered our knock. She seemed shocked to see white strangers. But undaunted, she led our small band through her house and into the misty open courtyard. There, in front of us, a fire danced in the darkness. Hanging over it was a huge cast iron pot. A couple of gnome-like men, straight from central casting, tended the hypnotic fire and stirred a weird smelling brew.

Our hostess motioned for us to sit down in the dirt within the crimson glow of the fire, as she went to fetch a round gourd cup. Then, pulling out an earthen jug from beside the fire, she topped off the chalice and offered it to me.

"Ees millet beer. I make. Try."

I gingerly sipped some, not knowing what to expect.

*Not bad. It tastes like musty fermented juice.*

"Mmm, good." I said, passing the gourd to Duchess.

"Ah, it's wicked!" she declared, smacking her full lips.

"Ees not reedy yet," our hostess explained, her eyes widening as she grinned. "Geets better," she added, pointing a crooked finger to the bubbling cauldron on the fire. "Zat's freesh one!"

In no time, we were joined by a group of twenty musicians and dancers who'd come from as far away as Senegal for the president's visit. As we passed that gourd around and around between us for nearly an hour, getting refill after refill, I don't know whether it was the potent brew or the magical setting, but we grew giddy with anticipation. And I swear that fruity home brew got better as the night wore on.

After a few gourds of the beer, the musicians, illuminated by the quivering firelight, started playing 'koras,' traditional stringed instruments and 'balafons,' African xylophone slats atop different sized gourds. Their friends swayed and dipped in soulful, animated dance to timeless Sahelian tunes.

Finally, bolstered by enough millet beer, our troupe joined in their ancient celebration. Egged on by their gracious applause, we timidly tried to mimic their ancient steps, as one tune melded into the next. Gradually, the dancers movements and gyrations mysteriously morphed into the sweeping and clawing, pacing and prancing of animals. Old men dipped like birds. Young women glided like gazelles. Others sat spellbound, entranced by the music. We were swept away to another time. It was a cosmic dance of life, an evening of pure magic.

The next day, Nigel planned to hire a boat to float a group on a great journey down the Niger. But Cheryl and I, talking to a boatman, learned the water level was too low to carry even a narrow-drafted pirogue to Djenné and warned Nigel. But as usual, he collected $20 from fifteen overlanders for the trip anyway.

By then, we certainly knew better. Sometimes you have to trust your instincts. So, we and a couple of others journeyed by truck the short distance to the fabled 9th century sandcastle-like city.

*If we're wrong, there will be other float trips. If we're right, we'll have saved ourselves a major headache.*

65

Well known for its impressive multi-storied mud mosque, Djenné was once one of Africa's most important learning centers and a major stop on the Trans-Saharan trading route during the 1300s and 1400s, the same heyday as its sister city, Timbuktu. Now that its glory days are gone, it has to settle for being simply picturesque. But it does that well. Its towering minaret mosque, two-storied adobe buildings, talented craftsmen and bustling marketplace effectively hearkened back to those legendary times.

Several hours after our arrival, the rest of our group straggled into town. They were absolutely livid. The river float had turned out to be another scam. The pirogue owner received his money up-front, then the overlanders were paddled several miles downstream 'til the river virtually dried up.

"I gees yoo have to walk to Djenné. Eets only forty kilometers," the boatman explained. "I can't refund your money. Zee owner has eet!"

In desperation and fuming, the overlanders hiked to the main road where they finally flagged down a truck and paid handsomely for a lift to Djenné.

Nigel was pathetically apologetic, as usual.

Another important African lesson was learned. Don't pay anyone for goods or services until they're in-hand or supplied. They'd learned the hard way.

In the morning, after spending the night sleeping on the hotel's star-canopied rooftop, we set off for what was to be one of the most spectacularly rugged and unchanged areas in all Mali, the Dogon region. Shortly, we pulled into Tily, a small traditional village of multi-story mud houses with straw roofs set at the base of a sheer, towering red rock cliff. There, we met our guide, De Gaulle, a gentle, well-educated man who might have passed as a small town Southern preacher.

"Zee Dogon people believe all objects, beings and phen-om-ena in nature have souls," he explained. Then he quickly set off to show us where some of them dwelled.

Hiking up a narrow, craggy trail, we arrived at small adobe huts, or fetish houses, built right into the hillside. Painted with cosmic symbols and decorated with animal skulls, those simple shelters house the Dogons' ancestors whom they believe never die. Their spirits continue to play a vital role in village life, overlooking the arid plain and their extended families. Also set among those mysterious dwellings lived the keeper of the dead and protector of the living, the Ogun.

We met the wise one hundred-thirty-year old holy man and his wife as they sat in the deafening solitude of his darkened hut. No, I didn't see his birth certificate, but he looked his age. De Gaulle explained that the Ogun's role was indispensable. He had the power to tell the future and was the seeker of answers. He might ask for help from the fox, who'd then leave tracks in the sand in certain patterns. Or, since the Dogon people worshiped Sirius, the Dog Star, they could meditate for thirty minutes while peering at it and miraculously discover the truth.

*If only our problems were so easily answered.*

Finally, De Gaulle explained that serenely mystical man had never bathed. "He ees washed by snakes which lick his skin clean!"

After that brief, fascinating encounter with an authentic living oracle, we continued our strenuous hike over the mountain. Two sinewy men, well past their sixties and wrapped in tattered white cotton pants, accompanied us. On their heads they balanced plastic water jugs weighing nearly eighty pounds each. Still they smoked and joked as their reedy bodies set a frantic pace. We struggled just to keep up with them, as we whizzed past giant baobabs and glided across the arid Sahel for several hours. Finally, we reached a few desolate mud huts and our destination, the village of Djuigibombo.

Exhausted and flushed with sweat, we poured into a small courtyard where De Gaulle's friends expected us. Millet beer was already waiting and they prepared our feast of rice, potatoes and fresh chickens. As we lay sprawled across woven straw mats in the mud block courtyard, a refreshing breeze soothed our sizzled skins. Then we stiffened to the screech of a scrawny chicken, as its neck was the first one rung in our honor.

The following day we woke at dawn and, after a breakfast of fried millet balls, set off on a seven-mile hike. Children energetically waved to us with minute hands from simple mud huts. With protruding bellies and herniated navels, their smiles seemed oblivious to their abject poverty.

De Gaulle showed us the intricately carved wooden door and raised female motif of a menstruation hut until an old grizzled woman came outside yelling and shooed us away. Nursing mothers, babes at breast, curiously peered from open doorways. Coy maidens peeked up from their work at the village well, giggling and flashing flirtatious smiles.

It all seemed so simple, so far removed from our way of life. For better or worse in the Dogons, people had little contact with the Western world. We were the oddity. Then we realized De Gaulle's dilemma.

*How can he share his village's traditional lifestyle with travelers and not risk ruining it by exposing it to foreign ways?*

Hours later, exhausted by the scorching midday sun, we straggled into Enndé, a village similar to Tily. It was tucked into the base of another scraggy cliff, dotted with more ancient fetish houses. The entire area had painfully suffered from drought for the past several years and its effects were obvious. The dust was choking and flies relentlessly swarmed our sweaty heads. However, wiry teenagers still approached us with hand-carved slingshots and homemade knives with handles carved in the shape of the Ogun's wife. Several little boys begged for English books to read and others scrambled after our empty soda cans.

Scrawny goats scavenged flecks of grass. Bony Brahmas pawed with their noses into the Sahel for water. Baobabs stood as silent sentinels with outstretched arms, watching, waiting for rain.

# Chapter V
# Voodoo Wakes, Python Snakes

*"Being well dressed does not prevent one from being poor."*
~ African proverb

*T*HE FIRST DAY OF SPRING ARRIVED. No birds chirped. No flowers bloomed. No trees bore fruit. Spring seemed as inconsequential as our barren, forgotten surroundings.

Most of the overlanders, as in the season past, still filled their days with marathon sleeping, music blaring, mindless chatter, and measureless games of '21'. Little had changed. We just attempted to give each other more space for our mutual survival.

After hours in the ghostly solitude of the plain, we reached the smudge of an indistinct border marking entry into Burkina Faso, one of Africa's poorest struggling nations. Only one small, adobe hut and two rusty chained oil drums separated us from what the world once knew as Upper Volta. The border official was out to lunch. His stamp was locked up.

*What new gyration will it be today? Will he tear apart our truck? Carefully study twenty-three passports, looking at each and every stamp? Or invent some new frontier torture. Little will surprise me.*

As we awaited the answer, Bear, Clara, Chester and Peggy set up the tables and started to prepare a simple lunch of fresh baguette and tomatoes tugged out from secret hidden recesses of the truck.

Suddenly, like ants at a picnic, more than thirty villagers appeared out of nowhere. Reed-thin children, if they wore anything, were dressed in tattered rags. From underneath shabby shirts, swollen bellies protruded, betraying acute malnutrition. Boys stared hungrily at our simple fare. Young mothers gazed quietly in awe, babies suckling at breasts. Yet no one uttered a single sound. There was no "Cadeau, cadeau, mister?" No pulling at our sleeves. No attempt to sell anything. Only profound amazement. They looked like they'd never seen anything like us before, a truck like ours or people as pale and pink.

For pregnant moments they just stood there waiting and watching. They were so polite, so patient, almost as if waiting for a meager scrap of food to fall unnoticed to the ground.

We studied them too, not knowing quite what to expect. Why did they scrutinize our every move? Maybe we should give our meager fare of tomatoes and bread and fruit to them? But we'd just bought that cheap, simple fare from their neighboring village. What made it so special?

Naively we shared ripened mangoes with a few of the younger boys. Immediately, they wrestled over the prized fruit. It flew into the air. Then it was grabbed from one hand and wrenched from another.

More than just food could set tensions off. When Bongo tried to bury our trash, a few scraps of food and empty tins, there was a virtual riot. Ten eager boys dug up the cans faster than he could throw dirt on them. To top off the high noon insanity, Sprout chose that uneasy moment to give away an old reeking pair of tennis shoes. As we left to meet the border official, she tossed them into the frantic crowd. They were tugged this way and that and passed around like a football. A fight broke out. Finally, it ended with one joyous boy waving a tattered shoe, as another scored its mate.

We'd learned another sad lesson. There was little use in feeding a few without feeding the many.

That evening, we pulled into the capital, Ouagadougou. It stood in stark contrast to the scores of simple, mud hut villages we'd passed the previous eight weeks. Ouaga ('Waga-doo') was a calliope of motion and sound, an oasis in a land otherwise barren of Western extravagances. Streetlights cascaded light along frenzied paved roads. First class hotels welcomed wealthy, foreign businessmen dressed in three-piece suits. Garish monuments commemorated the people's continual struggle. Chic black sedans dodged and wove down swarming streets. Cacophonous mopeds sputtered past thousands of shoppers with their day's booty balanced in baskets on their heads.

We set off in search of Burkinabé, carved treasures, in the city marketplace. Street merchants hustled scarcely seen visitors with wooden carvings and colorful materials, batiks, and the traditional pebble games played on wooden boards called 'bao' or 'woaley'.

However, instead of handicrafts we discovered a mini-supermarket. It was a desert wet dream, an air-conditioned fantasy. Fresh peanut butter. Spices. Wonderful fruits: ripe mangoes & papayas, firm bananas & crisp green melons, sweet strawberries & avocados. French Brie and Camembert. Wines and whiskey. Delicious paté. Real French vanilla ice cream, and even fairly recent issues of foreign newspapers. All at prices nearly ten times the original. It was all too decadent given the poverty in the surrounding countryside. But to weary overlanders, who'd had little contact with an outside world, it was paradise.

That afternoon while ten of us treated ourselves to a dip at the hotel pool, (doubling as a bath for us), Sprout phoned her parents in the States. After half an hour, she approached the hotel cashier to pay the charges.

"Sept cent quarante dollars, mademoiselle, s'il vous plait," the cashier declared matter-of-factly, speaking through thick glass.

"Could y'all repeat that in English?" she replied in her lazy drawl.

"Of course. Seven hun-dred for-ty U.S. dollaires, pleeze."

"D-dollars?" She just stood there awestruck. "Not CFAs?"

"No, mademoiselle. We only accept dollaires for zee telephone."

Outrageous! Sprout had him recheck the charges then spoke with the manager, but they refused to budge from an amount several times their per capita income. She ended up putting it on her parents' charge card and it would be months before they'd find out how completely she'd 'reached out and touched' them.

After an otherwise inconsequential two-day stay, we sped toward Togo. As feared, we were still struggling to make up for those two lost weeks in Tam. Overland companies were relentless when it came to schedules, and we were told in no uncertain terms that we had to arrive in Harare, Zimbabwe by a certain date to carry yet another unwary group back to London.

Fortunately, in the wild, surprises come quite 'naturally'. Breezing through the border and into Togo, we immediately sighted our first African wild game. Right at the edge of Keran National Park, three towering elephants nonchalantly grazed not a hundred yards off the edge of the paved road. After over six weeks of desert life, it was a magical moment. And, unlike American reserves, there was no sign warning us, "Do Not Feed the Animals."

Entering the park via the international highway, we had exactly ninety-two minutes to drive from one end of the park to the other–no more, no less, according to park rules. If we took more, it meant we'd stopped. If we took less time, we'd been speeding. In either case, there was a heavy fine.

So at the gate, we carefully synchronized our watches with the ranger and set off. As luck would have it, we soon realized it was wise we didn't spring for the park admission. Even with twenty-three sets of eyes desperately searching for anything that moved, we didn't spot any more wildlife except a few scampering baboons. Of course, midday was the worst possible time to sight game anyway. Most animals sensibly dozed in the shade.

*Only mad dogs and overlanders are out in this searing sun.*

Leaving the park (right on schedule), we continued southwest into lushly verdant mountains and remote villages. Those Togolese 'Kabyé' homes were distinctively different: grass-like and not adobe, with thatched cone roofs rising to a point in the center. Perhaps more surprising, especially after Burkina Faso, was the look of general prosperity. Many villages were even equipped with sophisticated pumping systems, probably courtesy of the Peace Corps.

Over the next day, the weather became increasingly humid and tropical as we wended over the mountain ridge. Plumeria trees speckled hillsides with polka dots of pink and white. Guava, mango, papaya, palm and coconut trees grew to jungle-sized proportions in that steamy climate.

As evening set in, we sprinted toward the Cascades, waterfalls that promised a moment of private, hedonistic pleasure. All day, we fantasized ultimate relaxation with the gentle sound of waterfalls lulling us to sleep. Rumor had it we could even catch a refreshing jungle shower in the early morning.

Well, Henry, true to form, wasted no time en route to our mountain nirvana, driving like a maniac on narrow, winding roads through unlit villages. He sped around each and every corner throwing cards, bottles and cameras careening across the inside of the truck like unguided missiles. Abruptly, he slammed on his brakes as we slid into a massive four-foot hole in the road. Then, he gunned the engine and tore off again. It seemed like he got an especially perverse thrill in rushing up behind cyclists. Waiting until he was almost on top of them, he blasted his powerful horns and sent them sprawling into the bushes.

His antics took on a new meaning when we learned he couldn't see at night. His eye had been skewered with a radio antenna like a kebab on a previous trip in eastern Africa. However, now, no amount of cautions could slow him down. He only cranked up the stereo. Our warnings were drowned in a power-crazed passion ignited by heavy metal. He was possessed, a demon unleashed on the back roads of Togo.

*So much for the serenity of the mountains.*

Hours, yes hours, later, as we zoomed down another cow path, someone dared to voice what was on everyone's mind. "So just where are these falls?"

"Oh, they're just up there a bit," Nigel promised, vaguely waving into the darkness. He had no idea. "We'll take showers in the morning since there are a few crocs up there, too."

Turned out, our mountain hideaway was far from bucolic. In the never sur-prising advice of our 'experienced' guides, we were to pitch our tents at the edge of a fish-breeding pond, not beside those thundering falls. Although it was already pitch black, we could tell we hit a new low in campsite selection. Sure, we'd roughed it, already camping in dust-choked gravel pits, among desert dunes, over hotel septic tanks and on decks of whorehouse ships.

*But now, a malaria-infested swamp?*

Of course, everyone was already in the habit of changing into long pants and shirts at nightfall. It was comical to watch twenty-three of us modestly hunched behind truck seats or crouched in low tents as we struggled into bulky protective clothing. After applying a liberal dose of the industrial strength insect repellent DEET to any exposed parts, we'd attempt to survive another night of ravenous attacks. Nevertheless, swamp camping screamed for trouble.

As we set up our orange day-glow tents along the reedy bank, the whirring of bat-sized, malaria infested mosquitoes echoed through the stillness of the night. Swarms circled for the kill. Then en masse, they dive-bombed our exposed heads. There was no doubt in anyone's mind. From the feel of the golf ball-sized welts popping up on our faces, they had more success in breeding mosquitoes in that pond than fish.

Swamp camping also added a new, skewed dimension to the art of 'free ranging', or going to the toilet in the wild. There was no running water, no hole and no seat. There was just you and your tissue, nature and your imagination. In the desert, the only problem was finding a tree, because they were so scarce. Stumbling on one, you'd undoubtedly discover twenty-two others had found it before you.

Swamps definitely added new depth to the challenge, especially when certain sensitive areas hover perilously close to the dark ground. Only then do you remember you haven't doused DEET on *every* possible inch of your body. Unfortunately, Cheryl had spent her day trying to control projectile vomiting–along with the 'runs'–a very tricky combination.

Still, as everyone frantically dodged and swatted, I chuckled at how steamy overlander trysts had already turned our journey into a Togo love connection–stranger still, given our overpowering odors and total lack of privacy. Overlanding did make strange bedfellows.

Pooky, our shy, elfin woman, mistimed her move on Nigel and became Bongo's mother/lover instead.

*If you can't love the man, love his shadow.*

To everyone's surprise, Fluffy, our Saharan suntan model with the poofy hair, and curly-headed Zippy moved in together amid the romance of the dunes. The oddest couple of all became ol' Trotsky and Peggy with their identical, matching cornrows.

*But seriously, how romantic can it possibly get when you haven't showered in weeks? Hey, married couples know these things, right?*

As we dozed off, our silent black veil echoed with the monstrous barking of retriever-sized bullfrogs.

Rising in the still-dark coolness of the next morning, everyone hiked back to the famous Cascades. True to form, they'd existed only in some travel writer's vivid imagination–obviously long before the current drought. After all that, our 'thunderous' falls drizzled with a pathetic bladder-infected trickle. Dejected, we hurriedly packed up and headed on toward the coast.

Before long, we arrived in Lomé, and it was an unparalleled pleasure to pitch our tents alongside the cooling Atlantic. It had been so long since we'd seen so much water or comfort. A stiff afternoon breeze blowing in off the ocean helped moderate the sultry, ninety-five-degree weather, while the campsite even offered cold showers and a shady open-air bar.

Cheryl and I quickly headed for town, seeking a welcome break from life in that stifling overlander chrysalis. Those moments were so rare and we looked forward to them with undisguised relish. In fact, I was already counting the days until our arrival in Nairobi and setting off on our own.

The marketplace or Grande Marche was an easygoing treat. It was enormous, occupying three blocks of three-story buildings right in the heart of the city. The market was chock-a-block with thousands of people doing their daily shopping. On the first floor were a huge variety of fresh meats and fish, stacks of fruit and heaps of vegetables. Mound after mound of colorful spices were piled high in conical mounds on tabletops, while the second and third floors were chock full of fabrics from throughout Africa and as far off as Holland. Colorful batiks and intricate wax designs far surpassed anything we'd seen so far. All the incredible materials were sold by the 'pagna', about two-meter lengths, with the entire roll being about three pagnas in length. Many were geometric. Some featured smiling African presidents or wild animals. Others were abstract, while East African fabrics had Qur'anic quotes encircling the edges. All boasted a uniqueness and flair difficult to duplicate in the west.

Lomé was a fascinating oasis that offered enough exciting city life, movie theaters, lively restaurants and well-stocked shops to sustain and relieve swamp mauled travelers. Cheryl and I also made it a point to explore the delicious spicy local seafood, reconfirming the culinary connection between America's Deep South and southwest Africa. After reaching our fill of Creole food and dense crowds, we headed off to discover the mysterious voodoo market in Bé that we'd heard so much about.

We ambled down streets jammed with thousands of Togolese, Senegalese and Ghanaians shopping and selling almost anything imaginable. One small cart, not larger than a pretzel vendor's stand, sold probably three hundred different items, from combs and candies to cassettes and cards, from perfumes and peanuts to condoms to razor blades. It was all right there.

Still, it was a plodding, sweaty hike to Bé down alleys swarming with running children and pecking chickens, bleating goats and local soucous music, street stalls, carts, cars and thousands of people swimming upstream through the thick afternoon humidity. People moved slowly and deliberately in that stifling heat. With reggae blaring in boom box beat, if you closed your eyes you could be in the Caribbean. Still, for all the overpowering chaos, the people were kind and reserved.

There was none of that Marrakech, "Lookie, lookie." We were greeted with miles of grins from large women in American t-shirts, men sweeping streets with palm fronds and engaging bare breasted girls balancing baskets of fruit on their heads, as they threaded their way toward the marketplace.

After asking several bewildered passersby for directions, Cheryl and I eventually reached Bé and its intriguing market. The voodoo stand was indeed magical, wilder than expected. There were weird fetish objects to cast a spell and objects to break them or fend off bad luck. Wart hog tusks sat glistening in a pile; monkey brains and bleached white bones; tiny bird skulls; strange skins and body parts, unrecognizable except to the initiated. It was all fascinating, especially when we realized that this was the same voodoo that African slaves had carefully stowed away on their voyage to New Orleans and the New World, much like America's other settlers carried more puritan beliefs.

Togolese voodoo was far more complex than Hollywood's bloody chickens or dolls bayoneted with pins. It was a way to ask for wealth or pray for a sick child. It was a coin in the fountain of fortune or a way to 'see' a lost relative. In its natural state, it often blended with Western faiths to create something powerful and tangible, something the locals could easily believe in.

We ached to see more. As we walked back to camp, we were wondering if we might be able to actually witness a ceremony while we were there. As if by magic, we soon caught the unmistakable sound of a drum pounding down the street. As we grew nearer, we heard singing and shouting and saw people drawn toward the music. Racing round a corner, my curious partner and I followed the rhythms. We peeked into shop after store trying to discover its source, as we wove our way in and out of the crowd. Finally, we gingerly poked our head through an open doorway in the direction of the chanting. The high-ceilinged room had the look of a church with pews down either side. We stood in rapt awe as about thirty women dressed all in white, clapped and swayed to the beating of the drums. One woman, as if in a trance, danced up and down the aisles of the room, sweating, flying and rushing from side to side in a frenzied dance.

Suddenly, she raised her head and her eyes met ours! She stared at us just for a moment then smiled with deep compassion.

We started to back away from the door to leave, yet the other women, sensing we meant them no harm, made no sign that we should go. So we stood there, transfixed, trying to blend into the wall, while taking in the flurry of excitement unfolding before our eyes.

Then, just as quickly as they'd started, the drums stopped. The chanting ceased and we respectfully backed out the door.

It was a short drive to Cotonou from Lomé, just 120 miles due east. After a night camped in the yard of a local guesthouse, we set off for Lake Ganvié. We were filled with anticipation because we'd been told was one of the few sites that even other African travelers would go out of their way to visit.

Lake Ganvié was first settled back in the 18th century by the Tofinu tribe. Once their land no longer supported farming, they moved to that swampy lake region, constructing houses right over the lake. There they were protected against the Abomey warriors, who were prevented by religious ban from going out onto the water.

Today, the people of Lake Ganvie´ are supported entirely by their fishing, fish breeding, the sale of their artwork and, of course, tourism.

Eager to see this "floating village," we loaded into two pirogues with our lanky polemen and pushed off toward the center of the lake and bamboo houses.

Floating markets with fish, fruit, vegetables and grains were carefully wedged between the shore and the village. On one shore, a young girl and her brother cut and stacked reeds to repair their house. Women paddled past, their cigar shaped pirogues heavily laden with fish and spices from a trip to the market. Pigs passed by too, paddling in the murky water.

As we floated toward the village, teenaged boys screamed, "Youuu! Heyyy! For one ci-gar-ette, we weell zrow ze net. You take photos, okay?" Holding cigarettes in the corner of their mouths like big-city gangstahs, they threw their net spiraling into the air, again and again. Then one kid who'd been clowning for our cameras threw his lithe body so far with his cast that he tipped the pirogue until he and his buddy flew out into the rank water. Popping up, they grinned from ear to ear.

Entering that 'village' atop the lake, we passed house after bamboo house on stilts, lashed together in rows over the water like a lake-top Venice. Coasting toward one, we went inside for a quick look at its unique construction. It was fascinating but unsettling to watch through wide chinks in the floor as the lake waters rushed by just several feet below.

Hung throughout this house were examples of appliqué, their local specialty, depicting animals in a patchwork of brilliant colors sewn onto a dark background.

As we absorbed the primitive art and ambiance, another revelation quickly dawned upon us. Although Lake Ganvie´ was an interesting diversion and boat ride, it was yet another tourist trap. Everything was perfectly orchestrated for visitors. They knew we were coming in advance and tried to peddle us food, drinks and artwork from nearly every house. Even as we floated back to shore, toddlers waved from doorways, crying "Cadeau, cadeau!" We were just wealthy observers from afar, another industry to supplement their fishing. Another easier, less-cunning harvest.

Nighttime offered little relief from the oppressive humidity of the past few days. The air was still and rancid with the odor of rotting mangoes. It was so hot that even the crickets couldn't muster a chirp. Some overlanders slept out under the stars, beneath the truck, or strung hammocks in trees, trying in vain to catch a breeze.

We hadn't brought a separate mosquito net, as we had one attached to our tent and another to the bivy sacks covering our sleeping bags. So we stayed in our tent with the flaps unzipped, tossing and turning in fitful sleep throughout the night.

Finally, about 3 a.m. there was a sudden 'cr-accc-kkkkk' and the sky lit up like noon. The heavens let loose. People sleeping out under mosquito nets suddenly found themselves awash in a sea of mud. Some managed to crawl under the truck. Others, in a dazed stupor, ducked for cover, falling over tables, tripping over tent lines and lunging for zippers in the darkness.

"At least," I lazily muttered, "the breeze has returned."

Finally wrangling a spare day, we convinced Nigel to drive us to the nearby town of Ouidah, Benin's original port city. It was the infamous village from where Togo and Benin's blacks were shipped as slaves to America, Brazil and Haiti in the 1800s. Coincidentally, it was also the center for Benin voodoo.

After what we'd experienced in Lomé, I looked forward to perusing the Voodoo Museum housed in the old Portuguese fort. My imagination was sparked. Unfortunately, when we arrived, the museum was under renovation. Its collection of skulls, bones, ghost clothes, paintings and engravings would have to wait for another time. Disappointed but not defeated, we drove down dead quiet streets to the Python Temple.

*Is this going to be the real thing? Or another sideshow for culture starved travelers?*

That afternoon, six of us who were interested in learning the fine art of caressing pythons, approached the concrete compound of squat buildings set around a courtyard. There, a grizzled, stooped fellow gruffly greeted us and led us inside the maze to a small building brightly decorated with mystical inscriptions. Then cautiously, he slowly creaked open a plywood door to a concrete box. Inside, we spotted four or five six-foot pythons used in the voodoo ceremonies.

"I let zem loose at night to feed," he cackled, in a voice that was a cross between Maurice Chevalier and Gabby Hayes. "Een morning zey usually return."

"What if they don't?" I wondered aloud.

He shrugged a sort of 'such is life'. Then grabbing the largest python in his hands, he ceremoniously handed it to me. As it undulated between my fingers, a mixture of cold and hot, wet and dry, its sinister eyes and sneer sent a slight tinge of terror down my spine.

Later, of course, the crusty caretaker who'd already charged us admission expected a gift as we left. Nigel rolled him a cigarette, insisting that the old fellow take a drag. The Python Man tried it, wheezed, coughed and shot us a grisly glance. Since he looked disappointed with just his nicotine gift, we slipped him a plastic pen, Africa's second currency, before leaving the concrete temple.

In Africa, a plastic ballpoint pen or piece of gum was the perfect cadeau or best way to conclude a deal. Need to bribe your way through a roadblock? Want jungle slime scrubbed out of your clothes? Maybe you'd like your monkey meat ground at the market for the perfect patties? The pen was mightier than the dollar.

Cigarettes worked wonders, too. Once in Mali, Sprout was interested in offering a t-shirt and hat for a goat skin bag. The man repeatedly refused to trade until I suggested she include a couple of cigarettes. Regardless of our Western 'political correctness' about smoking, he couldn't refuse that offer.

As we explored the denizens of the Python Temple, Bongo, ever the clown, enjoyed a perverse game of taunting the local kids in the heat of the courtyard.

"Catch. Come on. Catch," he screamed like an animal trainer, as he flung pieces of ice cream into the hungry crowd.

The kids leapt into the air yelling. But by the time they'd fought over the sweet treats, the ice cream was mere puddles in the dirt.

Nigel and Henry, ever the leaders, just stood and grinned.

Since the Voodoo Museum was closed, we set off to search for the real thing, an authentic temple. Driving down a small dirt road, we eventually stumbled onto a snug, white concrete-block building with colorful designs blanketing each wall, veiled and overhung by a thick awning of trees. Two crude murals depicted a massive bull tied to a tree. Another showed an immense snake, a man and whip. Its facade was even scribed with the date of its first use–1700 something. By sheer luck, we had stumbled on the oldest active voodoo temple in all Benin.

Timidly, a few of us gingerly poked our heads through the open door, scanning the dusky interior bathed in dim candlelight. In front of us, a towering red dirt termite mound altar rose, nearly as high as the corrugated tin roof. At its base lay scattered bits of bizarre sacrifices, ancient and mysterious objects with spikes that had been driven through them. A small gourd held a palm oil concoction. There were scraps of children's clothing. Decay and pools of candles left from past ceremonies surrounded bits of blood-covered coconut. Then we heard a clear, strong voice addressing us from the corner in the darkness.

"Bonjour. Ça va? Entré."

We stood in awe, a little frightened, intrusive, not quite knowing what to say. Shuffling into that dank, foreboding room, we awkwardly faced the altar, now flanked by a young, wiry fellow the color of darkness, dressed in ordinary street clothes.

"Thank you," we cautiously whispered.

"Yooo have questions?" he asked, scanning our puzzled faces.

"Are you a v-voo-doo p-priest?" Prudence stammered.

*Looking for something or someone to make cornrows fashionable?*

"No, I am ze Guar-di-an of ze Temple."

Dropsy, our security guardian, quizzically chirped, "How long you been a Guardian?"

"Since I was a child. My fa-thair was Guar-di-an of ze Temple before me," he replied. "I have been here on-ly for one year, since ze death of ze last Guar-di-an."

"Do you make sacrifices here?"

"Oui, I sacrifice ze goat or ze cheek-ken to help make weesh come true."

Hefty Chester was turning green and looked like he was going duck out any minute.

"Why are there children's clothes on the altar?" I asked.

*Can't be sacrifices...*

"Sometimes, ze women zey come to me. Zey want me to pray for ze sick child. And zey bring me ze ba-by's clo-zing to use in ze cer-e-mo-ny."

"Is that blood up there?" Maxie asked, nervously twitching and pulling her bandana off her head.

"No. Eet's oil and pey-pairre."

There was a collective sigh of relief.

Cheryl continued, "How many people here in your village practice voodoo?"

"Nearly ev-ery-one. Some aire Christian too. But zey still need a leettle voodoo sometimes," he chuckled.

"What can ya' do here?" easy-goin' Slim asked sheepishly.

"I can bring ze good fortune," he promised. "I can make ze people well." And looking at Dropsy, he offered, smiling broadly, "I can even mix ze love potion for ze wo-man looking for ze hus-band."

On that optimistic note, we thanked him and headed back down the road to the truck, until we detected the faint thumping of drums again and people singing in the distance. Without missing a beat, or waiting for group 'consensus', Cheryl and I took off running down the road in the direction of the haunting music.

A few others followed, as Nigel yelled, "Hey wait, we're leaving!"

As we rounded a corner, suddenly, there by the side of the road was another voodoo ceremony in progress. It was joyous. Hands clapped to the beating of the drums. Handsome ebony people danced and swayed. Heavyset mamas took turns singing into a portable microphone. People shuffled, hopped and pranced in the dusty street, as we were welcomed into their midst with smiles and open arms.

One wizened man assured us, "Eet ees finally safe to celebrate."

The music grew in intensity and became more frenzied and animated as proud old fellows, dressed in their best suits, started bucking and pitching from side to side like men half their age. Gradually, the graceful dance transformed into something natural and primordial, ancient and primitive.

The only comparable movement we'd seen was at an Inupiat dance we'd witnessed in the northern Arctic in Barrow, Alaska where we'd lived for a year. There, at the world's edge, ancient men and women in parkas soared through the air like ethereal ravens, humpback whales or walruses.

*Now, halfway around the world, we're part of a similar spiritual dance, a primeval party, an enchanting celebration of life. Like their fathers and their father's fathers before them, these gentle people are celebrating the tenth anniversary of a loved one's passing, his final bold leap in life.*

*However now, it's destined to be shared with us*

# Chapter VI
# Baboon Platoons

*"If you tell people to live together, you tell them to quarrel."*
~ African proverb

*T*HE ROAD TO NIGERIA was fraught with delays. We wasted several days in Benin attempting to get truck insurance for Nigeria because it took a certain amount of greasing the right palms. However, crossing the border was another sobering test of patience. For two hours we nervously paced as our truck was checked and double-checked and passports were scrutinized. Finally, a bottle of whiskey traded hands and gates were flung open. The stakes had certainly increased since the old days when a beer or cassette could bribe us through.

Nigeria stood in uneasy contrast to Benin. Everywhere we looked were hordes of people. Even smaller villages were huge in comparison. Nigeria was already the world's seventh most populous country and it looked like half the nation was lining that pockmarked highway.

We headed directly north toward Kano, skipping Lagos's legendary crime, strangling pollution and stationary traffic. Sailing from one machine gun-toting military checkpoint to the next, we made great time winding our way back into the rain-starved Sahel. We were pleased to find that once outside the cautious reserve of the big city, back in a land of simple mud huts, we rediscovered the friendly curiosity made Africa so special.

As we passed one gracious lady gathering water at a well, she stopped pouring long enough to wave, then actually curtsied.

Arriving that afternoon in the metropolis of Kano, our never-ending search for the perfect campsite resumed. Unfortunately, Kano's only site was as far from perfect as we'd ever seen. Surrounded by walls topped with broken shards of glass and barbed wire, it had all the charm of a concentration camp. There were toilets, but no water. Brimming with human excrement, they offered a constant feast for man-eating flies. The showers, splotched green and brown with years of mold and blood, were rife with mosquitoes and worked only an hour each day. They'd trickle on at eight in the morning for thirty minutes and then again at midnight.

For one fleeting moment, we thought we might have a reprieve. Nigel suggested, "Hey, they have doubles at the Central Hotel next door for 150 naira. Why don't you join us and we can all check in there?"

"Great, that's reasonable," I excitedly answered.

However, when he and Sprout, Henry and Maxie and Cheryl and I showed up, their price instantly doubled to over 300 naira. The hotel desk clerk unabashedly explained, "Oh, 150 naira is the 'local' rate."

*'Local' rate?* We'd run into that before when buying food, clothes or souvenirs. Travelers could never hope to get the same price as locals in Africa unless the merchant was desperate for a sale. Still, I was surprised to hear that hotels played that game, too. We tried to reason with the functionaire.

"How'd you like it if you were charged a different price in Lagos than a person from Lagos?" I asked.

"I don't go to Lagos," he deadpanned.

*It's going to be tough to change his mind.*

"Well, we paid 150 naira last year when we were here," Nigel added.

"That was last year."

Henry demanded, "Prices have doubled since then?"

"For foreigners, yes."

That was it. End of discussion. Unlike business owners, hotel clerks never care if you stay or not. Makes no difference to them. After a useless thirty-minute debate on the fairness of 'tourist' pricing with the inflexible clerk, Henry, Maxie, Cheryl and I felt like we were 'beating a dead desk clerk' and returned to the compound. Nigel however cajoled and pleaded for the next hour, finally wearing down the clerk's patience to the point where he called the manager. Not wanting to deal with some sniveling, unshaven overlander in red leather boots, he eventually relented and gave them a room at the 'local' price. So Nigel and Sprout savored the next three days in the unrivaled luxury of an air-conditioned three star hotel.

Meanwhile, the 'real' overlanders salivated at just the thought of 'real' cold showers. They suffered long lines at midnight, just for a chance at a close encounter of the shrinkage kind in that memorable hall of slime.

Eager to make the best of an uncomfortable situation, my partner and I ventured into the thousand-year-old city the next morning, hoping to discover a treasure to justify our stay at the POW camp. Our ill-fated tour began at the Emir's Palace. The enormous mud walled complex was impressive, right down to the brightly uniformed soldiers in plumed hats who guarded the gate and blocked our entry. However, the Palace was for 'locals' only–or by special invitation.

We wandered to the Gidan Makama Museum next door, trying to satisfy our curiosity about the local architecture. Built in the 1400s, it allowed us a rare chance to inspect the fascinating local adobe construction from the inside out. After a photo capsule view of Kano's role in West African history, we ambled past the Palace to the adjacent Central Mosque that could hold over fifty thousand Muslims at prayer. But that, too, was closed to non-Muslims.

Following a brief stop at the colorful outdoor dye pits, Cheryl and I set off to explore throbbing Kurmi Market before the heat of midday became unbearable. With its thousands of stalls, Kurmi was reputed to be the largest market in all of Africa. Surrounding us were row after row of dazzling materials and batiks. Twenty or thirty shops featured hand-carved statuettes, trading beads and dazzling gold and bronze jewelry. I even spotted an impressive crocodile briefcase complete with spines down the front.

"Hey, the perfect 'power' briefcase!" Cheryl teased. "Let's pick one up."

However they refused to haggle over the price because they were in the midst of Ramadan–and it was on the endangered list, after all. Eventually my partner selected some bright red and yellow tie-dyed cloth at one of the many stalls. A bespectacled little man measured her and immediately set his antique sewing machine whirring. Moments later she had a hand tailored skirt and matching top. The material's bright yellow and aqua bull's-eye set squarely on her backside. Hypnotically, like some pulsating Cyclops's eye, I secretly chuckled as it winked and swung back and forth as she walked.

The only positive thing about our campground was its proximity to the air-conditioned hospitality of the hotel bar. In the hottest stretch of the late afternoon, we made it a point to retreat to the pub for a brew and opportunity to chat with the locals. For once, prices for locals or foreigners were identical.

That particular afternoon two Nigerians joined us, one from Kano, the other from outside Lagos. Robert worked for the local utility company and was the epitome of modern Africa. In neatly pressed shirt and slacks, he might have come from Detroit or Atlanta, except for the impressive set of facial scars running across both cheeks. The other man, Amos, was a businessman from the south. Dressed in traditional kaftan, he also had raised scars running diagonally across his cheeks like a set of cat's whiskers.

Of course, they were more than a little curious about where we were from, what we did, and why we were in their pub. We shared their curiosity, wanting to discover as much as we could about their life in Nigeria.

"Though Amos and I are from de same country, you know, our ways are ver-ry different," Robert immediately pointed out. "North and south Nigeria are like two separate countries."

"Well, your scars are very different." I pointed out. "What do they mean?"

"They're tribal. We can recognize other members of our tribe wherever we see them throughout Africa. See him?" He wagged a finger at the waiter. "I can tell he's from my tribe."

"They are also for beauty," Amos added, "Like tattoos."

"Our languages are very different too," Robert said. "I speak Hausa and can hardly understand dis guy!" he joked, pointing at Amos.

"Dat's because I really don't think you're Nigerian," Amos countered laughing. "We speak Yoruba and even eat different foods."

"Yea, I can't stand to eat fish." Robert grimaced at the thought.

"Ah, it's the best. Better than what you call food. And another 'ting, since we've started, I cannot stand the dryness here. I miss the ocean," Amos mused.

"Well, I'd die if I tried to live in dat heat!"

Their good-natured rivalry continued all afternoon. Although we initially steered a wide berth around political discussions, without much coaxing, they spilled their sad tale of Nigerian life and how much had changed since 1970's glory days. With fat oil revenues, the economy had boomed. Vast new highways were constructed. Bridges were built and there was prosperity. After the slump in oil prices in the '80s and political problems, the economy took a tailspin. Now, there was no way to support the roads and utilities that had been built. Blackouts, water outages and interrupted phone service were commonplace. Sleek freeways suddenly ended in mud paths, and travel to Western countries, once frequent for businessmen, was practically unheard. Both admitted the surging population was part of the problem and would only continue to make a bad situation worse. One in five Africans lived in democratic Nigeria. Within thirty years, it would become the world's fourth largest nation.

"What we do den?" they wondered in unison.

The following day, we headed north across the sun-baked plateau of Jos and one hundred miles east to the Yankari Game Reserve, Nigeria's foremost location for sighting big game. Weary from exploring big cities, we were more than ready to see more of the four-legged variety of Africans.

After a day's drive under the constant, withering glare of the merciless sun, the refreshing pool at Wikki Warm Springs in the Park invitingly sparkled. The twenty-five foot wide natural swimming hole was nestled in the shade of a canopy of overhanging trees. At one end, a small cascade constantly replenished the healing waters. To the other, spread a cluster of tangled vines and verdant pond vegetation. No time was wasted in chucking our clothes and racing down the slippery hill to the alluring lake below. What incredible pleasure it was to soak in warm, bilharzia-free waters for once.

Bilharzia, an invisible killer, was something we feared more than stampeding rhinos or hungry lions. It's widespread throughout most of the continent. Bilharzia, or schistosomiasis, one of the continent's most debilitating diseases, is contracted in lakes or slowly moving rivers and transmitted by snail worms which enter your body through the skin and lay eggs in your veins. Over the years, if left untreated, the effects are extremely painful and cause dangerous complications. Not a pretty way to go, by any means.

Thankfully the only things we had to watch out for in our giant African hot tub were the aggressive baboons. Those wily creatures with crewcuts and bulbous butts were only slightly intimidated by humans. During the day they hid in the shade of the branches shielding the hot springs. We heard them bark occasionally, and watched them watching us. When you weren't looking, they'd tear down the tree, scamper across the bank and snatch your camera or clothes before you could raise a yelp from the sleepy mist of water.

We found out just how fast they were that night. Part of our dinner routine was keeping a careful eye on the large male baboon that'd circled the truck from a distance since we'd arrived, especially since one of our treasures that evening was a perfectly ripe pineapple. It had been weeks since we'd had that sweet treat and it was a welcome addition to our usual Spartan fare of bread and tomatoes. Well, Slim, our Kiwi barkeep, no sooner placed our prize harvest on the dinner table than that baboon bounded at least twelve feet, snatched the pineapple in his massive canines and tore off down the road. Not to be out maneuvered by an ape, Slim ran off after him at full tilt.

At about 6 foot 5, Slim had a long sprinter's gait. Still, the baboon, even with a gimp paw, ran rings around him. He evaded Slim for a good ten minutes, running through the campsite, as the rest of the cook crew tried to head him off. It seemed to be just a game for him. The ape would drop the pineapple teasingly. He'd bark a taunting laugh and let Slim get just close enough before he'd snatch it back and bolt. Finally, after another ten minutes, the baboon tired of the chase. In resignation, he dropped the precious prize from his mouth and scampered off, dragging a withered paw behind him.

Slim returned the hard fought-for fruit to the cheering cook crew, but a little too late. The pineapple was ringed by a huge set of teeth marks and had a large chunk missing. He'd won the battle, but the simian had won the war.

"Ahhh, don't 'ya jest haite thet," Slim groused, rubbing his cowlicked head.

The baboons spied on us long into the evening but didn't attack again. They were content to just tip over trashcans in search of tasty morsels. However, early the next morning, we discovered just how relentless they could be.

Shortly after sunrise, I woke up to a strange growling and grunting. Peering out our tent flap, I saw a platoon of about twenty good-sized baboons sweeping across our campsite, fanning out in military style. We'd been warned those aggressive apes were feisty enough to tear through our tents and plunder anything they could lay their paws on. But surely, not with us inside.

Henry was waiting for them. He'd brought a 'proper' super high-powered, shiny aluminum slingshot all the way from London for just such an occasion. He shot first at one, then another. It was enough to scare them off. Quickly they re-grouped and moved in from another side. He fired. They retreated. Then finally, they swooped down, kamikaze-style, all rushing in at once, picking up anything that wasn't tied down before they left.

Since all the baboons seemed to be at the top of the hill, giving the campers a run for their breakfast, I couldn't imagine a better time for another long soak. Picking up a towel, I slid down to the hot springs that doubled as a communal bath for the locals. The pond was still. No baboons were in sight. Confidently, I hung my towel from an overhanging branch, stepped down into the clear water and ducked my head into the warm soothing springs.

As I surfaced and shook the water from my ears, I heard, "OOOOOHA GRUUUUNN! GRUUUUNN!" Rustle. Rustle.

*I must be hearing things. It's just the wind and trees.*

Then it came again. "GRUUUUNNN!"

As I looked around, three local teenagers sped across the wooden foot-bridge, spanning the twenty-five-foot placid pond. I'd heard an elephant–and it was very near.

Quickly I grabbed my pants and joined the kids in hot pursuit. Scaling an old stone wall, we followed that unmistakable rustle in the head-high grass. There, not fifty yards away stood a beautiful female elephant grazing in the swaying flaxen grass. We all froze in awestruck wonder, afraid to move and risk the possibility of chasing her off–or having her charge. Although she certainly knew we were there, she paid us no mind.

"GRUUUUNNN!" came another deeper trumpeting behind us, back towards the lake.

Scampering back down the hill to the pond, our view became more and more obscured by heavy undergrowth. So we took turns perching on each other's shoulders to peek over the thorny thickets. Yards from us stood a massive bull elephant bathing in the warm current, just downstream from where I'd been minutes before.

We cautiously inched closer, not wanting to risk a charge. Finally, we were so close we could see his massive, alabaster tusks glistening in the rays of morning light. We paused, barely breathing. At just that moment, sensing our presence, he threw his head back, spraying a shower of water through the trees. Then casually sauntering away, he climbed the bank and disappeared across the opposite shore into dense undergrowth.

*In Africa, nature can be lurking around any corner–or hot tub.*

More intentional game spotting continued all morning, as we loaded the truck and set off across the small dirt roads of the reserve. Cheryl and I commandeered the rooftop seats. With our heads in a constant 360-degree swivel, we tried to spot elusive game before passing them. Between our continual turning and constant ducking to miss three-inch long barbs from overhanging acacia trees, we were dodging and weaving like prizefighters. Meanwhile, Chester pulled out his equally massive lens and Perfect Couple, of course, kept a 'perfectly' detailed list of birds spotted.

The earthen hues of that dry, grassy savanna made it especially difficult to spot game. The wildlife so perfectly blended into the groundcover. Often you were on top or past the game before you knew it. The bird life, surprisingly, was a little easier to see. One of the first we spotted was a brilliant lapis blue Abyssinian Roller, who eyed us from a nearby branch while devouring a still-wriggling scorpion. Awkward looking storks glided overhead. Guinea fowl in black and white polka-dotted plumage scurried single file in search of food, as white herons perched atop baobabs beside uninterested vultures.

Then we started spotting larger mammals. Cape buffalo, with their horns comically upturned like a bad perm, stared at us in stony silence. Our nemesis, the baboons, scampered for the security of the treetops and threateningly barked whenever we glided to a stop. Monkeys peeked curiously from high atop spindly branches, while statuesque waterbucks cautiously observed us for just a moment before bolting for cover.

*This is our first taste of African big game and I'm famished for more.*

Chester's usual "Hot, damned hot" weather forecast continued over the next two days as we sped toward Cameroon. We'd become accustomed to cool morning air, but now it disappeared, just like the pools of water seductively appearing on the road that evaporated as we grew near. Finally, we rolled into Cameroon's border town.

Mora was in the midst of Ramadan, the highest of Muslim holidays. For a month the devout gave up eating and smoking from sunrise to sunset. Although the holiday made traffic lighter, it also meant that shops and even border posts kept more unpredictable hours than usual.

As we waited for the border hut to open, Maxie, our kitty-wallah and even tightfisted Prudence opened the food storage bin. For some strange reason, they chose that particular moment to carve a huge, ripe watermelon and loaf of French bread right out in the street. As they gorged themselves, pink, sweet juice dribbled from the corners of their mouths and fell to the ground leaving tiny craters in the dust.

Pious old men looked on in disgust. Shrouded women angrily glanced away. Children nervously giggled. Yet still they continued slurping, oblivious to their lack of tact and offense to thousands kneeling in prayer just behind them in the square.

*So much for cultural sensitivity.*

Clearing the border that afternoon, we continued trucking on toward Waza National Game Park in northern Cameroon, where we anticipated spotting even more game. Waza wouldn't disappoint us.

Reaching the front gate of the park, we picked up Benjamin, our sixty-year old guide who had a horrific set of facial scars running lengthwise down his weathered brown face. They looked less deliberately planned than those on the Nigerians we'd met.

*Are they tribal, or feline?*

Waza was wonderful. Nature abounded. In just moments, from the truck's top deck, we quickly spotted more storks, cranes, vultures and rollers than we'd seen all day at Yankari. There were herds of waterbucks and Cape buffalo. We were watched by wary jackals, sheltered in camouflaging brush. Thompson's gazelles mutely gazed up from their grazing, as Sable antelopes, nearly suspended in midair, effortlessly loped across grassy plains. Giraffes poked their heads above thorny acacia trees as they searched for tender leaves or pods to nibble. Families of warthogs defensively postured with tusks thrust upward. With a snort, they'd back down and dart off across the grassy prairie; their tails rigidly raised like antennas with fuzzy balls stuck on the ends. Like Neanderthal pointers on steroids, their stiffened tails would lower and extend straight out from their massive hairy bodies.

Then rounding a bend in the road, just in front of us, lay a herd of elephants, larger than we'd ever imagined. There must have been well over a hundred bathing and feeding around a pond. We carefully glided to a stop—as quietly as our enormous overland Dutch oven could.

Thirty soaked pachyderms merely glanced up to acknowledge our presence and then went right back to bathing. Those magnificent creatures trumpeted water from their trunks into the warm air and across their backs. Several younger calves imitated the rest, spouting water, dipping down into the refreshing pool, then emerging to snuggle next to their mothers. That process continued for about ten minutes while another seventy elephants pulled down leaves, pushed over trees with Herculean trunks and munched grass in the surrounding savanna. Then in very orderly fashion, the elephants in the pond started lumbering toward shore while another thirty or so meandered single file into the water. Transfixed, we stood and observed them over an hour through binoculars and cameras until exhausting our film.

*Yes, there's certainly is a distinct advantage to having a 'proper' guide–someone able to actually track animals, short of nearly running them over.*

Because this was lion country, we were all anxious to spot our first feline and we didn't have to wait long. Without much difficulty, Benjamin found a fresh set of tracks in the dust beside the road, not far from the elephants. Since he hunted lions daily, he knew their general haunts. Following that trail a short distance down the road as it veered off to the right, we headed directly into tall golden grass that stretched for endless miles.

Nigel ground the truck down into its lowest gear.

*Now's not the time to get stuck.*

As our belching truck lumbered farther into the high grass, Benjamin hopped out of his seat. His eyes narrowed to beads as he searched right and left to follow the still-warm trail the lion had left. We sweated bullets of anticipation, cautiously leaning out the windows, each wanting to be the first to spot the cat. Yet she couldn't help spotting us first. It was impossible to sneak up on a lion in that heap of a rattling wreck.

All of a sudden, Benjamin repeatedly pointed to our right, excitedly whispering, "Der she is. Der she is. Over der."

Not more than twenty-five feet away, a lioness crouched in thick, shoulder-high grass. Her golden muzzle dripped with crimson blood, as the carcass of a small, freshly killed antelope rested firmly between her massive paws. She glared at us with apparent hostility through one wary yellow eye. The other was swollen, red and infected, perhaps from a recent, less successful battle.

We coasted closer and closer. With every squeak of our brakes, her fury mounted. She growled, baring fangs as though she'd like nothing better than to bring down our massive gray intruder. As we coasted closer, she grabbed her limp prey in massive jaws and silently carried it farther into the grassy cover. We advanced. She retreated. Again. And again. Finally, seeking respite from our prying eyes, she turned, stretched her neck, cocked her head and growled one final time. It was over. Snatching the limp antelope in her jaws, she fled deep into the dense flaxen grass she called home.

Between the wild game and daily fifteen-hour drives, we were exhausted by the time we reached Chutes de Telo near Ndgoundere. We pitched our tents on a grassy knoll not far from the top of the falls, and looked forward to spending several days bivouacked in solitude. It was a long overdue chance to relieve a lot of pent-up frustration. Plus, a surprise birthday bash was planned for Nigel.

*There's no better way to kick off our holiday than with a shower au natural under those falls.*

Skidding down the hillside through vine-laced trees and vibrant tropical flowers, Cheryl and I raced to be the first to reach that spectacular pool. The water poured from overhead, falling in a transparent liquid sheet hundreds of feet. Two huge granite boulders, once part of the hillside itself, rested placidly in the water. They were ideal ledges to crawl upon and stretch out like lizards in the toasty rays of the sun. A rainbow arched across the face of the waterfalls in a heavenly lei.

My partner and I stripped free from our dusty clothes, plunging naked into the brisk waters of the tropical pool. Tenderly we hugged under the falls, lost in our own private paradise.

At sunset, Nigel's birthday bash went haywire. Curiously, no one bothered to tell him about it, so he spent all afternoon sequestered in his tent. At dinner, he was shocked when presented with his makeshift birthday cake: a loaf of bread covered in chocolate icing with a banana candle stuck on top that Cheryl had cleverly prepared. Always the easygoing sort, Nigel was more than ready to join in the debauchery. However, because Henry and his gang had started partying hours earlier, almost all the beer was gone. Of course, in the bush, it's never as easy as just heading to the local market for more.

As usual, Nigel didn't say a word. He just ambled off to bed in sullen disgust. With him gone, the insanity broke loose. Music blared. Rum was swilled. Henry, our miscast 'co-leader', danced and played 'bouncy, bouncy' on the truck seats with Dropsy, our klutzy security-wallah. Before long, he was dancing with mild-mannered Willie. We knew it was all getting too weird when Prudence, Dropsy and Peggy, the cornrow-headed Canadian, cornered baboon-chasing Slim behind a tree, tackled him, stripped off his pants and waved them through the camp.

"Ah now, thet's a worry," he sighed, a little too enthusiastically.

*Never have so many become so drunk on so little.*

Then Henry made a fatal mistake. Cornering nurse Clara behind a bush, he attacked her, trying to take off her dress. Bear heard Clara's screams and stormed over like his namesake, hands beating in the air, yelling, "Not with my wife ya don't, ya bugga." Bringing his ham-sized fist back, he round-housed Henry squarely on the jaw and sent him sprawling back into the dirt.

That had been far too long in coming.

# Chapter VII
# Ubangui Anguish

*"Only when you have crossed the river, can you
say the crocodile has a lump on his snout."*
~ African proverb

*N*O ONE SAID MUCH THE NEXT MORNING, especially Henry. He'd lost something more valuable than his eyebrow. He'd lost what little respect for him remained.

The overlanders took their dirty laundry to the pool below and beat their clothes on the rocks for hours. It was questionable which was worse–everyone's dirt or frustration. We each knew that no matter how much we were all on separate agendas, we were still stuck with each other for two more months. The tough hill terrain of the Central African Republic (CAR) and vast jungles of Zaire (Democratic Republic of the Congo) lurked just down the road. Having extra hands to pull, push and dig us out of the jungle muck just might come in handy.

It was a painfully slow drive to the CAR border. But by then, that was expected. Our sealed highway suddenly deteriorated into a dirt path just outside Ndgoundere. As if to test us further, we were chased by ominous clouds that threatened to impede our progress even more. There was no escape and they eventually exploded. The resulting deluge turned our dusty donkey path into a muddy mire.

By the time we eventually limped into the border, the CAR customs post was long-closed. So there was no choice other than to pitch our tents in a 'no man's land' between borders. Unrelenting, the rain continued to thunder and pound on through the night.

The sun reluctantly rose the next morning and with it our hope for a drier day. We crossed the border without event. After those heavy storms, we were relieved to find the roads still firm, allowing us to make up precious time in our race against the impending rainy season.

As we hurled from side to side down that primitive highway, we were surprised to see the white exteriors of mud brick dwellings painted with slogans and colorful characters of horses and hunters, boxing athletes and wild animals. Crossing rickety wooden bridges, we waved to children who bathed or pounded their wash in the streams below. We passed strong-shouldered women pounding grains or cassava in wooden bowls. Some braided each other's hair. Others breast-fed tiny, brown babies. Miniature goats bleated and bounded through soggy yards. Men stood on wooded beams and repaired thatched rooftops, or patched walls with a muddy plaster. At one point, we drew alongside a wrinkled fellow with an ax balanced across his head, singing, as he walked down the pitted road. He carefully cradled a small hunting dog under one arm and lugged a long spear in his other hand.

*It's life, much as it ever was.*

Bangui was entirely something else. Spacious, tree-lined avenues led to cacophonous markets and supermarchés boasting expensive French cheese, imported produce, wine and fancy pastries. The market's fluorescent glare stood in stark contrast to the sellers, hustlers, gun-toting military and beggars just across the street. Still, any hope of invading that import supermarket for long-awaited treats was tempered by their exorbitant prices: $20 for a kilo of potatoes, $20 per pound of cheese, $6 for a spool of dental floss.

We camped at a site outside town, just past the infamous Kilometer-7 Market, a brew of subtle attraction and utter repulsion. It was a modern scene of peasant squalor, reminiscent of the artist Hieronymus Bosch. Hundreds of stalls crowded suffocating streets. Music blared from every corner. Vendors yelled, "Touriste. Hey touriste!" Heaps of charred animal parts baked in the noonday sun, while monkey limbs were hawked by the kilo or the basket. Amid it all were hostile glares of contempt and obscene gestures.

Still, we'd looked forward to arriving in Bangui and gathering our mail. It would be the first news that we'd received in months. This was before e-mails and the Internet brought the world so much closer. So early the next morning, we all drove directly to the post office while Henry applied for visas at the Zaire Embassy.

As we eagerly hovered near the counter, the clerk studiously searched each cranny and pigeonhole looking for envelopes to match our strange sounding names. For nearly ninety minutes, we sweated and paced in the oven-like stillness of the reception area, until finally she announced, "C'est tout!"

"But where are ours'?" ten of us pleaded in unison.

"C'est tout. Fini. `A demain."

Well, we checked back tomorrow, tomorrow and three more 'demains'. Some letters were finally found. Four of us expecting care-packages from home were completely out of luck. Nigel was missing a birthday box, Sprout some peanut butter and pancake mix, and we were just looking for some word, from someone, anyone, that remembered we were still alive.

*Personally, I've never felt more alive. But the rest of the world, is it still there?*

When Henry returned with our visas, we discovered that food wasn't Bangui's only expensive product. Our visas cost a whopping $65 U.S. each, when typically they only cost $10-20.

*Has America suddenly cut off foreign aid to Zaire, and this is their way of getting even?*

For many, Bangui was a necessary health stop. Since that one fateful night of swamp camping, the group's health had deteriorated. Many were pretty ragged. Pouting Duchess had been weak for weeks. Unable to keep down solids, she alternated between chills and fever. Chester suffered similar symptoms of shivers and shakes throughout his smaller than usual 300-pound frame. Flinty's chiseled Errol Flynn-like face was the pallor of a melon and he was weak with the sweats, while tiny Pooky complained of aches and a malaise that even Bongo, her boy-toy drummer, couldn't cure.

They all went down to the local clinic for testing. After several days, it was announced that Duchess indeed had malaria and was placed on an intravenous drip until she could be flown back to England. Chester, deciding to tough it out, opted for malarial treatment. Everyone suspected that hepatitis was causing Flinty's jaundiced look. So he was given his own plastic plate, bowl, silverware and cup sketched with skull and crossbones. However, for some strange, sadistic reason, he continued to cook for our group. And Pooky? Well, she was prescribed medicine for a viral infection and got well 'straight away'.

Often you run into weird, but welcome coincidences traveling. One night during our Bangui stay, back at the campsite we happened to share a table and talk with two U.S. Marines, who'd dropped into the camp bar for a beer. By chance, one of them came from my small childhood town and the other had attended my Southern alma mater.

*How strange, here in the heart of Africa.*

Well, to celebrate our twist of fate, they invited Cheryl, whoever else, and me to join them for a swim at the Embassy compound. With tempting offers of real hamburgers and volleyball, we were delighted to accept. Plus, we were curious to see what type of plush accommodations our tax dollars bought. Most of our weary group was equally eager to take them up on their hospitality, even rabidly anti-American Henry. So, the next day, we headed out to the safe confines of the Embassy and were duly impressed.

Located along the banks of the Ubangui River, their sprawling ranch-style house was surrounded by a twenty-foot high barbed wire fence. With an Olympic-sized pool and barbecue, they were capable of fending off any potential invasion of insurgents–or tropical boredom.

As the others swam and played volleyball, my tanned partner and I chatted with Joannie, a diminutive, dark-haired Peace Corps volunteer from the Midwest. She'd been working out in the unforgiving bush for the past several years and was counting the days until she could leave. I sensed her timely departure came with much less idealism than her arrival. Africa sometimes had that effect on people.

She'd been living in a secluded Pygmy village. The kids taught her Sangha and she in turn tried to teach them hygiene to little avail. It was nearly impossible to change generations of village health habits.

"To complicate problems even more," she sighed, "foreign women have absolutely no status in the village. Much of my problem is that there's no sense of personal possession within the tribe," she confided, brushing sweat from her forehead. "If they want it, they take it. Several times I've been robbed and have even caught villagers climbing through my window to steal things."

We were a little shocked at her bitterness. Still, not too surprised, given her years of frustration.

"But that wasn't the worst," she added, lighting up a cigarette. "I had an English couple, some friends, visit me in the village. As they were leaving, I took a picture of them." She took a long drag. "Well, when I finally got the photos developed, one of the village women, someone I'd thought was my friend, demanded I give her a picture of my friends or…"

She stopped to blow smoke toward the ceiling fan.

"Or?"

"Or she'd cook my dog!" She slowly shook her head. "I've had enough. It's really time to leave."

Sadly, it was another case of good-intentioned Westerners headed to 'deepest, darkest Africa' to teach the 'natives' without bothering to understand a culture much older than our own.

All in all, it was a day rich with comparing our stories as 'travelers' with those of people who'd lived in CAR for years. As different as our experiences were, we could certainly empathize with their sense of emotional isolation. Whether spending a year or half a lifetime in a place like Bangui, according to them, you always remain a foreigner, an expat. You're prevented from getting too close and banned from digging too deeply, only able to just scratch the surface of a culture so richly exotic.

The volleyball game eventually ended after the overlanders knocked the ball over the fence for the fifth time, sending it sliding toward the murky Ubangui. We headed back to camp with months-old copies of some 'gossip rag', eager to learn all about Big Foot's alien love child.

It had been ages since we'd last eaten in a real restaurant and our steady diet of tinned fish, wheaty biscuits, veggies and bread had the pounds melting off the overlander men like no diet we'd tried before. We were all on our last belt loops. It was baffling to me how the women were actually gaining weight. Our diets and exercise were identical. On some days, breakfast was four-day-old fried bread and weak tea. Others, we'd feast on one pineapple and papaya split twenty-some ways, or those tiny foil-wrapped cheese wedges each split into three portions, even though there were cases of juices and cereals aboard. It just didn't make sense.

*It's odd. Everyone maintains stoic stiff upper lips as though slow starvation is part of the African experience.*

Why, the Perfect Couple even went so far one day as to gush, "We don't eat this well at home!" nodding their heads back and forth in their bizarre water ballet-like synchronized routine.

So, the night before we left the city, we decided to treat ourselves to a feast of exotic local dishes at a restaurant.

*Hopefully, we'll have better luck than Nigel and Sprout had last night.*

As they walked to a downtown café, two 'policemen' cornered them on the sidewalk and demanded to see photo IDs. Well, Sprout had one, but Nigel unfortunately didn't. For an hour the cops interrogated them in an attempt to extort 18,000 CFAs. At last, after some fast-talking and Cornish convincing, Nigel was finally able to talk them down to 8,000 CFAs or about $28 U.S.

*No, our dinners are bound to be better.*

Everyone dressed up in their overland finest, except for the Perfect Couple who whined, "We always get si-ick when we eat out. We'll just stay he-ere and have a boiled potato."

For the rest of us, it was surprising how excited we could get at even the smallest luxury: a shower, a cold beer, sleeping in a bed, a meal other than bread and potatoes. They were pure "luxxxurry."

That restaurant certainly fit the bill. Small candles along a narrow wooden table romantically lit the room. Though the dining was buffet-style, an attentive waiter shuttled mouthwatering cuisine back and forth from the kitchen. And what a glorious spread it was. We savored tasty bits of barbecued antelope. Succulent boa constrictor basted in spicy sauce. Incredible crocodile Creole. Wild boar in sweet and sour sauce, then something peculiar we suspected might be turtle. It could have been most anything, but it was exquisite–and didn't taste at all like chicken.

I always laugh at the way people try to describe a dish, then finally end up saying, "It tastes just like chicken," whether it's snake, crocodile, or buffalo.

*No, this is definitely not chicken.*

Since the waiter spoke no English or French, he drew a sketch of each animal and placed it next to its steaming dish. Fortunately, the cook was a better chef than the waiter was an artist.

"Whatever it is, it's brill-i-yant," Dropsy proclaimed, fanning herself with one of the drawings.

For once we all agreed and had at least one good meal before heading into the dense jungle ahead.

There was every intention of leaving Bangui after four days. We had our visas, enjoyed at least three cold showers–the mosquitoes in the stalls were an extra bonus. We savored a meal in a restaurant and went swimming. We'd even struck and packed the tents, food and cooking gear and were all sitting on the truck waiting to go, just like the family dog when anyone mentioned the word 'r-i-d-e'. But we couldn't leave quite yet. Arrangements still had to be made to fly Duchess home, while Flinty and Pooky had more tests.

Worst of all, Sprout finally had had enough. Even her buoyant boy-toy, Nigel, couldn't entice her to stay with the group any longer. It was a sad day all the way around, especially for Cheryl and me.

"Now we're completely on our own," I whispered, with more than a little trepidation.

Hoping to snatch some victory out of a day of defeats, I returned to the post office one more time, thinking our errant envelope had maybe just been mislaid.

*Maybe it's just sitting in one of the large cardboard boxes stuffed with mail in a back room?*

Well, the post office staff was sympathetic to our plight. "But your box is only six weeks late, monsieur," the clerk reminded me.

According to them, that would make it almost on time.

Together, we checked every overflowing box of mail we could find, even in a storeroom with piles of wayward letters dating back over a year. However, with no luck. As a last resort, I left our forwarding address and an entire pack of cigarettes with the clerk to ensure a little extra attention. In CAR, that was no light bribe. He eagerly promised to send it–if he ever received it. Nevertheless, to this day, our mail has never been found.

The following morning, Duchess cast off for the comforts of England, disgusted Sprout headed for Paris, and the rest of our brood, properly medicated, stereo blaring and cards shuffled, set off for the tranquil splendor of Kembé Falls. It was a relatively easy drive on well-graded dirt, although it took most of the day.

Upon arrival, as usual, I surveyed the primitive wooded site and chose what I thought was the best spot to pitch our tent. As I'd been camping since my early teens, I was constantly perplexed at the sites our 'leaders' chose for camping. One night it was a river 'wash'. If it rained, Henry and his groupies were bound to become one with nature–or 'swim with the fishes'. Another night it was a gravel pit. That was a favorite choice among overlanders. Still another, it might be a malaria-infested swamp, or atop some foul-smelling septic tank. Their choices were incomprehensible to me. Plus, by that point, quite honestly, my frazzled partner and I tried to bed down as far away from that group as possible, since we'd seen and heard enough of them during the day.

Well, I no sooner started staking down our tent than Nigel backed the massive, belching truck to within ten feet of where I was setting up. He shut off the engine, then noticing my irritation, laughed and walked away. At that moment, to make matters worse, Trotsky and Perfect Husband proceeded to toss all the packs and sleeping gear onto a ground sheet right outside our door.

"Hey, what do you think you're doing? Can you please toss those to the other side?"

They shrugged and continued heaving forty-pound packs, luggage and black plastic bags nearly onto our tent.

Well, I totally lost it. Draining the soda I'd been drinking, I flung the bottle with all my might against some nearby rocks where it exploded with a loud bang into a million pieces.

The camp grew quiet. Trotsky was stunned. Shaking a ratty head, he asked, "Hey, why'd you do that?"

*He just didn't get it. Then again, I had yet to see any of those coddled groupies show any emotion at all on this trip.*

So, I unloaded with a battery of reasons in a barely restrained fury, but knew for certain that it fell on deaf ears.

In fact, with a concerned look, he snorted, "Well, you know an animal might get hurt on that glass."

*Animals? Is he serious? I'm not too worried about the animals. They face worse each day. No, I'm worried about us–and you so-called 'overlanders'.*

That bottle went sailing to scream "Don't screw with us anymore!" and I figured it was safer to hit the rock with the bottle than his thick head.

Of course the falls were less than spectacular since the rainy season hadn't officially arrived–but they were running. Already there was a swift current in the Ubangui River above the falls. So, in addition to our warnings about bilharzia and river blindness, we added the very real threat of crocodiles.

*If there's any way to make one of my eyes look right while the other looks left, now's certainly the time to try.*

There is a certain knack to bathing in African streams. You need to find a spot where the water is deep enough to sit, but not so deep that you have to tread water. Also, because of all the dreaded snail diseases, you need to be in quickly moving water. However a fine line separates 'quickly' from the kind of swiftness that sweeps you off the bank and over a set of two hundred-foot falls, or into the mouth of a smiling croc faster than you can say 'meaty morsel'.

And then, what to do with your soap? In some parts of Africa, soap is as rare as a paved road, especially a body soap that can't also be used to wash clothes, scrub a hut or bathe your camel. And, well, soap on a rope is certainly out of the question. You try to gingerly place that treasured sliver on a rock near the water. Inevitably, no matter how well you chose that stone, as soon as you put your wet soap down, every decaying leaf, minute insect and mold is instantly embedded in it, and then on you when you wash.

I thought I'd found the perfect location perched on a ledge, anchored between two larger stones, just twenty-five feet from the top of the pounding falls. That was until a slight, dramatic movement just upstream caught my eye. As I hurriedly wiped the suds from my eyes, the slippery soap shot out of my hand and cascaded over the falls performing a half-twist in just 3.5 seconds–to no cheering crowd.

Later that afternoon, in the shade of a small bamboo bar upstream, we relaxed with the locals sipping cool Bimbo beers and watching crocs frolic in the Ubangui. Because it was my night to cook, I couldn't spend much time there and headed back down the dirt road toward camp. That night's feast of haute cuisine was spaghetti. We usually tried to fix pasta in our cook group, as there was so little that could possibly go wrong. After all, Slim, Willie and I were cooking together at that point, and we needed all the help we could get.

Food had become a weapon of mass distraction. For months, Prudence had been cutting back on our rations with her usual, "We're saving it for Zaire." She'd heard rumors about a food shortage there, so we were preserving the hundreds of pounds of bulk food that we carried on board and buying more local food. That initially made sense. However, when we saw less and less appetizing local food, unless we counted the charred monkey limbs and wriggling grubs, logic dictated we needed to dip into our dried and canned reserves. Well, not Prudence. No, she was the gourmand who suggested thickening tomato sauce with white flour instead of opening a small can of tomato paste. She was saving the fifty-cent can for 'wherever'. Zaire? Tanzania? Who knew?

So that special night, against my better judgment, I was forced to concoct pasta, on her insistence, using only instant onion and chicken soup base for the sauce. It was a solo venture since Slim and Willie, the personable Kiwi duo, showed up late, then only tended our puny wood fire. The skies already grew dark as massive thunderheads rolled in from the west.

*We'll have to hurry, if we're going to get everyone served before this deluge breaks.*

As luck would have it, within minutes, we were in the midst of a torrential, tropical downpour. Dinner was as ready as it would ever be since the rains were quickly dousing our feeble flames.

"Aw-raite!" Slim screamed in his Aussie twang. "Cum un' git ya tucker!"

As I ducked inside the truck to grab my rain poncho, the others scrambled to the soggy fireside. Rain streamed down their ruddy faces as great dollops of Ubangui spaghetti was plopped on their plates. By the time they left the fire, their red plastic plates were already swimming in more rainwater than sauce. Then out of the drenched darkness came one gargled groan after another.

"What's this, some kinda joke!" Maxie growled, as her matted bleached hair fell and dripped down her face like a wet octopus.

"Awwwyecch!" others chimed-in.

Prudence failed to warn me, as I threw together that insane concoction, how concentrated they were. I'd added five times the correct amount. It was salty enough to give a fish hypertension.

Still, I must admit that a satisfied grin did cross my lips.

On a more positive note, the pounding rain did an excellent job of watering down the sauce, as the intrepid overlanders gagged down dinner amid the relentless storm of another African night.

104

# Chapter VIII
# Jungle Trance, Pygmy Dance

*"Do not call the forest that shelters you a jungle."*
~ African proverb

BY HIGH NOON THE FOLLOWING DAY, after crossing a Swiss cheese swatch of dirt road, we reached the watery crossroads to Zaire and our old friend, the muddy Ubangui. In decaying, decrepit Mobaye, where insects successfully feast on man, we were part of a scene reminiscent of a low budget *African Queen*. There was the crusty river captain and his run-down boat, an equally dilapidated market selling only fermenting mangoes and dried grubs, and the open-air butcher shop on the banks of the murky river. Men in tattered t-shirts sold chunks of raw beef and Cape buffalo swarming in a black veil of hungry flies in the midday sun. Heaps of horns and rotting testicles lay littered and rotting on the fetid field.

Eventually, the ferry that was to tote us across the Ubangui loped into the dock and Nigel cautiously inched our truck onto the tiny craft. It was a tight fit. One could have just as easily fit the puny riverboat onto our overweight lorry. Then, issuing a stern warning, the river pilot cautioned us not to take photos of the dam as we passed, or for that matter even show our cameras. Otherwise, the nervous river sentinels would take us for spies and blast our ship with heavy artillery.

We were soon underway and shortly rolled onto the opposite shore without a major international incident. The toughest part, we imagined, lay ahead. Zaire's reputation preceded it. We'd both marveled and worried about it since our arrival on the continent. On one hand, we'd heard about its legendary intense beauty, the friendliness of its people, its endangered gorillas and disappearing Pygmies. Yet then on the other hand, we'd also been warned about its terrible roads and dilapidated bridges, the near impossibility of travel during its rainy season, and its share of mindless bureaucracy.

Well, our fragile craft no sooner landed than the first obstacle confronted us. The half-ton pickup that landed just before us was stalled. Huge oil barrels stacked ten feet high overhung its sides like giant insect eggs ready to rupture at any moment. Meanwhile, the truck perilously leaned in the mire on the hillside above the river. It completely blocked the road leading past the customs office to the main highway. There was no way around it.

For nearly an hour, we sat there and watched as the driver rocked his truck back and forth, gunning his engine, trying to climb that small hill. However, his treadless tires were useless on the rain-slicked slope. Finally, out of desperation, a few of us offered to machete a quick path to the right of the truck, through to the main road.

*We've crossed the Sahara, so it can't be any harder than sandmatting.*

Well, we'd no sooner started our task than the truck driver made another feeble attempt to climb the slope. Linked by a thin, taut rope to another larger lorry, it chugged and strained about fifteen feet up the embankment. Suddenly, both trucks started to skid back toward the two nervous drivers' assistants, who quickly tossed rocks behind their rear wheels then dove out of the way.

As that mayhem continued outside, Nigel and Henry trudged through the mire of officialdom. Seems the chief medical inspector was upset because the address penciled in my passport didn't match the address on my yellow immunization booklet. I was called before him, as he sat stuffed into a miniature, rusty school desk in the stifling heat of a cramped, windowless office. The slow 'swoosh, swoosh, swoosh' of the fan overhead did nothing to cool the room. It only agitated the pesky river flies and kept them from landing on his sweaty, furrowed brow.

"Why two dee-ffer-ent add-ress?" he demanded.

"I just recently moved."

He just stared at me through narrowed eyes.

I continued, "As you can see from the dates, monsieur, the yellow booklet shows vaccinations from this date and this other one."

With that stifling heat, I knew if I didn't get out of the room soon, he was going to have a real medical problem on his hands.

"But two deefferent place?" He flicked the mole on the tip of his nose.

He still didn't understand until I opened my pouch and flashed him my driver's license. It was suddenly all clear. That plastic coated card with my photo was OFFICIAL looking, so it must be correct.

"Ohhh." He leaned forward and stamped the entry paper with a lethargic "thump," disappointed we'd skirted paying a hefty cadeau.

By that time, our truck had made it around the stalled lorry, now up to its sides in muck. Our papers were in order and a green uniformed customs official was examining our truck with a fine toothed hair-pick. Up until then we'd been lucky. Through all those border crossings, we never had to unload all the tables, plastic bins, tents and, worst of all, the back locker and its sixty bags. However, that nitpicking inspector was thorough. He'd already examined the interior and inspected our overhead nets where we stored a hodgepodge of cassettes, books, cameras, food, insecticide and rain gear.

*He could make us strip everything out of the truck. That could take hours.*

Then he headed for the back locker. Now, not coincidentally, I'd helped pack the bags that day and our growing cache of souvenirs. Knowing we were passing through a border, I'd planted a surprise, a little booby trap, to help dissuade all but the most determined official. Earlier, I'd inadvertently learned if you stacked all sixty bags just right, when anyone opened the door, even just a crack, a wall of packs ten feet high would threaten to avalanche out onto your head.

As Nigel inched the door gradually open, the officer, seeing the mound of moving canvas careening toward him, hastily decided all was in order. So we were finally waved on our way–and after only four hours.

It was a relief to finally arrive in Zaire, these days, after years of war, known as the Democratic Republic of the Congo. For four months we'd heard that their roads were some of Africa's worst and we were ready to face the challenge. Imagine our disappointment when we discovered its roads of torture were actually paved.

*Wait a minute. Are we too late? Has this all changed in the past year?*

As we easily drove down a sleek two-laned highway, we marveled at neat rows of Western style houses, new multi-story hotels, an airport and a palace.

*A palace? Ah, that explains it. So this is the president's hometown. A president can't have visiting dignitaries traveling around town on dirt roads, especially when they've given the country billions of dollars in foreign aid.*

Our dreams of jungle life weren't dashed, only postponed. A few miles later, just outside Mobayi, the pavement abruptly vanished. Creeping vegetation surrounded and engulfed that meager swath through the forest, and we were back on pockmarked, one-lane dirt roads bumping toward Bumba.

Bumba was a port city. If we timed it right, we'd be able to catch the legendary riverboat down the Congo River to Kisangani. That ship was one of the major forms of transportation through central Zaire. We'd heard that people crowded on board with their livestock, goods for sale and families for the several day float to the big city. Meanwhile, everyone camped out on the upper deck, sharing stories, drinking warm Primus beer and listening to the infectious rhythms of soucous music punctuated by the peals of goats.

*Given our past luck with boat trips, don't count on miracles.*

Over the next two days, we slowly inched our way down that verdant jungle trail, passing houses built of simple adobe mud over wood with roofs of either thatched straw or woven leaves. Hordes of children greeted us, as they rushed out screaming, "Bonjour!" and "Donnez moi une stylo!"

"Ah, pens are the second currency here, too," Cheryl laughed, reassured.

Those friendly folks tended coffee trees and subsisted on what they could grow or raise: bananas, mangoes, chickens, goats, pineapples and manioc or cassava root which they dried, pounded into powder then baked into a loaf. Many of the men also hunted. We passed them walking into the jungle, armed with only machetes, as they went in search of porcupines, monkeys or wild-eyed wart hogs.

We did our share of searching too, as our eyes scoured the road, eager to avoid sliding into giant crevasses capable of completely swallowing lesser trucks.

After dodging those craters for two days, we spent a restless night in Lisala, camped in another guesthouse yard. It was unmemorable except for the objects that were stolen right out from under our tent's flysheets as we slept. Losing a tent sack, mallet and tennis shoes, although not necessarily valuable items, were still reminders of our own vulnerability. It was unnerving to realize that someone actually had the nerve to unzip your tent fly and sneak something out–with your head just inches away.

In the morning, not a trace of the culprits was found. But later, several wiry boys approached me, trying to pawn off an expensive compass and flashlight they'd probably recycled from a previous camper. It was supply and demand, jungle style.

Finally, the afternoon of the second day we pulled into Bumba, weary, but otherwise unscathed. Nigel checked on our riverboat connections, while we headed for the market to stock up on food. What a shock that madhouse was after the pastoral serenity of the countryside.

Every Bumban huckster and salesman began a full-court press. We were easy targets. Some overlanders shopped for used blue and white Zaire flour sacks that they hoped to have hand-tailored into distinctive shirts, vests and dresses in Kisangani. Meanwhile, Cheryl, Bear, Clara and I were relegated to finding food. That turned out to be an almost impossible and certainly unappetizing task.

Women in brightly colored 'kangas' swayed past us carrying fried whole monkeys, their tails wrapped up over their backs to form a basket-like handle. In the meat stalls, piles of primate parts set stacked, waiting to become main course at someone's evening meal. Then there were the stalls specializing in fried grubs. Or, if you preferred, you could buy the fat, white, wiggling larvae alive, eyes bulging as they squirmed 'round and 'round in a bowl.

Since I had no blue-ribbon recipes for ape with me, we settled for more tinned pilchard fish. It was nothing new. We were eating them at least once a day. That wouldn't have been so bad. However, under Prudence's constant supervision, the contents of three small cans were invariably smashed to a briny pulp. Then, once it resembled cat food, we indulged in a feast of about three canapés each.

After our unsuccessful shopping spree, we re-boarded our 'beast' in search of blackmarket gasoline. Petrol was notoriously difficult to find in Zaire. However, following a hot tip, we ended up in front of a squat, ivory-colored, concrete-block house. Nigel ducked inside and, after some intensive haggling, he returned with the smiling owner who carried a bucket and plastic funnel. There was no choice of three grades of gasoline. No air pump. No little green tissues to clean your windshield. No giant Slushee machine. No self-service pump—or any pump for that matter. That explained the bucket. There was one large oil drum and for over an hour they refilled that bucket then poured it 'polepole' through the funnel and into our tank. It was like trying to refill a well with water–one cup at a time.

Finally stocked up, we headed to the local campsite perched along the Zaire River where we'd spend the night, hoping to catch that boat in the morning. We pitched tents facing the murky river. The weather had been clear all day. For once, we left our rainflap off, hoping to catch a breeze and find respite from the baking ninety-degree temperatures with 90% humidity that transformed our tent into a day-glow steam bath each night.

*Maybe there'll be a break in the weather.*

You need to be very specific what you wish for. About 1:30 a.m., the skies let loose with a downpour so intense I thought we'd go floating down the Zaire without the boat. The torrential rain quickly submerged our entire dome. A river flowed underneath it as well. I couldn't even begin my frantic bailing until Cheryl finally pranced outside in the buff to batten down our rainflap.

That downpour continued well into the next day. Weary weather, combined with news that the boat trip was a 'bust', dampened our spirits. No ships were scheduled to arrive for two more days, and then it was only a navigational boat. So, more than a little disappointed, but not too surprised, we loaded everything again, mustered our enthusiasm and continued toward Kisangani.

Over the next several days our progress grew slower as the road deteriorated further. In one three-and-a-half hour stretch, we only managed to cover a bone jarring fifty-five miles. Although the road itself wasn't all that muddy yet, we had to constantly skirt deep gullies that ran down either side that was left over from the previous rainy season, as we avoided holes capable of snapping our springs, as easily as we did our morning wheaty biscuits.

'Bridges' were frequently mere logs wedged across swollen riverbanks. Often, we'd have to slam on the brakes, climb down to inspect, test and usually repair parts of those shaking structures before we dared to cross. At one point, we even stopped for two hours to help some local men armed only with primitive adzes remove a tree as large around as a house trailer, totally blocking the road.

For a silly diversion, we staged a 'Stuck in the Muck Contest'. The object was to guess the first time we'd get totally bogged down in the muddy road–so deeply we'd have to dig out. Well, it wasn't long before Bongo won, and we all gained a bit of instant enlightenment.

*Digging out of concrete mud is no easier than sandmatting.*

Still, as bad as the roads initially were, they became far worse. At points, one side of the road rose three feet higher than the other that doubled as a riverbed during the frequent rains. The challenge became balancing the truck between the two sides without completely tipping over.

Yet, even with all those obstacles, we were still impressed by the rugged beauty and pureness of it all. One day, we encountered hundreds of brilliant butterflies. From a distance, they appeared as brightly waving lapis banners, as though a mirage. Approaching, you could almost touch their silky wings. One of those lovely creatures even adopted me as we hiked down the road and rode along on the brim of my hat for thirty minutes or so.

Our 'Walking Zaire' program, as Cheryl and I called it, grew out of a need to have some private time; time away from the group after four long months together. Plus, we wanted to discover the jungle, unfettered by the womb-like truck and its stifling insulation from nature. It turned out to be one of our better decisions. People saw and treated us differently once we removed ourselves from the 'flash' truck and were just simple travelers, walkers with only the dirty clothes on our backs.

There were no more demands for cadeau. People approached us out of curiosity, smiling and asking, "Where are you from? What are you doing here? Where are you going?" Children ran down to meet us, yelling, "Mbotay!" Gnarled men stopped work just long enough to shake hands. People actually wanted to have their photos taken and you didn't have to feel like you were intruding on them, sneaking a shot or stealing their soul.

One day, after walking about two-and-a-half hours down a dirt path, we encountered a handsome young man in his twenties surrounded by three young women and their babies. They gathered around his feet as he sat on a hand-hewn bed and read to them from a tattered book. It was a scene of great love and tranquility, and I just had to stop and speak to him.

He paused and rose to greet me in French. We introduced ourselves and then very tentatively I asked if he'd mind if we took a photo of him and his wives to remember them and preserve that very special moment.

Initially he refused, somewhat shyly.

However I asked again, promising to send them a copy of the photograph. Well, they'd probably never had a family portrait. Delighted, he agreed. I took their shot and later, true to my word, sent him their photo that spoke volumes to me about a family's love–one that transcends any culture.

From our daily tramps, we also got a much clearer look at the smaller details of everyday life that we'd normally miss from the fleeting window of a truck. Right down the road from that fellow and his wives, we discovered a pole sporting two skulls stuck in front of two houses.

"Wonder what that's all about?" my partner hesitantly asked.

As we grew near, a young man in a torn American t-shirt hailed us. "Dees," he said proudly, motioning to the skulls, "dees ees wart hog." He made a grunting sound. "Dees ees ape I keell not long ago," he added, doing his best chimp imitation. Patting his large belly, he laughed, "I am goood hun-ter, you know."

*I like that. Life in the jungle is reduced to the simplest of things.*

Some days, I'd take off completely alone and walk for an hour in the jungle, studying the scenery, chatting with people and taking more photographs. People really opened up to this wide-eyed stranger. Snowy-haired ladies approached to show off their grandchildren. Teenaged girls flirted, giggling at my odd appearance, and white-shirted, clean-scrubbed schoolboys shared their hopes and dreams of travel.

Then all too soon, our truck loomed on the horizon. As it grew larger, throwing dust all over those gentle people who'd just shared their wealth of kindness with me, I grew sad. The illusion of being the solitary traveler and citizen of the world quickly vanished. Again, I was only part of that bizarre group, now so jaded by Africa that few even noticed or returned the waves and genuine smiles coming from locals. These kind, simple people were more curious about us than we were of them. Most of the overlanders were strangely content to play cards, read and listen to music all day.

*How tragic. Why do they even bother to cross Africa? Is it just some kind of finishing school for them–Mummy's notion that they should go 'off to see the continent' before settling down?*

We finally pulled into Kisangani, a sprawling metropolis by Congo standards, straddling the Zaire River. It was a shock to be back in the daily rush of a major African city again. In some ways, it was a disappointment. For two weeks, I'd been content with camping in bamboo-shrouded jungle clearings, appreciating the friendly hospitality and curiosity of the simple people. Yet in other ways, big-city comforts were a welcome change.

Our group immediately checked into the Olympic Hotel, their rear courtyard. We, on the other hand, thought it foolish tle comfort. So, for the equivalent of $6 US, we rented a high-ceilinged room with private bath, ceiling fan and real bed. Although less than standard anywhere else, there it was a decadent luxury. It had been months since we'd slept on anything other than the ground, and it was miraculous how little things like running water, a bed and cooked food could revitalize your body.

*We'll need all our strength in the coming weeks.*

We eagerly looked forward to exploring Kisangani, especially legendary Stanley or Boyoma Falls. With little trouble, Nigel hired a guide, Pierre, who promised take us not only to the cascades, but also to the village of Wygenia to meet those people whose lives centered around the falls.

Early the next morning, our motley troop headed off with Pierre for the short trek through the frenzied town to the cataracts. He was the perfect guide to tell us all about the famous site, since he'd grown up in the tiny village of eight hundred that earned their livelihood fishing at the falls.

Now we were accustomed, when thinking of African falls, to imagine sheets of thundering waters careening over mountain cliffs to smash against rocks hundreds of feet below. Stanley Falls was something else altogether. Perhaps they were only 'falls' to Henry Morton Stanley, for whom they were re-named. He was the same 19th century reporter from the *New York Herald* who set off to find Dr. David Livingstone, the Scottish missionary and explorer. Stanley was also the one who, after running into the first white man in the heart of the vast jungle, was credited with the timelessly brilliant observation, "Doctor Livingstone, I presume?"

Stanley Falls more closely resembled rapids on the murky Zaire River. Its rushing water ran past and under a series of wooden and bamboo platforms supporting many cone-shaped baskets. These perfectly engineered fish traps were woven from nearby river reeds and varied in size. Some were narrow, perhaps only three feet long. Others were so massive it would take three heavily muscled men, sweating and straining with a rickety pulley, to hoist them up when full. But they were very effective. Sardines and even the larger, more prized capitaine fish inadvertently swam into them with the water as it flowed past. Each family had their own set of baskets and lowered them in the river five times each day. As some worked on the bamboo scaffolding, younger sons, apprentices in the family business, sat on the banks and repaired or created more of those unique reed traps that ensured life for the families.

Observing that finely honed operation made us all the more curious to visit their homes. So we eagerly climbed into a long, canary yellow ten-person pirogue and set off down the swiftly moving river to the village of Wygenia where the fishermen lived. Pulling ashore, Pierre led us past mud and straw huts to the rear of the village looking down upon the waterway below.

Hearing a slight rustle behind us, I wheeled around to stand face-to-face with the chief, dressed in a simple loincloth. Impressive looking gold medals with blue and yellow ribbons hung as a garland against his bare, mahogany chest. His spotted leopard skin headdress was fringed with brilliant bird feathers reflecting the rays of the sun.

Smiling, he welcomed us, then grabbed two wooden batons. Striding over to a log drum sitting in the clearing, he beat out a message announcing our visit to the Wygenians. At least, that's what Pierre told us. He might have said, "We have a group of live ones here. Quick, bring all your souvenirs to sell."

For as we walked back to the pirogue, we were again politely shown an assortment of wooden carvings, necklaces and masks, including one from a circumcision ceremony. We'd come to expect a certain amount of merchandizing by then. Besides, I personally felt better picking up a gift from them and supporting the village directly, than dealing with another salesman in the marketplace.

After canoeing the short distance back upstream, my partner and I walked with Pierre back into town. As we passed a fellow with a grinning baby chimpanzee tethered to a pole beside his house, Cheryl sweetly remarked, "Oh, how cute, a pet chimp. It seems pretty cruel though to leave him tied out in the yard like that."

"No," Pierre replied laughing, "eett ees to eat…."

"To eat? But he's just a baby!"

"No, not eat yet. Zey raise heem 'til he geet a leettle older and geets too mean. Zen zey have heem for din-naire."

Such were the realities of everyday life in the bush. It's all a matter of culture. Personally, I've met quite a few charming calves, yet we eat them without feeling too disgusted. The allure of Styrofoam packaging and in-store music makes it all more palatable for Western tastes.

The next day, after handing over our flour sacks to local tailors to have shirts made, we explored the front streets and back shops of Kisangani. There was the usual central marketplace that stretched nearly a hundred yards on either side of the road, offering row after row of scrap lumber stalls covered with burlap roofs. Each had its specialty. One sold only fried bats; another boasted crispy monkey parts. One had rows of tomatoes lined up. Several sold freshly ground peanut butter spread onto banana leaves in dollops. Some displayed stacks of cassava roots and piles of papaya. Another peddled peppers and only peppers. Then, there was one stand that carried all the little household items impossible to find anywhere else. It was the original jungle discount store with its plastic combs, playing cards, bottle stoppers, can openers, pens & paper, ointments, mirrors, aspirin, envelopes, razors, matches and cigarettes sold by the piece.

Oddly enough, in Kisangani's market, there were two or three entire rows devoted to selling only used American clothing. They were all the rage–so much so, they made it difficult to find traditional fabrics. Those leftovers from twenty years of our garage sales and charity donations all ended up right there in the heart of Africa. There were corduroy bell-bottoms and flowered shirts from the 1960s, blue jeans with embroidered patches, shark skin suits and high collared Nehru jackets, filmy negligees, baseball caps and t-shirts from New Jersey schools, even platform shoes, looking no better now than they did way back then.

*It's yet another shocking reminder of how hard it is in a 'global village' to escape the web of Western influence, a global kudzu.*

The next morning, we collected our various hand-tailored flour sack shirts, vests, dresses, hats and t-shirts from our Pygmy laundryman. It was hilarious to witness–twelve rugged overlanders all dressed in their coordinated outfits, like reps of the Zaire Flour Conglomerate. Dark-haired, rosy-cheeked Pooky and Bongo looked more unusual than ever in their matching flour sack shirts and skirt combos, sort of like an African Raggedy Ann and Andy.

I have to admit, for some time Bongo's outfits had been a constant source of amusement. I remembered the duds he and his pal Flinty had bought in Algeria. Dressed in ankle-length flowing robes like house frocks, with hiking boots and sunglasses, they looked like Saharan transvestites. No one bothered to tell them that Algerian men wore pants beneath those outfits.

115

So, I don't know who laughed harder–the locals or us? Then again, after four months together on the road, you found a laugh anywhere you could.

Loading up again, we set off for the wilds in search of a Pygmy village and okapi reserve near Epulu. It was slow going as usual. The roads became progressively worse with each passing rain-drenched night. However, after creeping along all that day and all the next morning, we finally reached Epulu.

Epulu consisted of a small village and game reserve ringing the banks of a river with the same name. Large billowing violet jacaranda trees and emerald rolling hills fringed the winding river, replete with rapids, small cascades and the obligatory crocodiles. The rippling of the water and coolness of the mountain setting was very relaxing. Our serenity was only broken by the occasional human-like, bloodcurdling screams of hydrax, those tiny, mutant prairie dogs.

At one point, Cheryl hilariously joined them, throwing back her head and letting out a shrill, "Aaa-hhhhh!" in answer to their doleful cry.

*There's nothing like a little primal shriek to completely confuse the still-prim overlanders.*

Some of our companions used that occasion to go down to the river and beat their clothes. The 'twap, twap, twaps' of wet jeans slapping against rocks was only interrupted by occasional swats at the whopping flies.

Later that afternoon, we walked to the reserve and instantly spotted four gentle okapis. To my untrained eye, they resembled antelopes with brown and white stripes on their hindquarters. There, deep in the African wilds, American mammalogists had established a park to preserve and study some of the last remaining members of that endangered species. They'd been successful in breeding and raising newborn okapis in a protected environment, safe from their only natural predators–leopard and man. Their only slight nuisance was the rowdy chimps, their neighbors.

Those chimpanzees and other monkeys were confiscated from visitors by the reserve guards. Apparently, travelers had bought them from villagers to save them from the dinner table, only to lose them upon entry into the park since they were illegal to keep.

Small chimps frolicked childlike in the trees, swinging from branch to branch or just hanging upside down from the lower limbs. Others, like Jean-Pierre, a more aggressive three-year-old, ran back and forth on his tether trying to snatch sunglasses or cameras from unsuspecting passersby. Occasionally, as Cheryl discovered, the chimps would team up to create mischief together.

One young elfin ape, running free, dropped down in front of her and started untying her shoes.

"Ah, isn't he cute," she playfully cooed.

However, it was just a ploy to distract her while Jean-Pierre quietly sneaked up from behind, grabbed her leg and wrestled it back and forth, trying to throw her to the ground.

After lunch, in the ponderous heat of the noonday sun, we and our armed guards set off for the Pygmy village. No, our escort wasn't there to protect us from the simple Twa people. They were worried about leopards. For generations those Pygmies had hunted and survived along the banks of the Epulu River. Of course, that was until the relentless encroachment of visitors and farmers alike drove them back farther into the heart of the dense forest.

We hiked in silence, moving in single file for over an hour, trudging through cornfields, wading across streams, trekking among small clusters of miniature thatched houses, sliding down mud-slicked paths. Finally, we entered the thickest of smoke-ringed jungles. Suddenly, we heard the low, distant beating of a drum, and yelling back and forth across the shadowed jungle to either side of the trail. As we looked around, we could just barely discern dark, childlike faces peering at us from the brush to either side and to our rear, while others sped down the path to confront us.

Those reclusive forest people led us along the vine-choked path to their secluded village, consisting of ten bent-twig-framed huts interwoven with banana and other large leaves. The green, dome-shaped houses formed an elongated circle with small, smoking fires dotting the central courtyard.

Standing just barely three feet tall, those lithe jungle dwellers were dressed in ragged cutoff pants, while many of the girls wore tattered skirts of once colorful African fabrics. The Pygmies seemed to range in age from the newborn to maybe fifty-five or sixty. However, it was difficult to judge their age, as few spoke any French and no one uttered English. One man, with whom I could communicate, looked ten, but was nearly twenty.

They were very friendly and seemed unaffected by all our questions and photo taking. Tiny, teenaged girls warily approached to stroke my beard and trade for my red, cotton kerchief. They offered necklaces of large polished black seeds, charred decorated wood, black and white speckled guinea feathers, teeth, tiny horns and patches of dik-dik hair–all strung together on thin strands of woven tree bark.

We learned that much of their daily subsistence depended on these dik-dik, miniature antelope about the size of large rodents. The horns, teeth and hooves were destined for ornamentation, and hides became clothing or arrow quivers.

I was eager to chat with a small, bearded forest man who crafted bows, arrows and quivers for their village. His work was exceptional. The miniature wooden bows measured about three feet in length. Around the center of the shaft were thin twisted strands of bark wrapped into a grip. They were different from others I'd seen, whose shafts were encased in the gray fur of a monkey's tail. The string consisted of a thin strip of bamboo, anchored to both ends of the shaft. Arrow designs varied. About two feet in length, the more elaborate ones had small metal tips and gracefully shaped leafs instead of feathers. On others, the tip of the arrow shaft itself was sharpened to a point, with a screw-type ridge encircling it. Those were often dipped in an effective poison.

After watching him for awhile at his task, I knew his finely-crafted weapon would always remind me of my time with them. So we traded back and forth in sign language for awhile. Finally, a dollar and a Swiss Army knife, boasting a miniature saw, sealed the deal.

Before long, it was time to begin our own hunt for the elusive dik-dik, and together we set off into the darkness of the canopied forest. After trudging through wet, leafy jungle for nearly thirty minutes, our child-guide finally stopped abruptly. He motioned for us to get down. We crouched, eager to hear the little deer.

*By the way, what do dik-dik sound like?*

Meanwhile, our guide set off to string a fine net in front of us, about fifty feet across. In a few moments, we heard shouting in the dense forest a hundred yards ahead. It grew louder and nearer. The Pygmy bowmen herded and charged the dik-dik between them toward the net. The rustling sound grew closer and closer. We still couldn't see them, but it sounded like they were almost upon our blind. Then it suddenly stopped.

They'd escaped–for now. For just a moment there were sad expressions on the boys' faces as they re-gathered their nets and moved deeper still into the undergrowth. That procedure repeated itself again and again, as we pushed still farther "in search of the dreaded dik-dik."

*Is this the African version of our own legendary midnight snipe hunt? Are there actually such things as dik-dik?*

Then it happened. Torrential rains began again. We hurried back with our hunters to the shelter of their village. Half our group hastily set off with their gear, back to the comfort of our truck, not wanting to spend the night with our tiny hosts. Cheryl had stayed behind the entire day, since she was at wit's end and just needed to spend a day alone, lost in her thoughts. Their early return was bound to surprise and ruin her peace and quiet. As for me, I wouldn't have missed a night at this 'Pygmy Palace' for the world.

With our group halved, the Pygmies began to relax a little more. Young mothers sat under the dry canopy of the leafy huts and breastfed babies. Some wove bark baskets. The oldest woman in the family, an impish lady probably in her fifties, but looking twice that age, pulled out an eight-foot long banana stem pipe and started puffing away on a little jungle ganja.

As the nappy-headed men cooked a dinner of beans, rice and forest greens over their fire, they enviously eyed our simple dinner, one no fancier than theirs'. So we were more than happy to share our meager soup of plantains, tomatoes, cabbage and beans.

By the time supper was over, the rain had eased up. The men, along with several of us, sat around their fire for hours on six-legged stools, sharing stories in sign language and laughing in the enchanted stillness of the forest.

As it grew late, I wandered over to join Clara and Bear beside the women's fire at the other end of the tiny village. In the eerie light of that flame, young maidens danced and strutted to the mysterious repetitive notes plucked on a banjo-like stringed instrument. First, they'd flutter forward with their butts sensuously thrust out, then back. Backlit by the fire's glow, I couldn't see faces, just shadows shuffling in the primeval hollow. The smoke from the fires mystically swirled around those lights and the magic of the moment was intoxicating.

When the rains began again, five of us headed for the shelter of one of their igloo-shaped huts. Its warmth and dryness was a welcome relief, as the village was soon awash in a sea of mud.

119

*How different will their lives be without the occasional contact with outsiders? The Pygmy fellow I talked with assured me that they welcome visits. Of course, I figure that's because of the cadeaus, sweets, food, cigarettes or t-shirts we bring. Or the little bit of money that trickles down to them from the government. I'm certain of one thing, though. These forest folk are becoming as rare as the okapi—with no scientific group anxious to step forward and protect them.*

As I nodded off to sleep, the only remaining sounds were the gentle patter of rain on our leafy hut and sweet 'peep-peep-peep' from tiny chicks inside the basket that lay by my head.

Life was already bustling in the village by the time the sun's first rays filtered through the jungle's dense canopy to the darkened floor below. The women fixed another meal of beans and greens, as grandma lit up her favorite pipe.

We, too, caught the feverish pace of early morning, rolled up our sleeping bags, left a few small gifts with our cordial hosts and started the trek back to the rest of the group. Although we'd have preferred to stay longer, the government purposely limits visits to one day—minimizing the impact while maximizing the profit.

The next several days for us were a series of never-ending skirmishes, as we battled our way down 'roads', reassuring ourselves that those jungle paths couldn't get any worse. Yet time and time again, one lesson that we learned was always to expect the unexpected. Our meager snail's pace of fifty miles a day was quickly halved, as we snaked and struggled our way out of one deep rut—only to fling and flail ourselves into still another. It was tedious work and our efforts never quite seemed to match the road's challenge.

First, we'd try pushing. Twenty-one of us would hunker down behind the mud-splattered vehicle, grabbing onto anything we could lean against. Then, with a "One, two, three, PUSH!" we'd strain against the full weight of the truck. The wheels would spin into the red slime, slinging it back into our faces, slopping us from top to bottom, as the truck only dug itself deeper into the murky mire.

*If this massive tortoise flips over onto its side, we'll really be stuck with no way to turn back over.*

Borrowing on our Saharan experience, we pulled off the twelve-foot long metal sandmats from either side and slid them underneath our sludge coated tires—only to bury them, too, in the swallowing muddy quicksand.

"Maybe branches will work better," Nigel reasoned, laying down wood and stones in the three-foot deep ruts.

Those, too, were quickly sucked into the bowels of the road. Finally, we resorted to digging. By then, the truck was stuck in muck up to the top of the wheel wells. Each spade full of ooze only led us nearer the conclusion that that hole would be our last. It seemed our destiny to disappear into some abyss in the Congo Triangle.

Then, suddenly, through nothing short of divine intervention, we were freed again.

After nearly six hours of bumping and grinding against those road ruts, we saw an apparition—our worst nightmare realized. There, in the center of that one-lane road was a transport truck overturned on its side, like some caisson horse dying on the battlefield. It effectively and entirely blocked our path. Motor and palm oil seeped from its belly, filling the ruts with a black and orange psychedelic punch.

Over the next hour, while the driver of that truck and curious villagers debated how to upright their vehicle, we whacked at trees and cleared brush alongside the road, hoping there might be just barely enough clearance to inch past.

Although we put heavy chains on our tires, driving up that muddy embankment was like tap dancing on ice. Each time we bogged down, we ran through the entire routine again: lay down stones, place logs on top, dig out the truck and try again. Eventually, Henry would characteristically gun the engine, lurch overtop our makeshift bridge and dig deeply into the boggy mess on the other side. Then, the whole grand exercise in futility would begin again.

The hard work never grew any easier. As darkness finally enveloped us, black flies began their merciless attacks and the fierce nightly rains began right on schedule.

Eventually, however, after nearly five hours of grinding gears and smoking tires, we limped the final few feet up that small crest. Caked with mud from head to soggy foot, bone-tired, we immediately began our nightly search for a gravel pit to call home.

*Would all this be happening if we were traveling by ourselves?*

We knew it was possible. We'd talked with a daring couple back in Bangui and ran into them again in Zaire several times. Karl and Marian had driven all the way from their small Appenzell village in Switzerland and headed toward eastern Zaire. He was a crack mechanic with a good vehicle and they were well prepared. However, we lost track of them after Kisangani and it wasn't until months later that we met again at their cozy home. Of course, they had their own personal horror story to tell.

"So, how was your trip, Karl?" I asked, hoping for the best.

"Don't ask. You remember how bad the Zaire roads were? Well, when we were in the east, one day, I hit one rut too many. Suddenly, my back was on fire. It was so painful. I couldn't even drive."

"Ah, no. What'd you do?"

"Marian had to drive me to a bush clinic off in the mountains, and she could barely press in the clutch in our huge truck. Well, the doctor told me I had a slipped disc and they flew me back to Europe for treatment."

"That's terrible. Would you ever consider driving back to Zaire?"

"It would be great to go back," Karl told me, lighting up his meerschaum pipe, "but we'd never attempt to drive through Africa alone again. There's too much that can go wrong."

Still, I envied them. They were on the trip of my dreams, while I was left with this bad overland imitation, the fake Rolex of the African jungle. But soon, God willing, all that would change.

The next few days ran together like the floods down that muddy road. There, in the fly-plagued, malaria-infested, heat-wracked, steam room of the tropical jungle, a place even many locals seemed to avoid, nothing differentiated one day from the next. Time was only marked by the various ruts and craters that pocked that pitiful road–and pitted voices of reason against struggles for self-preservation. Finally, after days of seeing no one, except one lone, long-distance Primus beer truck, we rounded a bend and spotted a small wooden sign thrust by the roadside. It proudly proclaimed, 'Ligne de L'Equateur– Mustari Wa Usawa'.

*The Equator. We've made it!*

It was a small victory. However, if 'polepole' travel taught us anything, it was to take your wins when you may.

We mugged our way through the obligatory group photos in front of that sign, while Nigel and Henry, ever the fools, stood on their heads against the post. For those intrepid overlanders who'd never crossed into the Southern Hemisphere before, there was a ceremonial dousing. Bear eagerly poured a precious jerry can full of water off the roof, soaking Bongo and Pooky, Peggy and Trotsky, Fluffy and the Perfect Couple.

Then catching our second wind, we pressed higher into the mountains with equally high hopes. There was a welcome weather change. The air was sweet, fresh and cool. Even the mosquitoes seemed to stay behind at the Equator's imaginary line.

After pausing in the rugged, wild west town of Butembo for a few supplies, we continued into the densely forested mountains. Although we were plagued by the usual misdirection, we eventually located Hotel Italia, in all its ragged glory. The 'hotel' had four rooms and two concrete, outhouse-sized cells lit only by candlelight. If you were very careful not to move too quickly and blow out the flame, you could wallow in a cold water bucket bath.

Yet those simple pleasures washed days of mud and mishaps back into the forgiving soil. They anointed us with faith in preparation for our next challenge.

*top to bottom:*
Snow-covered Atlas Mountains. (Morocco)
Ancient hunters' glory is set in stone. (Algeria)

*top to bottom:*
Fulani-style ear piercing, Mopti. (Mali)
Dogon fetish houses (Mali)

*top to bottom:*
Tranquility and goaty essence of an oasis. (Morocco)
Hustle and bustle of Djenné marketplace. (Mali)

*top to bottom:*
A real charmer, Djemaa el Fna. (Morocco)
Dogon village door with animist figures. (Mali)

128

*top to bottom:*
Chutes de Telo, where overlanders go wild. (Cameroon)
Overlanders have this effect on people. (Morocco)

*top to bottom:*
Even in the jungle, there's time to read. (Zaire)
Village life, much as it ever was. (CAR)

*top to bottom:*
Dance of the "Monkey Men." (Mali)
The ones that didn't get away, Stanley Falls. (Zaire)

*top to bottom:*
Getting "small" with Pygmies. (Zaire)
Morning breaks in a Twa village. (Zaire)

*top to bottom:*
Mischievous Jean-Pierre gets ready to strike. (Zaire)
Rare "mzungu" sighting. (Zaire)

*top to bottom:*
Gorilla my dreams, Djomba Sanctuary. (Zaire)
"She has her mother's eyes." (Zaire)

*top to bottom:*
Silverback, undisputed king of the mountain. (Zaire)
Our worst fears realized, middle of nowhere. *Photo by Cheryl* (Zaire)

*top to bottom:*
Wygenian chiefly welcome. (Zaire)
Hippo: head and snout above the rest. (Zaire)

*top to bottom:*
How many lions can you spot in this picture? (Tanzania)
Gitega Drummers, the soulful beat of Africa. (Burundi)

*top to bottom:*
Wacky wildebeests, Ngorongoro Crater. (Tanzania)
Antelope: the other "red" meat, Ngorongoro Crater. (Tanzania)

*top to bottom:*
Wildebeest watching, Ngorongoro Crater. (Tanzania)
"If we stand really still, no one will notice us." Serengeti National Park (Tanzania)

*top to bottom:*
Jr. Masai welcoming committee. (Kenya)
Fashion statement, Ngorongoro Crater, Tanzania

*top to bottom:*
Ribbon of pink takes flight, Ngorongoro Crater. (Tanzania)
Masai life in the winds of change. (Kenya)

*top to bottom:*
Disappearing snows of Mt. Kilimanjaro. (Tanzania)
Ecstatic Cheryl atop Gillman's Point, Mt. Kilimanjaro. (Tanzania)

Thundering power of Victoria Falls. (Zimbabwe)

# Chapter IX
# Gorilla Stalk, Volcano Walk

*"You do not teach the paths of the forest to an old gorilla."*
-- African proverb

*I*N THE MORNING, we set off toward Goma and the mountain gorillas we'd dreamed of photo-stalking for so long. We made good time for a change, considering the primitive road conditions, until we finally rounded the highest ridge in that verdant pass. Facing Lake Edward, shimmering like a vast opal in a setting of stone, we careened down that last mountainside, relieved to be clear of the jungle and back onto the flat, dry plain.

Wild game surrounded us once again everywhere we looked. Antelope and stoic Cape buffalo grazed amid gangly storks and cranes lining our parade route through Virunga National Park. The volcanic brothers Mount Ruwenzori, Nyiragongo and Karisimbi cast monolithic silhouettes on either side.

Although we were out of the rainforest, the incessant showers were still hot on our trail and showed little relief. The skies beat an incessant machinegun burst against our windshield as we inched through shanty towns and mud hut villages into Goma. Main Street was a swollen canal, where a gondola would have been more practical than a landlocked truck. Normally, it would have made sense to keep on driving through that cheap Venetian imitation. But Goma was our last chance to stock up on much-needed supplies and to reserve a guide to take us up into the sequestered domain of the endangered gorillas.

Tracking down the Institut Zairois pour la Conservation de la Nature, we soon learned it would be days before we could begin our search for the endangered and well-hidden mountain giants.

"Do the gorillas take credit cards?" Fluffy asked with a pout.

145

*No, not even traveler's checks.*

We were forced to bivouac in the high-priced government campsite. Cercle Sportif was probably once a first-rate campground, but it had deteriorated into a marginal tract not too different from all the rest. Grass grew where there were once tennis and basketball courts. Sure, there was a bathroom—but no water. Still, true to form, for just the right cadeau, you could enjoy a bucket shower right in the privacy of the outdoor basketball court.

Two days later, and not a moment too soon, we set off on our quest for the mysterious mountain gorillas. To better our chance of spotting them since there were only about four hundred left, Cheryl and I split up. One of us went with each group. Nine, including my irrepressible partner, would trek three hours to remote Bukima, while the rest of us hiked back to the older site at Djomba Gorilla Sanctuary.

Wild, pristine beauty surrounded us as we drove to the base of remote Djomba to establish camp. Towering green peaks sprouted out of ripe clusters of lush vegetation. Massive pyramidal volcanoes rose off the verdant floor suggesting its prehistoric past. Churning, whitecapped rivers cascaded over mountainsides into translucent pools below, and its beauty didn't end with nature. In that gem of Africa, the people were the luster to the stone. Wherever we went, we were delighted to meet people so fresh, so unjaded by the stifling caution suffered today in so much of our Western world.

Relaxing around camp that night, our last minute doubts and anxious antic-ipation mingled with the singing of rambunctious young villagers. Nigel and drum-beating Bongo made up and taught them a silly song, one deeply steeped in the traditions of Africa. The 'Donnez moi' ('Give Me') song had simple words that the children quickly learned and, realizing the joke, thought it was as funny as we did. Nigel would sing "Donnez moi une sty-lo" ("Give me a pen") and the giggling kids would all sing his verse repeatedly, "Donnez moi une sty-lo, Donnez moi une sty-lo," in munchkin-like voices. They loved it, since it was one of their time-tested lines to use on travelers. As Bongo tapped out a simple rhythm, Nigel would follow with another round of "Donnez moi," asking for bonbons, a gift, a cola, some money or a gorilla. The kids marched and laughed around the fire, singing verse after verse.

As we finally nodded off, two little girls sweetly harmonized a traditional folk song, a melody to make the angels look down in envy.

In the morning we awoke with all the anxious anticipation of kids on the last day of school and wasted no time in setting off. It was a short, invigorating hike up the steep mountainside through early morning mist. Reaching Sanctuary hut, we quickly divided into groups of five and six, the largest allowed in the reserve at any one time. We'd heard that there was a new month-old baby gorilla in one of the families and each secretly hoped we'd be the ones to find her.

Our guides, Pascale and Michel, soon joined us. The first, a heavyset, deep ebony fellow, carried a machete to clear the brush and thorny vines from the dense undergrowth, and his wiry, lighter companion had a rifle slung over his shoulder in case we spotted any leopards–or locals.

"Ain-ny per-sone we see up zere, zey aire poach-aires," he threatened in his lazy patois French, "and zey weell be shot wit-out warn-ning."

*This is serious business.*

Clambering up the rolling hillside, our band trudged and hacked our way through underbrush for about thirty minutes, as we stepped over logs and looked for hidden signs of the quiet giants.

"Zey on-ly nest in an area one night," Michel whispered. "Zen zey move on."

Upon closer inspection here and there, we noticed signs of chewed branches and piles of still-steaming dung, until suddenly Pascale stopped.

"Look. Over zere!"

We cautiously poked our heads around a small bramble thicket. At first, I didn't see anything until my eyes adjusted to the leaf-filtered light. But then, yes, there he sat, our first gorilla, a giant tuft of black fuzz, lounging and eating in the sun. As we excitedly watched, that young three-hundred-pound male threw back his head and yawned, examined us, lumbered out of his bed of leaves, then returned to the more serious task of eating. Tiring of that, he turned, walking on knuckles to within a single breathtaking yard of us.

*Is he going to rip my arms off as easily as he'd stripped the branches off that bamboo tree?*

I instantly looked down assuming the non-aggressive posture Pascale had taught us.

However, this adolescent male didn't seem the least bit upset by our presence and continued ambling into a clearing not thirty feet away. Slowly, yet deliberately we followed, cautious not to make any sudden or threatening moves that might alarm him. We stepped into the small cove of trees where two female gorillas lay sleeping like children in the grass. Not ten feet away, in the shadows of a gnarled overhanging tree, stood the colossal silverback himself.

He towered over six feet tall, as massive as a refrigerator. Jet-black, except for a metallic mane of shaggy hair running across his back, he sized us up, as if measuring our intentions. Inadvertently, I found myself standing right in his leafy bed, peering at him face-to-face, amazement-to-scowl.

*If he's going to charge, this will be the time.*

Instead, he continued his cold, penetrating glare. Then turning, he slowly retreated into the shadows of the alcove. We could feel his eyes still riveted on us, as each wondered what to do next. Yet nothing happened. He didn't charge. The others didn't run.

So, after a few moments, we turned and circled his shaded chamber to see if there was a better view from the other side. Rounding the thickly vined alcove, we discovered three young male gorillas playing and sleeping in the covered entrance. To their left, several feet away, a shaggy older male grazed on leaves, while another brilliantly coated male lay behind him dozing in the streaked sunlight. We'd struck it rich, having stumbled onto almost the entire family of eleven.

*But where's the mother and her newborn baby?*

For thirty minutes we knelt in that grass, watching and photographing the family in their lair as they ate, played or slept in the sun. They generally ignored us and seemed blasé about our presence. That was most surprising. We'd expected them to take off deep into the mountainous undergrowth upon spotting us. Chimps or baboons would have.

*Obviously, but these are intelligent creatures in a protected environment. They've learned that people are no threat.*

Feeling foolishly brave, I cautiously inched closer to catch a portrait of one solitary brooding male at arm's length. Anxious at first, he finally relaxed, frolicked and played in the sun. Rapt, I was touched by his measured glances filled with such curiosity and intelligence.

*Does he know why these odd beings are taking photos of him? Why others pop up here every few days?*

148

All at once, there was a sharp, frantic rustling in the bushes behind him. Branches inexplicably snapped, while his companions shot furtive looks. We were just six feet from the family. Before we could retreat to safety, something approached from the thicket. It was the young mother gorilla with a tousle-headed baby whose walnut-sized hands bravely clung to mom's hairy chest.

At first Mom was shy, silently sitting, munching leaves behind the protective young males. Then, after the massive silverback reappeared and assured her safety, she crossed to squat beside him, just three feet away from me. As she sat there, curiously eyeing us and stripping leaves from nearby trees, her tiny fuzzyheaded tike climbed off her chest and half swaggered, half crawled toward Prudence crouched beside me. At this, the mother quickly scrambled over and snatched the curious infant back into her arms.

*Intelligent creature. Knowing Prudence, I would have, too.*

However, the inquisitive baby climbed down again, this time headed directly toward me. Tottering back and forth, her tiny feet tramped through the tall grass. Finally, she paused just inches away. The pop-eyed, eighteen-inch high, thistle-haired imp stretched out her tiny hand toward me.

"I don't believe this!" I whispered to myself, as she caressed my beard then touched my lips with her slender black finger.

Mom didn't appreciate her curiosity. Grunting a low, menacing "HUH," she quickly snatched her adventurous toddler back. Then there was a similar grunt and grumble of "HUH, HUH, HUHs" from the males then encircling us.

It was just a warning. They meant us no real harm. Still, overwhelmed by the entire experience, it seemed best to head back. Besides, leaving their lair, we were shocked to discover we'd been with those docile giants for over ninety minutes, although it passed in an instant.

I was sullen and a little melancholy hiking back down that hill to camp. Rejoining Cheryl after her excursion, I learned that she was equally successful in her search and profoundly stunned by their majestic presence.

*How tragic it is those wonderful creatures are nearly extinct thanks to man's greed and carnage. Ultimately, how much is our very survival reflected by their own?*

Zaire was like that, a land of continuous contrasts. One day you're hunting with the Pygmies and another tracking mountain gorillas. Then, as if to tempt us further, eleven thousand-foot Mt. Nyiragongo volcano beckoned us with further adventure. After a little negotiating with the park service, and sustaining the usual bureaucratic shuffle, Bear, Slim, Flinty, Bongo, Zippy, the Perfect Couple and I set off to climb the imposing mountain. Lying near the Rwandan border, it was last violently active from 1978-79, but steam still curled from its craggy vent.

Initially, I considered it an easy hike and excellent opportunity to explore the natural volcanic wildlife and plants. Plus, it was a chance for some last-minute conditioning in preparation for our climb up Mt. Kilimanjaro in the next few weeks. Oh, how I was mistaken.

After meeting Jack, our nimble, black guide and our water porter at Kibati, we set off along the rugged lava trail in the heat of midafternoon. We'd heard it was nearly a five-hour rigorous climb to the primitive huts poised at the base of the summit. However, as we started a swift ascent through hardwood forests up this nearly perfect cone-shaped mountain, I discovered it wasn't the simple day-climb I'd imagined. Part of my problem was equipment, from my high-topped tennies to the full daypack plus sleeping bag and bedroll that caught on every low-hanging branch along the way. Normally, I'd trek much lighter. But since we planned on making our summit ascent at sunrise, I carried a heavy winter jacket although it was nearly ninety degrees. My pace was sure and steady, if not record-breaking. Since we were in a vast jungle where it rained almost daily, I just concentrated on carefully placing each footstep to avoid roots and camouflaged holes that could sprain an ankle in seconds–and ruin any chance of climbing Africa's highest challenge, Mt. Kilimanjaro.

Because we'd spotted rain clouds over the mountain when we left, the possibility of an impending cloudburst also weighed heavily on my mind, especially since our path already looked like it doubled as a streambed.

*If it rains today, this trail's going to turn into a slick slide to the rocky bottom.*

We beat a hasty pace up the mountain, as much as our throbbing hearts and wheezing lungs could handle. All of us were clearly winded after the first hour climb, but the worst was yet to come. Our gentle forest path suddenly transformed into a more difficult direct ascent straight up the craggy, shifting slope. Still higher and higher we climbed, never stopping or pausing, racing against time and the very limits of our bodies. About halfway up, each labored step became a maneuver around loose rocks and exposed roots. Yet, as I sweated and strained against the steep incline, our impatient guide and porter pulled farther ahead, oblivious to our slower pace. Normally their absence wouldn't have fazed me. But today, they had the rifle and we were still in leopard country. So the fear of ending up as kitty kibble provided a little added incentive to match their rush.

Nearly two-thirds of the way to the top, the terrain suddenly transformed again, this time to lava flows, ancient and newly formed. The landscape was daubed with giant lobelia that open to the sun each day and close at night. Volcanic cinder crumbled or shifted under our every cautious step, as black, foreboding rain clouds grew still closer.

Finally, after only three hours and twenty minutes since leaving the bottom, the stark hillside huts were visible, and with a final heave and burst of speed we arrived sweaty and panting at those dilapidated shelters.

Three tiny corrugated tin buildings crouched on the uneven hillside. Two were totally useless, with roofs, doors or windows missing. As luck would have it, however, the other one looked sound. So, eight of us, along with our guide and porter, settled quickly in for the night. At least its door, although not connected, could be propped against the frame to keep out frigid night winds.

*Time will tell if this roof will keep out the rain.*

No more than ten minutes after our arrival, that theory was put to the supreme test. With rain spewing down in torrents, the hillside quickly became a pathway for a raging river. Gusts whipped fiercely down the side of the craggy mountain and we were blanketed in a cacophonous clamor.

Fortunately Flinty, our time-tested keeper of the flame, lost no time in starting a fire in the center of the hut. Grasping the final bit of dying daylight, we arranged our bags around the flame with our feet toward the center like spokes in a wagon wheel. Although the wind fiercely howled outside, I was amazed how warm it became once we propped the metal door closed and snuggled deep inside our sleeping bags.

We needed to reach the summit in time for sunrise. So, like anxious grooms, we kept a waking vigil throughout the night, scanning luminous watch dials. Five o'clock finally came and we hurriedly bundled into heavy winter clothes for the final ascent to Zaire's barren rooftop.

It was slow going, as we created new switchbacks on the scarred mountain's face. Since our path was only partially illuminated by intermittent glows from flashlights, each step was painstakingly placed, otherwise we risked careening back down the gravely slope. Finally, as the first rays of sun painted the eastern sky with crimson reds, I spotted the top of Mt. Nyiragongo poking its head above misty clouds. Then, agonizing the final few steps, with a final burst of adrenaline, we set foot on her summit and immediately continued a dizzied scramble along her rugged rim.

To one side, a Danté-like inferno simmered at the bottom of the cone. Plumes of sulfuric smoke rose from inside the massive, dark interior. To the other, from the crown of Zaire over two miles up, we surveyed Goma's distant lights, the length of shimmering Lake Kiva and its volcanic brothers silhouetted by the sun.

By some cosmic miracle, standing together on the apex, all the personal and group struggles of those past few months seemed minute and dreamlike. The joy of travel had, once again, become the journey itself.

The next several days brought us to the bright lights and bustle of Bukavu. It was only a brief stop in a real town with real food, shops, bars and hotels with baths. We checked into the Hotel Canadien and Cheryl and I were one of the three lucky couples to win the room lottery. Yes, we'd be able to enjoy the well-deserved privacy of our own room, while everyone else camped in yet another dismal hotel yard and shared our bath. Although it was a dank, high-ceiling cell, it was the African equivalent of a 3-Star hotel, boasting a flush toilet and even bath water in the afternoon. It had been ten days since our last rendezvous with soap, so scrubbing came not a moment too soon.

Bukavu was probably the most modern and well-to-do city we'd seen in all Zaire. Its serene lakefront, with its many hidden coves ringed with exclusive homes, reminded me a little of America's Pacific Northwest. Her downtown shops were stocked the latest imported color televisions, refrigerators and modern Western clothing—objects only imagined throughout the rest of the impoverished country. However, you only needed to wander a few blocks off the main drag to find a seedier side of Bukavu. Ramshackle sheds housed throngs of ragged 'have-nots' eking out a marginal existence, living on dreams.

As the others relaxed in the bleary heat of the afternoon, Nigel and I set off in search of the blackmarket. Now, on any occasion, changing money on the African blackmarket had its downsides. First, in many countries there was a clampdown by the police. Sometimes, they masqueraded as moneychangers waiting to nab you. Other times, you were nagged incessantly by actual money merchants to exchange dollars, only to be double-crossed and turned into the police for a reward. Then, you always stood the chance of being robbed after making the exchange, of accepting out-of-date worthless notes, or falling for slight-of-hand hucksters who changed money in front of you, counted it out, then grabbed it back at the last moment to recount it. Palming that stack of bills, they exchanged it for another stack with smaller denominations. Then, nervously glancing around, they hissed, "The police are coming," as you both scurried off. Only later did you discover the switch.

So, given the hazards, we made it a point to only exchange money when there were two of us to watch each others' backs–and when the risks justified the rewards–such as when the blackmarket rate was two or three times the official one. The penalty for getting caught could be deportation or worse.

As luck would have it, a nearby barber shop, Bukavu's 'official' black market, could only change $50 of the $350 we needed. With much reluctance, Nigel and I sped off with the shopkeeper's friend in a hearse of a taxi. Shocks and suspension were unheard of options. To make matters worse, most of the wheels were attached with only one or two wheel nuts. So, fearing traffic death more than arrest, when we reached a roundabout, we jumped out, hopped into a cab and continued our jolting journey to the 'other side of the tracks'.

Within moments, the plush suburban shops and old colonial houses of the lakeside disintegrated into ramshackle clapboard houses, bars out of bad B-movies and fleabag hotels. They were stacked one on the other amid a cacophony of reggae blaring from tinny boom boxes. We tore down grimy alleys, weaving between locals and disinterested animals that dared to stand between us and our appointed rounds. Suddenly, our taxi slid to an abrupt halt. Piling out, we found ourselves stopped right in front of a policeman, with a well-greased machinegun slung over his shoulder.

A shot of terror crossed my mind. *Have we been set up?*

The stunned policeman just shot us a quizzical glance, as if to ask, "What you doin' here?" but he kept on walking.

The kid from the shop led Nigel and me into a nearby bar, the kind of joint with one rickety metal table and weathered ebony men staring through clouded glasses of flat Primus beer. The python-like bartender mysteriously muttered something to the kid, who signaled another fellow at the door, who limped off.

I was getting nervous with all the signals and whispers. The clock stood still until the fellow with the bad leg returned. We followed the kid up a winding dung-filled alley to a nearby house, its paint peeling as badly as my tropically fried nose.

The kid knocked on the mud-splattered door. It slowly creaked open, at first just a crack. Then it opened all the way to reveal an immense woman, as large as both of us put together, who burst through the doorway while sizing us up. Shooting the kid a knowing glance, she abruptly led us inside, bolting the heavy door behind her.

Inside it might have been any granny's parlor–except for the heavily muscled guy in the dirty wife-beater t-shirt, or singlet, drinking beer, belching and watching television.

Television? Nigel and I each raised an eyebrow, since we hadn't seen one of those in months. Then, with a perfunctory air, she guided us to the privacy of her back room. Turning, she quickly drew chenille curtains behind her.

"What can I do for you gentlemen?" she sighed, with a knowing twinkle to her eyes.

Well," I whispered, "we'd like to change three hundred US dollars."

"Okay honey, no problem," she promised, flashing a gold-toothed smile before disappearing into an adjoining room.

Instinctively, we both sensed something was wrong, very wrong. We waited and waited. Meanwhile, there was a lot of shuffling and banging behind closed doors, until she finally reappeared, glided over and began counting out crinkled bills.

*Wait. There is a problem. These are all large bills and next to impossible for us to exchange.*

"Can't you give us anything smaller?" I asked.

Madame rolled her eyes. Frustrated at being caught, she shrugged and disappeared a second time. Again, nearly ten minutes passed while we both nervously squirmed, until she finally returned with our booty. After she counted out a fat stack of bills again, licking her stout fingers between each new set of hundreds, I handed her six crisp fifty-dollar bills and we stood to leave.

"Would you like to stay," she cooed with a grin, "For une beer?"

"No merci, Madame" I replied, feeling as awkward as a kid buying his first pack of condoms. "Gotta run."

Stuffing the stack of bills into the bulging nylon pouches around our waists, we drew aside the curtain, rushed through the smoky outer room and back into the interrogating spotlight of the sun. For a long while, we tried to flag down a taxi. No luck. Finally, in frustration, we started walking down the crowded road, feeling about as conspicuous as a traveler caught in the wrong part of town, waving a couple of grand in the air.

*Good thing I've lost weight. Otherwise, I'd never be able to fasten my pants with this wad of cash.*

I kept furtively glancing over my shoulder to ensure that we weren't being followed by fellow in the bar, or by one of his cronies. Skirting past the cop we'd seen earlier, we held our breaths and nodded "Bonjour" as if nothing at all was unusual.

Meanwhile Nigel, head typically in the clouds, headed for a three-foot deep hole in the road.

"Watch out!" I yelled. He froze dead in his tracks, while I waved down a taxi jostling down that crowded street. It skidded to a stop in front of us. Without missing a beat, we piled into the jitney's back seat and, rocking side to side, ricocheted down the road.

After receiving the necessary visas and restocking whatever supplies we could, we headed on toward Burundi with little left standing in our way. Exhausted after an exciting month in Zaire, we were more than ready for a little change of scenery. By early afternoon, we rolled into Uvira, a festering frontier town just miles from the Burundi border. Although set on Lake Tanzania, it was as grotesque as the lake was pristine. Clouds of dust whirled and blew down nearly deserted streets. There was a certain ominous feel to it–the perfect setting for a coup. Soldiers waved machineguns and suspiciously eyed outsiders, while villagers spat and sneered with open contempt.

*Does this place smell like trouble? Or is it just the stench of rotten fish blowing in off that lake?*

Although we'd planned to spend the night, after that dubious welcome, we opted to backtrack three miles down the road and camp along the lake, just inside the border. Cruising to a stop in front of a small cluster of mud huts along the shore, Nigel hopped down. He asked the village chief if it was possible to pitch our tents beside his quiet village. After the weathered sage assured him it was fine, we began to unload our moldy tents and dust-filled bags.

"It'll be relaxing to camp here on the lake," Cheryl offhandedly remarked, in a rare case of premature optimism.

Well, no sooner did we open the back locker door than twenty anxious onlookers pressed in around us. There was something weird going on. A rancid air of aggression and resentment surrounded us. Then, it dawned on me.

*Here we are, white Santas in a huge sleigh parked right on their lawn. And if Uvira was any preview, I'm worried that we're in for one tense night.*

Our bags were quickly thrown from the locker and, with four of our larger overlanders standing guard, we grabbed what was absolutely needed from the bags, immediately stowing the rest back in the locked hatch for the duration of our stay.

Meanwhile, news spread quickly. The surly crowd swelled from twenty to over a hundred. Struggling to fix dinner and pitch tents in the fading light, we faced a security nightmare. Our cooks set out twenty canvas stools facing the table. Then we took turns sitting on them to patrol the food and keep the crowd cordoned off as much as possible. However, as much as scrawny Dropsy, our miscast mistress of safety, screeched, "Securrr-itt-teee!" reminding us to guard our food and the still-open truck windows, the unruly mob soon proved too much to control. They defiantly occupied half of the stools around the table and openly taunted us with, "May-be we steal your food. What you do zen?"

For awhile, we tried to ignore their comments, not wanting to land ourselves in a fight we couldn't win. Then, disaster struck.

"Ahhhh, damn!" Peggy squealed out in the darkness. She and Trotsky, cornrows flying, came scrambling into the dim campfire light. "Someone's nicked our tent. And everything inside!"

Immediately, several other overlanders rushed to check their own tents and discovered that many of their metal tent spikes were already missing. However, at least their tents were still there.

*Unbelievable. How can anyone sneak into camp and walk off with an entire erect tent with twenty people standing guard? Are we that unprepared and naive? Undoubtedly, so.*

Immediately, our security tightened. Overlanders were posted every ten feet around the perimeter guarding tents, stools, truck windows, tires and our booty of extra food that was covered under a tarp on the rooftop. As one might imagine, dinner was a complete farce. Everyone stood vigil at their posts, sneaking bites and paranoidly watching shadows glide in the eerie darkness.

Still, the crowd loomed larger. For the next several hours, tensions mounted. Wagons were gathered in a circle waiting for the next attack. Even Nigel, ever ridiculous in his baggy shorts with the seat ripped out, performing his nightly imitation of a barking dog couldn't appease the angry crowd. Odd. That scruffy-headed, barking and baying Cornish hound never failed to get a chuckle from villagers in the past. But no one was laughing this time. We were in big trouble.

Odd, but sometimes inaction is the best action. Turning in early, we hoped the crowd would follow our lead. Packing and locking the tables and provisions into the truck, everyone returned to their tents. There was no late night carousing. No passing of beers around the fire with the villagers, as we'd done so often in the past. The party was definitely over.

Surprisingly, that worked. The mob quickly lost interest and melted away into the night—but not before lifting eight more canvas stools from under our noses.

Cheryl and I'd struck our tent after dinner, deciding someone should sleep inside the truck to prevent break-ins. People ingenious enough to slip away with a fully pitched tent would have no trouble getting inside the truck with her three doors, ten windows and everyone's valuables. Meanwhile, Henry and Maxie lay on the roof to guard equipment, food and souvenirs stashed on top.

Sleep was impossible. We slept with one eye open and ears peeled for noises. In fact, every time Henry and Maxie rolled over and magnified booms reverberated through the hollow of the truck, I shot straight up yelling, "Who's that!"

The next morning, soft-spoken Nigel talked to the village chief, who assured us he'd do all he could to retrieve our tent and stools. Yet we didn't hold out much hope.

Wending our way down the road to the Burundi border, the lakeside show-down weighed heavily on our minds, as we struggled to remember all our positive experiences in Zaire. We focused on the smiling, open and gentle folks we'd met in that fascinating country.

*Maybe this tent incident and the crowd's attitude is just another poignant reminder of the severe needs and seething resentment in a land of 'haves' and 'have-nots'.*

As if some small consolation, entering Burundi was a breeze. There were no searches, no currency declaration cards to fill out and no customary four-hour wait at the border. It was like stepping through the looking glass. Roads were paved. There were real bridges instead of the usual rotted logs across streams, and even luxury beach resorts.

In true overland style, we set up camp just down the beach from a plush hotel on the shores of Lake Tanzania. Oh, how we'd dreamed of swimming in those cool, azure lake waters–and how disappointed we were to discover, once again, another African lake rife with deadly bilharzia.

Still, nighttime on that shore was magical, as a bright harvest moon cast its mystical glow over the inviting expanse of still waters.

That pristine fantasy was shattered the next morning when we were warned about the rash of robberies, muggings and recent murder of a foreigner in the area where we'd camped. So, again, we cautiously moved our tents even closer to the hotel.

*There's nothing like violence and fear to take the joy out of travel.*

As though to balance the bad news, we received word that our missing tent and some stools were already found. After his chat with Nigel, the chief warned the villagers that there would be no fishing on the lake until the items were returned. That ban struck home with swift frontier effectiveness. Best of all, there was no 'loss of face'.

So, quickly rejuvenated with tents and stools intact, we set off to Bujumbura to pick up Tanzanian visas and plan for our trip to the southern source of the Nile. As we tooled along the modern highway, we couldn't help noticing the striking difference in the affluence of Burundi compared with their brothers suffering just across the water. Bujumbura sparkled like a crystal on the edge of Lake Tanganyika. Street lights illuminated well-groomed lawns and large houses behind high security fences, and the latest foreign cars zipped down tree-lined boulevards past new multi-storied hotels and restaurants. Some homes and shops had telephones that actually worked. Stores were fully stocked with food. French patisseries boasted padded booths and glasscases displaying éclairs, and there was a booming central market catering to well-dressed locals.

We camped at The Cercle Nautique, the local yacht club. To discover a boating club in Africa was itself a surprise. It was quiet and unassuming, except for its marauding hippos. We'd heard that those 'river horses' that floated offshore often came in to feed on the grass after sunset. Still, we didn't really believe it until we discovered them munching away right in front of our tent. Cautiously circling them, we kept in mind an important piece of information: they remain calm—as long as you don't come between the hippos and the water. But if they feel trapped, watch out. They're faster than they look and more than one hapless camper has become a hippo hors d'oeuvre.

Later, while waiting for our Tanzanian visas to be processed, we set off in search of the source of the Nile and still another set of impressive cascades. Finding falls had become an overlander's hobby, just like playing non-stop '21' or working your way through the continent's variety of beers.

All morning, we drove through the green mountainous region just south of Bujumbura. Although it was only supposed to be about sixty miles to the Nile, we quickly traveled nearly twice that distance. Finally, half-expecting to see Tanzania's border any moment, we spotted a small sign that sent us careening off onto a winding dirt road farther into the sanctuary of the mountains. The surrounding hillsides grew dense with towering banana trees, impenetrable palms and mutant flowering vines. At last, we emerged through dense underbrush and suddenly stood face-to-face with a fifteen-foot pyramid marking the southernmost source of Africa's life sustaining artery, the Nile.

Sure, we'd found it much easier than Captain John Speke had done on his famous 1860 exploration into those 'mountains of the moon'.

*But where's the water?*

Not a drop was seen. We'd have to find our own.

Heading back down the road, the allure of Karera Falls hypnotically drew us farther into the emerald hills, deeper into the heart of the primeval forest. As the sun dipped close to the horizon, we arrived at the most spectacular falls we'd seen in all Africa. At least four different sets of cascades tumbled into the verdant tropical hollow. The most impressive was reached down a winding set of stone stairs. At the bottom, Cheryl and I discovered a brilliant turquoise pool cradled at the base of two immense sets of falls. It was garlanded with exotic flowers in exaggerated abundance down either side. Only twenty feet to our left was the summit of yet another thundering cataract, spewing water with volcanic fury two hundred feet to a flower-laden canyon below.

As the last rose-colored rays of the sun filtered through the trees, casting an idyllic rainbow arching over the falls, Cheryl and I set up our secluded camp. It was just far enough from the quiet upper pool to keep from getting soaked, yet far enough from the others to enjoy some well-earned privacy.

Dawn broke and we were saddened to leave the peaceful solitude that had come so unexpectedly. The last several tense weeks had taken their toll. Power struggles had matured into full-grown rivalries. Henry earned a band of die-hard partyers and Nigel befriended a few groggy groupies. The rest of us cherished our solitude and attempted to make the best of an often-impossible situation.

*Five months is just too long for any group to travel together, especially when their habits, hygiene and reasons for travel are so irreconcilable. I'm counting the days until we reach Nairobi; counting the days until we set off and discover the Africa of our dreams–unfettered and alone. It won't come a moment too soon.*

Two days later, we arrived at the Center for the Burundi Drummers in Gitega, Burundi's second largest town. We'd looked forward to seeing their electrifying performances of traditional dances and superb drumming since catching a preview of their talents back on Lake Tanzania.

Parking the truck at the bottom of the hill, we hiked up a grassy mound to the rustic corral where the dancers performed in front of rows of shaded seats. Sitting there, in anxious anticipation of the 'command' performance, we were joined by grinning local children, just as eager to see their favorite entertainers.

Nerve-jarring, pulsating drumming began somewhere out of sight. Then the drummers staged a magnificent entrance with the sixty-year-old 'Major' at the head of their exciting procession. Strutting across the grassy courtyard, he swayed and pranced like a Lipizzan Stallion. Elegantly decked out in a black and white beaded headdress that flew from side to side, he swirled his head to the infectious rhythm. A rainbow of colored beads bounced across his broad ebony chest, and his powerful fists clenched an intimidating wooden spear and imposing crimson and black shield.

Dressed in red and white tunics, the drummers numbered about twenty-five, ranging in age from ten to over sixty. Each carefully balanced a four foot long heavy wooden drum on his head, swinging it from side to side while dancing and beating an intricate cadence. Swaying into that courtyard to a haunting beat, they positioned the barrel-sized wooden drums in a straight line behind an even larger one dominating center stage.

Then, at last in place, one of the drummers struck a faster, more dynamic tempo, as the Major flew onto center stage, racing back and forth, bounding and dipping dramatically with arms outspread. Unexpectedly, he turned, swaggering toward us. Gracefully jumping straight up, he whirled four feet into the air. Again. And again. And still again. Teeth gleaming in an exaggerated smile, that half-man, half-bird soared as though the drums set him free. Then he plunged down to the earth in one ethereally fluid motion.

After finishing his airy bucking and swaying, he was replaced by one of the younger drummers, or sometimes two would move center stage. The spotlighted musicians beat the huge center drum with vigor and unbridled abandon. Broadly smiling, they rolled their sticks across and around their heads. Then they melded the gyrations, dips and wild arm flapping of tap, the graceful leaps of ballet, energy of jazz and dervish daring of breakdancing into moves like none I'd ever seen.

The spectacle continued for an hour with the Major returning after each drummer's solo at the center drum. Each time that he appeared, it was with greater energy, more frenetic tosses of his beaded head and higher, more impressive leaps into the stratosphere.

At the end, just as suddenly as they appeared, the drummers struck their familiar cadence, slid the heavy drums back atop their heads and strutted in single file out of the courtyard.

The Major flew off like some graceful heron, earthbound no more.

# Chapter X
# Whirling Wildebeests

*"Do not try to fight a lion if you are not one yourself."*
~ African proverb

THE FOLLOWING DAY, we set off through terraced emerald mountains until reaching the fertile plains of Tanzania. Crossing the border, we immediately set course toward Lake Victoria and the Serengeti to the southeast. It was just ten days to Nairobi, and I daydreamed of reaching that oasis. There had been so many bush camps and four or five days without fresh water to rinse the red African dust from our skin.

En route, we briefly stopped in the port city of Mwanza on the south shore of Lake Victoria. Parking our truck in the center of town near the post office, we fanned out to take care of business, most importantly the tedious task of changing dollars to shillings. By then, legally changing money should have been easy, but it usually turned into a lengthy torture.

First, you picked a number and stood in line. Upon reaching the front, you were given a form to fill out your name, address, nationality, place of entry into the country, and where you'd be staying. You then stood in another line to hand-in those. Then, you waited as tellers methodically moved through heaps of applications with triplicate forms. Finally, they began to call out numbers to then count out your money.

The procedure varied little from bank to bank or country to country. It was a grueling process, at best. But if you'd timed it right, and the banks were open and not on strike, and if it wasn't payday or a holiday, after an hour you'd end up with the local currency–at the official lackluster rate, sometimes half or one-third that of the booming blackmarket.

Of course, the underground economy was profitable for everyone. Locals used dollars or other hard currency as an inflation hedge or to buy precious goods like cars, televisions, refrigerators or cassette tapes at special stores accepting only Western currency.

As a visitor, even if you changed most of your money on the black-market, it was wise to have some bank stamped receipts to flash at the border. Otherwise, the officials would wonder how you visited their country for so long without changing any money—and that was sure to raise eyebrows.

After our banking was complete, some overlanders headed off for pastry and ice cream. Others went in search of beautiful Tanzanian batiks or carved wooden art. We discovered the main market and were instantly awed by the wide diversity of people.

Tanzania boasts over a hundred different tribes, the Bantu being the largest. However, we also saw many East Indians and East Africans from different tribes, judging by their dress and facial scars. There were also black-shrouded Moslems from Zanzibar and three dignified Masai women, the first we'd ever seen.

The trio, looking like ancient sages, leaned against the outside walls of a shop. There they sold intricately beaded chokers and bracelets, kaleidoscopic colored headbands and earrings, or medicinal bark and herbal concoctions. Their necks and foreheads were adorned with strands of brightly colored beads in huge hoops. Beautifully stretched four-inch long earlobes sported triangular beaded earrings with small silver medallions or arrows dangling from the bottom. One wizened woman wore a three-inch ivory plug, piercing her top earflap. Another had a wheel shaped disk nearly two inches across, wedged in her extended earlobe. All wore brightly patterned 'kangas', the local version of the kaftan.

After a few hours in that Tanzanian oasis, we re-boarded and continued toward the Serengeti. One of Africa's most renowned parks, its reputation comes well deserved. Stretching over nine thousand square miles, it boasts one of the highest concentrations of wild game in East Africa. Millions of mammals call that flat, nearly treeless grassland home. We were doubly lucky in our timing since it was migration season. One and a half million frenzied wildebeest and other game were already traveling west in search of grassy pastures to escape the dry weather of the plains. It was also their time for rutting and romance. Like true voyeurs, we looked forward to capturing it all.

It took several more days of bouncing up and down dusty cratered dirt roads to finally reach the entrance to Serengeti National Park. A large wooden sign greeted us at the gate, flanked on either side by sun-bleached Cape buffalo skulls.

Once we entered, wildlife awaited around every bend. Never before had we seen such abundance. Zebras stood stock still in the high grass, hoping we wouldn't notice, then whinnied and trotted off. Thompson's and Grant's gazelles leapt in a graceful, orchestrated procession across the golden prairie. Giraffes, placidly nibbling tender treetops, were hungrily watched by jackals, nearly camouflaged in the thickets. Massive vultures perched in thorny acacia bushes, scrutinizing the flat landscape for supper, as ostriches galloped past in a syncopated shimmy of feathers. Monkeys peered down from the security of scrawny trees. While baboons, as usual, barked their defiant disapproval.

Spotting a huge swirling cloud of dust off in the distance, we headed east hoping to encounter part of the great wildebeest migration. As luck would have it, they found us. Fifty crazed wildebeests suddenly swarmed across the road blocking our path.

Now to me, the wildebeest is one of the strangest looking animals ever created, seemingly made from spare parts. It was as though a cow, horse and Cape buffalo had one wild, lost weekend and that hairy hybrid was their offspring. Those shaggy creatures had a way of moving that was hard to duplicate. Dervish spinning and head crashing marked off personal territories, as they culled away as many willing females as possible. They'd run in circles. Two would turn and crash headlong. Then suddenly, they'd gallop off in another direction and repeat their head butting. It was difficult to tell if there was really a herd leader, or they'd simply whirled, spun and smashed heads so often that they were as lost as they looked.

*In many ways, they're like us.*

Looking through my binoculars, unexpectedly, I spotted a pack of five hyenas drawing closer and closer to one solitary wildebeest. He continued to eat, unperturbed. We stood there watching the drama unfold, torn between wanting to warn him and letting natural selection prevail. Suddenly, the creature thrust his hairy snout into the air and caught the scent of his would-be attackers. He snorted and pawed, then galloped off to the safety of the herd.

As the sun dipped, casting a brilliant red neon hue across the grassy meadow, two sculpted vultures perched motionless, silhouetted atop a spindly acacia.

Later that evening, as we relaxed around our tents, Cheryl and I were approached by four Bantu kids dressed in clothes as weathered as the plains they called home. The boy, using his best schoolbook English, stepped forward and boldly demanded, "Geeve me my pen." In many places throughout Africa, kids weren't allowed to attend school without them.

"We don't have *your* pen."

He tried again, changing his inflection, "Geeve *me* my pen."

"We don't have *your* pen."

We'd heard it all before. Somewhere making the rounds in East Africa was a textbook that switched pronouns. "Give me *my* whatever!" became the new battle cry replacing, "Cadeau, cadeau."

"What you want to say is 'Give me *your* pen,'" I coached.

He looked a little confused. Then he began a litany of "Geeve me..." phrases, similar to Djomba's 'Donnez Moi' tune. "Geeve me the time. Geeve me the soda. Geeve me your pants."

His sisters were mildly impressed with his command of English, but even more fascinated with our postcard of Masai women.

"Where do you live?" I asked the skinny boy.

"Over dere."

"Do you farm–grow vegetables?"

"Yes, corn, cabbage, tomatoes, cows, goats, an' chee-kens."

His sisters all nodded shyly, although they had no idea what we were talking about.

"That's good." We really looked forward to spending more time with villagers in the upcoming weeks. Preferably someone who could say a little more than, "Give me my whatever."

Finally, he said, "Geeve me *my* name."

His lesson had been too short, and I laughed, replying, "Give me *your* name."

"Joseph," he said, adding, "Geeve me *your* watch," as he tugged my arm. *Maybe he's learned his lesson, after all.*

Instead, we gave them bubble gum for their efforts. It was probably the first they'd ever seen, and they were dumbfounded when my partner demonstrated the secret of the perfect bubble.

Satisfied, they giggled and skipped off into an ebony night.

On our second day in the Serengeti, we headed southeast along the Grumeti River, across the Musabi Plain toward Ngorongoro Crater. We'd heard rave reviews from others that'd visited the fourteen-mile wide crater. A completely self-contained ecosystem, it was home to twenty-five thousand animals, almost every species found in East Africa.

*With any luck, we'll have the chance to see more lions and maybe even see the rare rhinos there.*

They inhabit the Serengeti, too, but since the park is spread out over some nine thousand square miles, it's easy for a hundred rhinos or even three thousand lions to remain far from the few scattered roads.

At the height of the sweltering noonday sun, we pulled over to have lunch–and tea. Setting up tables, we pulled out food boxes at a small rocky rise called Leopard Rocks.

*Leopard Rocks? Not everyone lunches in the Serengeti's prime big cat habitat. This is the true acid test. Does our smashed pilchard spread really smell like cat food?*

Afterwards, within a few miles of the crater, we began to spot tiny Masai villages, looking like cowboy corrals, dotting the steep surrounding hillsides. Stacked, crisscrossed wood and thorny acacia bushes encircled those simple mud huts.

Reaching Ngorongoro Crater, we slowly inched our way up to the ridge of its outer shell, then stopped the truck and got out for a walk. Gazing two thousand feet below to Lake Magadi, we were amazed to spot a pink, fluttering swath shimmering like miles of satin wrapped across that sea of turquoise–thousands of flamingos. It's also home to one hundred other bird species that are found nowhere else in the Serengeti.

As we returned to the truck, three Masai men and a woman approached us, apparently from nowhere. They were remarkably imposing. Standing nearly seven feet tall, the men wore large, beaded, triangular earrings with pendants, similar to ones we'd seen in Mwanza. One had a white, blue and red beaded headband from which dangled a small triangle in the center of his forehead. Another's elongated earlobes were fastened together under his chin. All were wrapped in red plaid capes covering a crimson toga-style cloth.

The statuesque woman wore a navy blue cape over a beaded, tan water-buffalo hide skirt. Poised, almost regal, she wore more elaborate halo-like beadwork on her neatly shaved head, while around her neck she wore circular hoops of probably sixteen strands of blue, orange, white, red and green beads.

*What a fantastic photo they'd make. But I've heard how sensitive the Masai are about having their picture taken. They've even been known to toss seven-foot spears through cameras–and overland trucks.*

We finally approached and asked if we could take their photos. They agreed, but demanded four hundred shillings from each of us, an outrageous sum. We'd never paid anything remotely close to that in the past. Truth was, in the past five months, I'd only paid for photos twice and that was the equivalent of about fifteen cents. We continued negotiations until a deal was finally struck. For one hundred-fifty shillings ($4 U.S.), all of us could take as many photos as we wanted before they walked away.

*That's fair–and involves no spears.*

We weren't surprised to learn that it was impossible to take our lumbering truck down the steep crater walls of Ngorongoro in the morning. That gravel path was just too narrow and we didn't relish climbing out to sandmat if we became stuck in the wetlands below. So Nigel arranged to have guides with 4 four-wheel-drives meet us about 6 a.m. for the journey into that Eden.

Later that evening, in stillness and bone-chilling temperatures, we quickly set up camp on the crater's edge. The sky was a sea of stars. For once, the music was silent. As I curled deep into my sleeping bag, the only sound I heard was a lion's distant roar.

The aroma of breakfast cooking and raw anticipation had us awake well before dawn. It was still frigid, but Nigel had cooked cowboy-style baked beans, stiff oatmeal and fried potato pancakes on the grill. Normally, that was enough to set biscuit-rationing Prudence into a tizzy, but nothing was said. Although we'd never used those rations she'd been "Saving for Zaire," our Spartan diet continued. Now, supposedly we were preparing for the latest rumored catastrophe–Tanzania's cholera epidemic.

Our four-wheelers rolled in at 6:30, but there was only one Land Cruiser and a dilapidated Volvo–a file cabinet on wheels. The third and fourth cars were nowhere to be seen. Why wasn't I surprised? Since wildlife waits for no man, we drew straws and Cheryl and I ended up in the gutless Swedish wonder, along with Pooky and Bongo, Bear and Clara.

From the moment we sat down on the bare metal floor inside the cab, (there were no seats), I sensed we were in trouble. As we pulled out and headed for the road leading down the steep crater wall, my worst suspicions were soon confirmed. That truck had no brakes–or shocks. The driver couldn't shut off the engine, since its battery wasn't recharging. The four-wheel drive was only two at best, and both tires were bald. Plus, I suspected the gears were nearly toothless.

However, John, our strapping seven-foot driver and guide, stripped what gears were left, as he shifted directly from third-gear to low, then coasted to a stop without bothering to use his nonexistent brakes.

*How will we ever get close enough to anything in this wreck?*

It would have been hilarious if it hadn't been so dangerous. That heap of moving junk rattled and shook, bouncing us off the floor, as we inched our way down the narrow side of the crater. To make matters worse, there was a blinding morning fog. We couldn't see thirty feet in front of us.

"We'll crash into an elephant before we see it," Cheryl screamed over the engine roar.

Through divine intervention, somehow, we made it to the bottom of the immense crater, fourteen miles across at its widest spot, and sprang clear of the foggy veil. It was positively magnificent below. It was much warmer than the ridge had been with just enough breeze to keep the mosquitoes at bay. Verdant grass waved high across the floor until merging with tall hardwoods. Its lake stretched as far as the eye could see. And if there was a better day for game spotting, I just couldn't imagine it.

As we jarred and jiggled across the narrow dirt path on the crater's floor, we quickly spotted several lions lazing alongside the road. John brought our rolling disaster gliding to a stop. There, just fifteen feet away, stretched three nonplussed females preening in the morning air. To our surprise, a young lion cub curiously poked his fuzzy head out of the safety of the camouflaging grass twenty feet behind them. Then another. And another. And one more–four in all.

We were speechless. Sure, we'd expected to see lions, but who'd have imagined we'd be that close, or find so many all at once, so soon. Those cubs were a special treat. Like the mountain gorillas, they showed no fear, totally indifferent to our presence. For awhile, we sat quietly studying them, then slowly advanced down the dirt trail.

Moving nearer the lake, there were zebras, ostrich, hartebeest and Grant's gazelles in such abundance that we lost count. There were jackals and fox, scores of Cape buffalo, and those comical trotting wart hogs, tails waving in the breeze like oversized antennas.

The lake itself was beyond belief. One solitary hippo grazed on shore, surrounded by thousands of brilliant flamingos, a splotch of gray in a sea of pink. At the slightest sound, those awkward looking birds, perched on pogo stick legs, suddenly rose up as a group, spreading their white, red and pink feathered wings and swooped off for distant shores.

"But where are all the rhinos, elephants and wildebeest?" I wondered aloud, hooked on the adrenaline of discovery.

Not wanting to waste a precious moment, we combined lunchtime pilchards and hippos. John drove us to an immense, jade pool inhabited by ten giants. At first, just their beady eyes and flared nostrils protruded from the murky pond. Then they'd submerge, resurfacing a minute later. Snorting against the water, they'd toss back overstuffed heads with wide, toothy yawns. As we sat enjoying those legendary, tutu-ed stars of Disney's film *Fantasia*, I was reminded of a story we'd heard in Zaire.

A traveler found a lake deep in the steamy jungle. It was a warm day and he was dusty and tired from his travels. So, he decided to take a dip. What he didn't realize was that hippos also inhabited that lake. He soon discovered his mistake after he was chomped on the backside. The bite was so severe that he had to be airlifted to the nearest hospital that could handle such a catastrophe–and that was in Uganda. Of course, there was a lot of red tape to get clearance to land because of their civil war. All in all, he was lucky to make it out alive, as they've been known to bite a human in half.

Sometimes remaining dirty means remaining alive.

That afternoon was even more remarkable. After leaving the hippo pool, we discovered a herd of nearly eighty wildebeest by the lakeshore. As we stood on the banks, completely entranced by their rutting ritual, each male defended his harem of at least ten females. They trotted around in circles, kicking with wild abandon, locking horns, leaping into the air and performing a helter-skelter dance.

Rolling farther down the road, we practically ran over yet another pride of lions. By the time the Volvo slid to a stop, we were just fifteen feet from ten full-grown adults: five males with great, shaggy manes and five golden females. They growled as we approached, but didn't attempt to move or attack. The three males kept gnawing the bloody remains of an antelope that lay pinned beneath paws the size of baseball mitts. With crimson-stained muzzles, they took turns ripping and tearing the flesh from its soft belly. Their companions, however, never took their eyes off us. We cautiously drove past, trusting our car wouldn't pick that exact moment to get mired in the wet grass. Then, circling back around the lake, we spotted two shadows off on our right, nearly hidden from view.

"John, take us nearer! Over there, quick."

He shook his head and refused. "I be fined if de ranger see me."

"But what about the other car over there?" The rest of our group was already looking at something.

Reluctantly, John inched us a little closer, either afraid of getting ticketed or stuck in the spongy lakefront. Soon, those shadows ninety feet to our right developed into a pair of the most magnificent creatures we'd ever seen–black rhinos. There were less than seven hundred remaining in the world, due to man's reckless poaching.

*These are so close that with binoculars I can look right into their heavy eyes.*

Understandably, hearing our cacophonous car with the fumes flaming out the back, they became nervous. So, we only had a brief moment before they stormed off.

"Come on John, let's follow 'em," Bear urged.

Hesitant, we set-off along the far edge of the lake toward their watering hole. Fording a small trickle of a stream that we could easily have walked across, our car hit a hole. Bald tires spun and we jarred to a stop.

"Oh, no," we sighed in unison. We'd thought we'd left that routine behind.

John rocked the car back and tried again to make it past the hole and up the three-foot embankment on the other side. Our wheels spun and black smoke poured into the mud, as we only dug deeper. We were stuck fast. A constant stream of water began seeping in through our doors. Then, to make matters worse, our engine cut off. It wouldn't restart. Defeated, we hopped out and suspiciously eyed the thick surrounding brush. Our other car had disappeared long ago. Of course, cell phones were an unheard of luxury.

*And here we are, deep in lion country.*

Within ten nervous minutes, we were joined by a quartet of other four-wheelers whose drivers hopped out of their cabs and then stood around eating, as though this was all a regular occurrence, their afternoon tea break.

*Is anyone going to do anything to get us out?*

Eventually, John borrowed a battery from one of the other cars, and with endless cranking restarted his beast. After a whole lot of concerted rocking and rolling, pushing and teeth gnashing, Bear, Clara, Cheryl and I rolled the car free. It had taken almost an hour.

We immediately started our ascent back up the crater wall to arrive in camp before sunset, because there were no headlights on the heap either. As we shimmied and shook our way up the trail, there were real doubts whether we'd make it out of the crater at all. It was touch and go, as we wheezed between first and third, and third and first gear for miles, all the way to the top. That heap slid from side to side, skidding perilously near the edge and deep ravine far below.

Ready to slide over the edge, I flashed back on the wise threat that my friend Pascal had yelled to an incredibly bad taxi driver in India years before, and I screamed at John, "Dead men don't leave tips!" above the engine's roar. Well, that was incentive enough to make him swerve in from the edge.

After forty minutes, much swearing and a few silent prayers, we reached the top, just as our beast let out a last "Pssshhheww-Kadonnk" and sputtered to a dead and final halt.

# Chapter XI
# Land of the Masai

*"By the time the fool has learned the game, the players have dispersed."*
~ African proverb

SAILING THROUGH THE PARK, then across sprawling fields of coffee and wheat, the next day we raced the short distance to Kenya. For the entire sixty miles to the border, 15,000 foot Mt. Meru and the snow-dolloped slopes of 19,300 foot Mt. Kilimanjaro (Kibo) were our constant companions. Towering magnets, they drew our eyes ever upward to their slopes.

To the people of Tanzania, Kibo embodies the soul of the nation, sending rains to the arid plain and fields. Locals even tell a legend about the mountain and how it was created from lumps of earth dropped by a small boy as he escaped evil spirits.

For us, it symbolized a tough personal challenge, perhaps the hardest in our lives. In two short weeks, my partner and I would attempt to climb that "Shining Mountain." We couldn't wait.

Our first day in Kenya was our last one with the other overlanders. It was only fitting that it was spent in pure drudgery, as we cleaned months of accumulated African dirt from every inch of the truck and repacked one hundred-sixty pounds of remaining food. All the rationing, all the bread, tinned fish and bad fruit had been for nothing.

*No, we didn't run out–not by a long shot.*

The next morning, an hour outside Nairobi, we swerved off the sealed road and onto a dirt trail leading a mile off the highway. There, a Western-garbed Masai in his forties, sporting elongated earlobes, welcomed us. Acting as though he'd just returned home after a painful absence, Stephen led us across the dusty plain for nearly another mile, as we passed grazing cows and a few bleating goats tended by young Masai boys. Our hike continued until the wooden walls of his village loomed directly in front of us. A six-foot high crisscrossed, stacked fence of interwoven branches and acacia bushes surrounded simple mud and dung houses.

"De wall becomes a fort and corral at night," Stephen explained. "As de sun sets, de boys herd de cows, de Masai's only wealth, through dat narrow gate. Den drag de thorn tree in, sealing de entry behind dem."

Eager to finally meet those Masai we'd heard so much about, we followed Stephen in through the entryway.

Spotting us, the villagers instantly rose to greet us. An ancient warrior with piercing eyes and multiple earrings on his long lobes stepped forward, crying "Jambo!" as he raised his gnarled hands in gracious welcome.

"Jambo sana!," we chimed back in the only Swahili we knew.

Stephen then introduced a dignified Masai woman with a shaved-head, wearing a beautifully beaded choker, nose ring and brass anklets. She herded about fifteen children, ranging in age from two to six, who smiled, laughed and mugged for our cameras.

Their timeless village had just four mud houses and small pen where they kept a few goats. Those simple huts, said to last twenty years, measured only nine by fifteen feet and were less than six feet tall–which seemed unusual, since most Masai adults towered well above that.

After Stephen briefly coaxed the strong, gentle woman, she was kind enough to invite us inside her home a few at a time to examine it more closely. By Western standards, it was tight quarters. Its doorway was so low that you had to stoop nearly double to enter. There was a sharp bend in the interior wall to the left within two feet, so you almost had to wriggle your way around the outside wall. Doing so, we immediately found ourselves in a cramped living area. It was dark, the only illumination emanating from a tiny cooking fire in the center of the floor where a green concoction bubbled and simmered. There were four small holes in the walls, through which trickled a faint beam of light and whiff of air. Even those were covered at night to keep out mosquitoes. Two feet to the right was a storage shelf built into the wall, while two feet to the left were two small separate beds: one for the man, one for the woman.

"After a woman gives birth," Stephen explained, "she and de man don't sleep together for another two years. It ees natural family planning."

Meanwhile, since the Masai are polygamists, the man just sleeps with his other wives.

"De tradition of male circumcision ees a major part of family planning, as well," Stephen continued. "De young men are initiated in a circumcision ceremony at eighteen, de girls at sixteen. After dat ceremony, de men train seven years to become warriors and den get married only when dey finish."

Reentering the courtyard, Stephen confided with a great deal of sorrow how drastically the Masai's life had recently changed.

"In de past, people in my tribe, dey live to one hundred-forty. Now dey are lucky to make it to sixty-five. De Masai practiced traditional medicine for thousands of years. And dey lived long lives on diets of milk or milk mixed with cows blood when dere was not enough."

"Why do they die so young now?" I wondered.

"People leave de old ways behind today. Dey turn der back on our medicine. Dey eat strange food. Some even go to Nairobi, you know, to make de money. Dey end up as security guards or waiters," he said, choking back his emotions. "It is very sad. Dey can't come back to de village and dey can't live in de big city. It kills dem."

It was a sad legacy. The Masai were one of the few traditional tribes remaining in Africa. Yet the lure of civilization encroached even there. On those windswept plains, tradition seemed ill-equipped to do what it had perfected over thousands of years–support an independent people and their modern desires.

Leaving Stephen, with that poignant image of the Masai struggle permanently etched in our minds, we covered that last stretch of highway into Nairobi. The lure of the 'big city' after all those months in the desert and jungle boggled our minds, too. That bustling, modern metropolis of over 750,000 was a 180-degree change from the bush and a vast difference from all those other major African cities we'd visited. Modern conveniences like telephones, electricity and streetlights actually worked. There were office towers and movie theaters, museums and markets, fish and chip joints and continental restaurants. Colonial-era hotels with flowered gardens existed alongside small, local hotels, which made up in hospitality what they lacked in elegance.

As we pulled into one of the more swank hotels in town and everyone else checked in, we checked out. Quickly grabbing our packs and all the artifacts we'd collected since Morocco, my beautiful partner and I left the group, hailed a taxi, and set off for dynamic downtown Nairobi–and our long-awaited freedom!

As we careened along, dodging cars and pedestrians, I thought about our past few months on the road.

*Although we've thoroughly enjoyed Africa so far, the hardest part has been traveling with this odd group. It's only reinforced my original notion that so much of the joy of travel is due to the sense of discovery, the adventure, the sense of accomplishment at the end of each day. It isn't where you're going. It's the process of getting there, the journey. It's knowing that by your own skill, luck or cunning you successfully travel from point A to B, eat local food without getting poisoned, find a clean room with running water. More importantly, you learn a little more about life. You chat with locals, share drinks, swap stories and lies. And because of all that, perhaps in some miniscule way, the size of the planet shrinks just a little bit more. And you learn that our similarities outweigh our differences.*

Without any trouble, we easily found a pleasant room in the center of town, perfect for what we had planned. They had hot water, friendly management to do our laundry and delicious aromas already wafted up from the Indian restaurant downstairs–all for just $6.50 a double per night.

Nairobi was scheduled to be our 'business' stop. We'd mail our souvenirs, get film developed, catch up on mail, get new Tanzanian visas and even find time to do some serious eating and partying. We started that night. Our 'last hurrah' as an overland group took place at a restaurant famous among African travelers–the legendary Carnivore Restaurant.

Waiters in white jackets formed an endless stream back and forth to the kitchen. However, most of the actual cooking was prepared over an open fire pit in the center of the room where huge slabs of flesh roasted and turned on spits. The overlanders were served by waiters toting chunks of charred meat, skewered on Masai spears. They worked their way up and down our banquet table, slicing off tasty bits of zebra followed by succulent hartebeest, then the more pedestrian beef, pork and chicken. Their procession continued for over an hour, until we were all ready to fall off our chairs in gluttonous fits.

Feasting, we excitedly compared plans for the coming month. Perfect Couple, Prudence, Slim the bartender, Maxie, hefty Chester, Bear, nurse Clara, Peggy and Trotsky would continue their safari on to Harare, Zimbabwe on the truck. Flinty, our adventurous fire-wallah, was anxious to climb Mt. Kenya.

Pooky, Bongo, Willie and Dropsy were all catching the train to Lamu Island, not far from Nairobi. The Middle East called Zippy, and Fluffy (along with her garbage bags) was flying home to London. Why, we were all amazed to even see a recuperated Duchess at our farewell bash, as Mummy had flown her thousands of miles from England just for the occasion. Sadly, our only absent companion was Sprout, who was 'gone with the wind'.

To our surprise, Nigel found a strange message waiting for him in Nairobi. He was ordered home in no uncertain terms. However, the biggest shock of the evening was Henry's appointment as group leader for that Harare leg.

*At least, our one-eyed wonder has driven that segment before–and there's no sand. Still, his promotion makes me especially grateful to be setting off on our own.*

A few addresses were exchanged along with vacant promises to write. We hoped to see Bear and Clara somewhere along the trail to Harare, but there were no tearful good-byes. There'd been no pretense of camaraderie so far, and it was too late to begin.

However, we'd come a long way since Belgium. Friendships had been forged or lost; loves bloomed or withered.

Peggy, our novice Canadian traveler, had learned how to use a squat toilet. Trotsky finally gave up on cornrows and reverted back to his Rasta-locks. Chester dropped about fifty pounds and finally bathed. Flinty survived hepatitis, while Duchess mastered malaria. Maxie and Henry were destined to long-haul cargo across Australia together. Although the Perfect Couple still feared eating out, Perfect Husband had bravely ventured into the unknown world of green vegetables. Prudence was still "Savin' it" for God knows where, and Nigel prudently considered changing professions.

For us, we were forced to expand our definition of 'patience' and had certainly grown together as a couple. For each of the overlanders on this 'trip of fools', travel had expanded and redefined who they were–and none of us would return home quite the same.

"Keep eating your potatoes," I joked, winking at the Perfect Couple, as we stood to leave.

They only half-smiled. Perfect Wife whispered, "Whatever did he mean by that?"

"And you, Prudence, keep savin' it!"

177

On the way out, Cheryl suddenly stopped beside Bongo and unexpectedly jabbed him. A shocked grimace shot across his impish face.

"You, you're such a punk!" she kidded.

"No, I'm not," he corrected her. "I'm a brat."

Yes, as Mark Twain once remarked, "There ain't no surer way to find out whether you like people or hate them than to travel with them."

Over the next five days, we took care of business. Our laundry, handled by Ali at the hotel, hadn't looked so clean in months. We even took in an American film at a theater down the street. In that B movie, the Marines liberated a small African country. Our all-black audience was enthralled, stomping, clapping and cheering on the 'good guys'. That film probably did more for Kenyan relations than any number of State Department visits.

Also, we finally had an opportunity to catch up on mail. At a local grocer, we found a perfect cardboard box for the assorted souvenirs we needed to mail back home. Still, we could have saved our time, since there was an independent service just outside the front door of the main post office. For a small fee, they'd box, wrap and tape packages and even help fill out the customs forms. Calling home was more of a challenge.

Placing overseas calls was a constant challenge throughout Africa. It was difficult to find phones, except in the telephone offices of major cities. You might have to call at midnight, because there are major time differences between North America and African nations. It could take hours for a call to go through, and then your connection was often so bad that you wasted $40 or more for three minutes of static.

Kenya's main telephone office sat right across the street from the post office. Seven clocks ran across the wall showing the times in Nairobi, Geneva, London, New York, Los Angeles, Honolulu and Tokyo. The time for Hawai'i was about five hours fast.

Tired of waiting under the cool whirring fan, my weary partner struck up an innocent conversation with an equally bored phone office security guard.

"I was noticing your clocks."

"Yes?"

"Well, I'm from Hawai'i."

He smiled broadly and raised an eyebrow, as if to say, "So, why are you here?"

"And," she continued, "your clocks show it's the same time in Hawai'i as it is in New York, instead of five hours behind."

"So?"

"Well, it's wrong."

"So?"

"So, don't you think you should tell someone?"

"Why? Someone probably wants it dat way," he reasoned.

Africa's like that.

Those days quickly passed and finally we set off to catch our train for exotic Lamu, looking forward to its unique Arabic atmosphere. An island in the Indian Ocean northeast of Mombasa, Lamu dates from the 1400s with the construction of their first mosque. In the next century, it grew in prominence as a port for both Arab and Indian traders sailing the coast from Mombasa to Zanzibar in search of slaves, spices, ivory, rhino tusks and fruit. Unlike other Kenyan towns, it remains influenced more by the Swahili culture, due to those early traders and rule by the Sultan of Zanzibar from the early 1800s until 1963.

We hopped aboard a Kenyan express train that evening, since it offered few stops and fewer problems. The coach turned out to be much more comfortable than expected, although we were both surprised to discover it was segregated—men in one compartment, women in another. Still, even second-class was very cozy with plush seats, screened windows and room service to make up your bed and bring your meals. Plus, there were only four passengers to a compartment. All in all, it was a vast improvement over our usual truck.

I shared my couchette with an American who'd been counseling Tanzanian youths, as well as a communications professional from Mombasa and a young Kenyan who never said much. Occasionally, he'd just throw back his head and laugh. We spent hours talking about life in Kenya and I learned more about the real country than any tour group could tell.

Freedom is such a precious and fragile gift of any civilization, especially when you live in one of Africa's only democracies. Even though Kenya's leader Daniel arap Moi was determined to remain "President for Life," groups in Nairobi were already actively demonstrating for a multi-party government and elections. This movement was gaining momentum and definitely seen as a threat. In some ways, it was similar to what we'd witnessed in Eastern

179

Europe before the Berlin Wall came down. There was the same acute frustration, the same vocal protests, the same police wagons. In Kenya, as in other countries where dissention isn't 'politically correct', the press and other media are slowly strangled and dissention is muted until one party or tribe ultimately gains full control. Meanwhile, a powder keg smoked—ready to blow.

Although our train left on schedule, by the time we rolled into Mombasa we were already thirty minutes late. Because we had a tight bus connection, we wished our new friends "Kwaheri," grabbed our bags, raced through the crowded station, caught a taxi to the overflowing bus office, and just barely grabbed the last two seats on an already stuffed coach bound for Lamu Island.

'Crowded' is an understatement. People three or four deep, grasping tattered boxes, were shoehorned into the aisles. Teenagers sprawled across the dashboard. We squeezed six people plus baggage into a back seat meant to fit five. At one point, a seventh sweaty person even tried to wedge his way onto our rear rumble seat. To avoid getting stopped and cited, every time we sallied past a police checkpoint, everyone in the center aisle squatted to avoid being seen. Yet as crowded as it was, people were quiet and patient. All in all, it was an everyday African comedy.

*Finally, this is the Africa I've imagined.*

Most of the passengers were women. Some were shrouded from head to foot in black Muslim robes with only their faces peering out. Most carried children on their laps. A few non-Muslim ladies wore tangas, those tie-dyed brightly patterned cloths with Swahili sayings written on their borders. Otherwise, there were just a few older gents huddled in the back—and us—the only foreigners on the entire bus.

Along the road to Malindi, our bus played tag with others along the narrow two-lane highway. Our driver 'counted coup' as he zoomed past one truck after another at breakneck speeds. Passing one, the passengers would cheer in unison, "Yaaaa!" Then they'd turn and crane their necks backward to watch the ensuing chase.

After Malindi, a lively coastal town, the paved road suddenly evaporated into dust. The air was thick with a powder that flew in through the windows and the open rear-ceiling hatch, enveloping us in a rusty haze. It was a long five hours, but it was all somehow more real—a slice of African life—and we reveled in the ordeal.

On that leg, Abdul approached me. He was an older mustachioed Lamu resident garbed in a starched white suit and matching brimless fez, who took great pride in warning us about the boys on the Lamu docks.

"Dey sweep you off to dere lodges as soon as you land. And charge you much more. Dey receive commission, you know." In hushed tones, he conspiratorially whispered, "Now, I have a house in town where you could stay for much less. Other Americans stay dere all de time."

*That's got possibilities. Staying with locals usually gives us an unusual opportunity to talk with families and gain real insight into the area*

"We'll look at it," I promised, hoping to eliminate the usual room search.

"You two stick with me when we land," Abdul advised with a wink.

Around 4 p.m., we pulled into the creaky docks opposite Lamu Island, then piled everyone into a small motorboat. There were nearly sixty of us in all, a shoulder-to-shoulder mosaic on that overburdened launch, with water lapping perilously close to its top.

It was a fifteen-minute ride up current to the tiny isle, but it passed quickly. The Indian Ocean transfixed us, glistening and desirable in the hot sun. When we arrived, just as Abdul had warned, the docks swarmed with local teenagers offering to help us, guide us, or take us to "a good, cheap place."

For once, we ignored their pitches and tagged along behind Abdul through a maze of two-storied whitewashed buildings with brightly painted shuttered windows. The doors on the houses stood eight to ten feet tall, thick and intricately carved. It reminded us a little of the Greek Islands. Mysteriously, there were no cars, no people—just the occasional donkey cart. It seemed odd that those narrow cobblestone streets were nearly deserted that time of day. However, as we found out later, no cars are allowed on their island.

Abdul's home was, in actuality, a well-appointed guesthouse. We entered the lodge through heavy doors and found ourselves standing in an open courtyard flanked by a large wooden dining table and reception desk. Lush tropical foliage formed a canopy against the sun's rays. On either side of the entry were two two-story, thatched-roof buildings of rental rooms.

Abdul graciously served us a refreshing mint tea. Then, we began the first round of negotiations. As in the rest of Africa, there was no set price for accommodations. It always boiled down to what the owner thought you were willing to pay. At first, his thought was double ours.

"Since we paid one hundred-fifty shillings in the big city of Nairobi, it's only fair we should be able to find a room here for that price," I reasoned.

"Yes, but look at dis room. See dat private bath with shower, a double bed, ceiling fan. And we serve you very nice breakfast."

"Yes, but we can find another room here for only a hundred shillings."

"Maybe, but not as good as dis."

*He might have a point.*

Abdul then led us to the rooftop where they had pillows and thick rugs for lounging on the terrace. After a little good-natured kidding back and forth, and a lot more tea, I began again.

"Well, I know it's your slow season and we're willing to stay a week."

"Pay in advance?"

I nodded.

"Without breakfast?"

"No breakfast."

So, we finally settled on one hundred-fifty shillings, $6.50 US, for that slice of island paradise. It was a great bargain and everyone was happy.

Lamu is a fascinating, quiet town. As the birthplace of the same Swahili language used throughout east Africa, little seems changed over the past century. Arab 'dhows', sailing ships based on a centuries-old design, still loaded their precious cargo at their dock and plied those same waters. With sails capturing the wind as in ages past, they carted precious cargo down the African coast.

The village also epitomized that often-heard Swahili word, "polepole!" It's more than a word. It's an attitude, philosophy and way of life. It's the not-too-distant cousin of mañana. That's Africa. Nothing rushes. No one hurries. Everything eventually gets done in its own good time.

Our next week was spent in 'polepole' bliss. With no traffic, hordes of visitors, or greedy merchants shouting, "Hey, Ali Baba," we relaxed for seven days in hedonistic pleasure. Each day we slept-in late, then hiked forty-five minutes to a pristine white sand beach. En route to our private ribbon of serenity, we passed only five other discrete couples so spread apart that they weren't even aware of each other.

Evenings, we feasted on local seafood, ranging from lobster Thermidor to mixed seafood at one of twenty different restaurants for just $3-4 dollars.

Petley's Inn was the only place that served drinks in that conservative Muslim town, and it was only open a few hours each evening. Even then, supplies were so rationed that it was best to order two drinks at a time, since they might easily run out within any fifteen-minute period. It was an intimate, quintessential 'Rick's Place' sort-of bar, complete with ceiling fans, ferns and a clientele whose carefully worn chairs exactly matched their backsides. Its window opened out on a shaded central courtyard where enticing aromas wafted in from the restaurant next door. Some evenings local boys stopped by to sell warm stuffed 'samosas', those delicious nuggets resembling fried egg rolls, right through the window for about five cents each.

As small as it was, Petley's was the place to see and be seen. One night, we were surprised to run into Dropsy, our 'Securiteee' officer and affable Willie–together. They'd had a love/hate relationship for months, like a couple of twelve-year olds trying to deny a first love. At last, magically, they looked contented.

It was in Lamu, too, that we discovered an enigmatic indoor-outdoor theater. One night, after leaving Petley's, we followed the crowd out into a field where a film was being shown and paid 3-1/2 shillings each to enter through a concrete doorway. However, once inside, we were still outside. There was no roof. A crowd of about a hundred lay sprawled on the grass, very seriously staring at an old film flickering on a blank wall that doubled as the screen.

*That's Lamu: a tough Muslim exterior surrounding a 'polepole' existence–a wonderful African time warp.*

All too soon, it was time to leave our tropical hideaway and head back to Tanzania and Mount Kilimanjaro. As the boat shoved off, we sat on our packs, already nostalgic about a place that had revitalized our spirits and reminded us why we loved to travel.

Our coach ride back to Mombasa was long but more comfortable. Learning from our previous trip, we chose seats closer to the front, away from its rear tires. Although the driver's assistant desperately tried to convince us there was a mysterious seating chart and that we'd been assigned rear seats, it would take more than that to chase us to the back of the bus.

Funny, although we were in a country with electricity, flush toilets and Western goods, it was still Africa. The rules changed daily depending on the position of the stars, your nationality and the state of every man's personal little kingdom. We were always the 'mzungu', the white people, the outsiders.

We arrived in Mombasa by 3:30. Because the last bus to the Tanzanian border left at 4:00 and was due to arrive at midnight, we opted to get a room for the night. Besides, we still had to search for the best connection to the border. Several companies made the run, but we'd heard that some were much better than others were. In our search, we collided with a cockeyed rooster of a fellow in ragged clothes, baring the door of a bus company office. He was too unkempt for a street hustler, yet too well spoken for a beggar.

"Come with me," he confided. "Dis company is very good. I will help you," he promised, staggering up the creaking steps, leading us into the bus office.

It was a one-room, concrete block affair with flies as thick as the yellowed files on the office table. However, the sympathetic black lady behind the counter was friendly and knew exactly what we wanted. Although we had to rush back to our hotel, change money and hurry back with shillings, she stayed open well past closing, just waiting for our return.

The following day, our five-hour ride to Tanzania was easier than expected. The bus left on time and wasn't nearly as crowded as our last. Our journey was actually quite relaxing. Shooting west, we cut through Tsavo National Park, where we spotted a few lone giraffes and the ever-present baboons scampering across the highway. Finally about 1:00 p.m., in the sweltering heat, we pulled into a run-down, windswept café. As the last few passengers shuffled out, we remained glued to our seats figuring this was only a 'pit stop' and chance for everyone to wolf down warm sodas. Besides, we just couldn't lose those seats and wind up in the back again.

"Dis ees eet!" the driver exclaimed, dragging himself up out of his sweaty seat.

"This is the border? Where are the usual flags and official looking oil barrels?"

"Border?" he laughed, shaking his head. "No, dis ees Taveta. De border's just over dere," he said, pointing a chubby finger due west.

I didn't see signs of anything in that direction. Still, since he'd already shut off the engine and left us sitting there, it was the end of the line–whether we chose to believe it or not. We climbed down, hoisting our twenty-pound packs onto our backs. We looked for traffic heading that direction. Nothing. It was as though all signs of any moving vehicle, four-wheeler, 'matatu' (private taxi), oxcart or wagon had disappeared off the face of the earth.

We started trudging in the blistering sun, sizzling like two flies under a magnifying glass. Lugging full packs made the going excruciatingly slow. After thirty minutes and two miles, "over dere" remained to be seen. There was nothing. Once, two boys approached on rusted, rickety bicycles. For one heat-deranged moment, we tried to figure out how we could fit two travelers with packs onto one wobbly two-wheeler, that looked like it had been abandoned by colonists at the turn of the century.

Thirty minutes turned into over an hour and at least two more miles, until at long last the border hut rose on the horizon.

Thankfully, we cruised through Kenyan customs. Then again, they certainly weren't busy. There were only a few locals, who traipsed right through. We were the only two travelers. The last Kenyan official was very polite, asking about our trip and wishing us good luck on our climb up Mt. Kilimanjaro.

*That's very friendly.*

"Dere's just one small problem," he warned. "Dere's no way to get to de Tanzanian border."

"What do you mean? There are no buses, no cars? No way to get there?"

He shook his head and stared at the ceiling, as if to say, "This is Kenya. What's a person to do?"

"Well, how far is it?" Cheryl asked, still flushed from our trek. "We've already hiked from town."

"Oh, only four kilometers. I guess you could walk."

"That's only about 2-1/2 miles, Cheryl," I said, trying to convince us both. "We can make that."

"Do we have any choice?" she winced.

We thanked him, threw on our packs and set off for "over dere" once again. No, it wasn't far in the scheme of things, and normally we wouldn't give it another thought.

It was dusty and parched. Heat waves rose off the road. Pack straps dug into our shoulders. Still, we plodded on.

"A kilometer is a very relative thing here," I rasped, as we finally spotted the secluded Tanzanian border at Hololo over five miles later. It had taken us nearly ninety minutes and we were heavily panting. Sweat streamed down our faces, as red as that no-man's-land.

Again, we were the only Westerners at the post, and after filling out all the usual ridiculous declarations and forms, we were finally stamped in.

Then, the Tanzanian border official asked a question that set our soft-boiled minds to reeling. "Where's your car?"

*Car? Does he think we got this sweaty riding in a car?*

"No car," we shook our heads slowly.

"Oh, den dere ees a slight problem...."

*Oh no, not again.*

"Dere ees no transportation to Moshi."

"What? No cars, taxis, matatus? Nothing?"

"Well, a few private cars. You might want to talk to someone outside."

*There's just one car sitting outside. That limits our possibilities.*

"How far is it?" I wondered aloud, hoping it might be just one more "over dere."

"Very far, you know. Forty kilometers."

*Definitely too far to walk. Forty African kilometers could mean eighty real kilometers–or four hundred. Who knows?*

Thanking him, dejected, our packs suddenly twice as heavy, we trudged outside and started asking around. That didn't take long, since there was just one driver of one car.

"Excuse me, bwana," I began in my most respectful Swahili. "How much to take us to Moshi?"

Eyeing us carefully up and down, again, as if to measure our exhaustion or prosperity, the fellow smiled and in all seriousness quoted, "Thirty-five dollars."

"Thirty-five? You must be kidding! That's what we paid for a week in a Nairobi hotel. We'll give you five."

He echoed our laughter.

"Okay, ten, final offer."

He still shook his head.

"He thinks he has us," I whispered to my companion.

*And he might be right.*

Frustrated, yet hoping for the best, we threw on our packs and started meandering down that endless road to Moshi.

"Who knows, maybe he'll chase after us," Cheryl wished.

"Yea, right. This isn't some cheesy film."

Fortunately, we hadn't walked more than fifty yards when we spotted another pickup by the side of the road with two teenagers in the front seat.

"Oh, here we go again," Cheryl muttered under her breath as I approached.

I figured I'd use my best (and only other) Swahili and see if that helped.

"Jambo!" ("Hello!") I cried.

"Jambo sana!" ("And a big hello")

"Habari?" ("How are you")

"Mzuri." ("I'm fine, thanks")

"Mzuri sana." ("Very fine.")

"Ugh." (We all moaned together.)

Well, it did actually seem to help. At least, it added a little humor to our predicament. After we explained our predicament, the two young brothers started the bidding—this time at twenty dollars.

The man in the first car, now spotting his competition, tried to call us over to lower his price. Waving him away, he tore off with a screech of tires.

Before long, those young entrepreneurs quickly came down to ten dollars and a crisp green cotton kerchief that my clever companion had set aside for just such an occasion. So, climbing into their truck bed, we sped on down that highway.

Within forty minutes we rolled into Moshi, a city in the shadow of what must be one of the most spectacular natural sights in the entire world—Mount Kilimanjaro. That legendary mountain that had called to us for so long and from so far away, materialized from under misty clouds.

*Will she allow us to climb to her snowy summit? Or, will the heavenly altitude, unpredictable weather or our own sheer exhaustion defeat us in the end?*

# Chapter XII
# Challenge of Kilimanjaro

*"Anticipate the good so that you may enjoy it."*
~ African proverb

*I*N MOSHI, IT'S OPEN SEASON ON TRAVELERS. They figure you're in town for only one reason–to climb 'Kili'. You're either planning a trip or just returned from one. So we were constantly serenaded by aggressive young hustlers walking down the streets, driving by in trucks, and across dinner tables in crowded restaurants, crooning, "Hey, bwana! Wanna climb Kili?"

So, it really isn't difficult to find a trek organizer. Finding a reliable one, well, that's a different story.

Early the second morning at our Moshi hotel, we met their in-house trek planner, Mr. Winston, a pudgy, mole of a fellow in a plaid polyester suit. Mischievously smiling, he led us behind closed doors, as if we were secretly planning some invasion.

"Mr. Winston, if we hire you to organize our trip, could you get a Mr. Johnson, as our guide?" I asked, as soon as the pleasantries were behind us. "He comes highly recommended by our friends in Lamu."

"Sir, dat ees no problem," Winston assured us, stroking his thin mustache, "unless he is on de mountain already. Mr. Johnson is a very good friend."

We already knew that 'a very good friend' in Africa means you might have actually vaguely heard of the fellow.

"And you," I continued, "would you take care of all the other details: our food and supplies, lanterns, transportation to the park entrance, hiring porters and park fees?"

"Of course. Now, will you take five days to climb Kibo?"

"No. Six. We know it can be hiked in five, but we want to spend an extra day at Horombo Hut. That'll give us a little more time to acclimatize to the altitude before going on to the summit. Any problem?"

"No, no problem," he assured us. "However, you will have to pay for an extra day of park fees and more for food."

I remembered all the cautions our friends had shared about Mr. Winston, since they, too, had hired him. "Make sure you get what you pay for," they warned. "Negotiate hard. Don't let him nickel-and-dime you to death."

"Sure. That's fair," I figured. "No other charges, right?"

He shrugged, promising, "No, not'ing else!"

Once those guidelines were understood, the serious haggling began. Winston wanted $200 from each of us, plus park fees. We countered with $50. Eventually, we settled on $100 each, plus the standard park fees of $196 each. Others we knew had recently paid organizers as much as $400 each, plus park fees. So, we felt we'd done well.

"We'll give you half in the morning to buy food. The rest when we finally hit the trail. Okay?" We played it cautiously. We still didn't quite trust that fellow, but we tried to banish those doubts from our minds.

"Okay. Don't you worry about a 'ting," Winston replied, cracking a gap-toothed smile, as he scurried out the office door.

Those parting words rang off-key, like some tone-deaf karaoke singer.

Our trek was to begin the next day. It didn't give us much time to tie up loose ends. As we knew from past experience in Africa, even the simplest task could take forever. So that entire day we rushed around the sleepy village of Moshi, trying to find a canteen to replace one stolen off our pack on that launch to Lamu. We planned to sip high-energy glucose drinks during our climb and canteens were absolutely essential. However, it's difficult to find plastic containers in Africa, especially ones in convenient liter sizes. People never toss them out. They're far too valuable.

After scouring every single street, we came to a startling realization. There wasn't a single outfitting shop in the entire village. So out of complete desperation, we ran to the open market and found several used fruit juice containers. Quickly snatching up a couple, a determined Cheryl set off to find a sidewalk tailor. That part was easy, since they lined the street with their antique sewing machines. She quickly drew one fellow a sketch of a burlap holster that we could attach to our belts. Could he do it?

That little man, glasses as thick as magnifying glasses, scrutinized her crude drawing, asked a few questions and set his ancient manual sewing machine whizzing into action. Before you could say, "Asante sana," we had two canteens in burlap holsters.

That evening we met Winston again, who, not surprisingly, had discouraging news. "Johnson ees not available. He ees already on de mountain."

"Oh, no!" That was bad news at that late hour. "Don't you know any other good guides?"

"Don't you worry. I know another very good man to take you," he assured us. "His name ees Thomas."

We'd heard, "Don't worry," all too often before, and it usually meant just the opposite. Against our better judgment, we reluctantly paid Winston half the money as promised so he could buy supplies. Uneasy about that latest turn of events, we confirmed our departure the next morning. We were still on.

We awoke with such excitement, anxious anticipation and a little dread about what the next six days might bring. Still, it was a glorious morning. The mountain shone radiantly on the horizon. Clouds normally obscured her snow-capped summit by 9 a.m., but that day was a welcome exception. I considered it a good omen. All that remained was our packing.

Although we hired three porters, we needed to travel as lightly as possible. So we tucked most of our belongings into our large backpacks and left them with the hotel manager. Our sleeping bags and bivy covers, wool socks and gloves, down jackets, canteens, glucose powder, hard candies and gum, camera and film all fit in, or on, our small daypacks. We'd rent the rest of the heavy winter equipment necessary for surviving the summit's severe weather from a shop at the park entrance.

After meeting Winston at 9:30, we climbed into his old Peugeot wagon with Thomas's assistant, Samuel, a kind, muscular man, the rich shade of cappuccino. Perhaps our age, he already looked ten years older. The two of them had shopped at the market, but I only saw one box of supplies tucked behind the seats.

"Is this going to be enough food for six of us for six days?" I asked, hoping we'd left Prudence behind.

"No," Winston explained. "Of course, we'll pick up more supplies and send dem up to you after you start de trail."

That made sense. "So, where's Thomas?"

"He'll meet us at de park entrance. He had some business to take care of."

It took us nearly an hour to drive from Moshi to the park entrance. As we sped along, I couldn't tell if all the pieces were falling into place–or falling apart.

*We just have to stay flexible. This is Africa. It'll all come together somehow.*

When we eventually drove through the park's outer guarded gates, we were instantly besieged by eager porters, outfitters with worn-out equipment and an audience of general gawkers–but no Thomas.

Winston hurried off to inquire at the park office and soon loped back, shaking his head. "Thomas cannot make it today," he explained, "because of a death in de family."

Our hearts sank.

*Will we have to cancel our trek, so close to departure?*

"Don't worry," Winston again reminded us.

The wheels of the finely greased Tanzanian business machine started grinding away, as our outfitter scurried about, shaking hands, bending ears and negotiating for a substitute. Of course, there were several qualified guides hanging around, but knowing his dilemma they played hard to get.

As Winston struggled to find a capable replacement, we ambled over to the park's equipment office and were encouraged by what we found. The quality of the equipment hanging inside their tiny storeroom was surprisingly good, compared with the awful junk hawked outside. The temperature on Kilimanjaro's summit could easily dip below freezing. So we planned for the worst and rented heavy, knee-length coats with nylon outer shells, gaiters, nylon outer gloves, wool balaclavas, thick hiking boots, thermals and a ski pole each. However, no crampons were available. Normally, we'd have brought gear with us from home. But since we only needed winter equipment for that single climb, it was hard to justify lugging it for six months across the length of Africa.

Carrying armfuls of equipment out to the crowded parking lot, we found that Winston had already secured our guide. Patrick was a dark, shifty fellow in his mid-twenties. Already he had a less than charming demeanor, because he knew Winston was in a bind. Personally, I wasn't convinced Winston had ever worked with him before, but he was stuck and so were we. At that point, our only option was to postpone our climb and wait for Johnson's return.

So, by default, Patrick became our guide, Samuel, our head porter, and Galence, a lithe teenager, our other porter. Patrick insisted on hiring a third and fourth porter, since he didn't plan on carrying any gear–not even his own. We left that up to him, knowing that Winston had paid him a set price for his services, including any other porters he thought were necessary.

With all those details finally settled, Cheryl and I eagerly set off up the well-marked rocky trail, well ahead of Patrick and our four porters who'd follow us with six days worth of supplies, food and water in containers.

Now, Marangu Trail begins at about 5,900 feet. Although we felt strong and charged with adrenaline, we forced ourselves to set a slow and steady pace through that dense rain forest. 'Polepole!' became our mantra. We'd heard that people often failed to reach the summit because they set too fast a pace and didn't allow their body time to adjust to the drastic change in altitude. We were determined not to make that same, possibly fatal error. In fact, some folks we spoke with actually claimed that smokers had a better chance of making it to the top because they get winded sooner and are forced to a slow down.

I wasn't quite ready to believe that one.

Only an hour from that trailhead, we ran into Slim, our baboon-chasing bartender, Bear, Clara the nurse and good ol' Prudence, as they were racing down. They were as shocked to see us, as we were relieved to see them. I thought that the ladies looked fine, but the men, surprisingly, looked the worse for wear.

"Well?" I wondered, "Did ya make it, Bear?"

"Yea, all four of us did," he panted. "It was a little tough goin' though."

"The trail good?"

"Yea, no worries, mate," Slim croaked, his eyes heavy with huge circles. I'd never seen him look so exhausted.

"Take it 'polepole'" squeaked Prudence in her grating, all-too-familiar outback accent.

"Yea, we plan on it."

Bear proudly grinned, adding, "We reached Gillman's Point."

"Where's that?" my companion wondered.

"On the rim. It's another hour 'cross to Uhuru. You gotta reach Gillman's early to have any chance of gittin' to Uhuru 'cause you gotta git there and back by 9. After that, the snow gets too icy. You could easily slide into the crater."

"Naow, thet could ruin yer day," Slim joked.

*I can imagine.*

We wished them luck on their journey to Harare, as they rushed off to rendezvous with the others who'd skipped the trek. It was great to see them; encouraging that someone we knew actually had made it.

*If the weather's good, and the ice passable, we'll shoot for Uhuru Point. But since we don't have crampons for the ice, just making it to Gillman's will be a victory for us.*

Mandara Hut lay about four hours from the Marangu Trail head. As we continued up that well-traveled path toward our day's destination, we were never really alone. Besides passing porters with exhausted returning trekkers, we met German expats living in the Philippines, a Dutch couple and two English university students who sprinted past.

That trail was wide and well graded, canopied by ancient hardwood trees. The weather was clear and warm, but not too hot. Although we ambled along at a 'polepole' pace, even with our leisurely lunch break and frequent water stops, we easily reached Mandara Hut in just three-and-a-half-hours.

The campsite was much more polished than we'd expected. Then again, we were used to camping in gravel pits. Throughout the site were scattered twelve small wooden A-frame cabins, each sleeping six climbers. Another spacious two-story A-frame doubled as a dining hall with beds upstairs and two neat rows of picnic tables, benches and wood stove downstairs. The site even offered toilets, sinks with cold running water and a shop selling soft drinks and beers.

I was relieved when our porters and Patrick dragged into camp about an hour later and headed for a central cook shed. There, all the different expedition porters combined their food in a common pot over an open fire, creating a simple meal for everyone. So, on that first luminous night, most of us ten ragged climbers enjoyed the same bland banquet of potatoes, rice, carrots, cabbage, bananas and some nondescript meat.

Ah, but life is sometimes cruel. Just as we sat down to our carb-fest, exquisite aromas wafted in our direction. Across the candlelit dining hall, a group of rowdy Italians feasted on spicy morsels. Here was the rich culinary vision that we'd fantasized about for the past five months: real pasta with Italian sausage in a thick, simmering tomato sauce. They'd obviously done their own cooking.

"We should have them cater our next climb," I joked to my hungry partner, who unsuccessfully tried to contain her drooling.

As if on cue, the Italians started singing opera, uncorked an endless stream of Chianti and pounded their goblets on the heavy wooden table in time to their clamorous singing.

I was envious. "But how are they going to feel like climbing in the morning," I asked the Germans sitting beside us, sharing our boring fare.

"Oh, they don't have to. They're just here for two days. They'll spend another night, eat some more, drink lots more, then hike back down."

*There is a certain panache in that. But it's a bit out of the way just for a picnic.*

By 8 p.m., it was nearly freezing outside. The heavens shone brightly in a cloudless sky. We were fading fast and headed back to the warmth of our private cabin, while those day-trippers continued harmonizing in fortissimo Florentine voices long into the night.

On Day Two, we awoke to a dense pea-soup cloud cover enveloping our camp. A fine, misty spray clung to our nylon jackets and hair like the slobberings of a friendly dog. Still, once we were shown the trailhead, we wasted no time in setting off again on our own, while Patrick and the porters broke camp.

The first section of the trail began with a steep ascent for several miles up the pitch of a hill. Carefully wending our way through an expansive heath, our trek was slower than the day before, because we had to avoid nature's booby traps of slippery mud and concealed tree roots. Reaching the top of one massive mound, we caught our breaths in a beautiful alpine meadow dotted with flowers. Nevertheless, it was still foggy, gusty and brisk, so we didn't hesitate long and pressed on. That rolling grassland gradually transformed into sharply sloping, marshy moors. Fortunately, it had been relatively dry on the mountain for awhile. So those bogs weren't spongy enough to slow our pace. Since it was only about eight and a half miles to Horombo Hut, we continued our relaxed gait, pausing only when we became winded or felt our heartbeats accelerate too much.

*As long as we can continue to breathe through our noses, we're setting just about the right pace.*

We advanced on that soggy path, gradually ascending the slippery hillside, until we finally poked our heads above the blanket of clouds. Majestic Mount Kilimanjaro rose to our left with Mount Mawenzi to our right, forming a heart-pounding panorama. Those mountains appeared so distinctly different. 'Kili' rose gradually, almost mesa-like in the distance. She was topped with a dollop of pure white snow and cast a smoothly sculpted silhouette across the plains below. In contrast, distant Mount Mawenzi, her crown sharply peaked and jagged, attested to more recent volcanic history. With razor edges bare of snow, she cast a craggy monolith in a deep lapis sky.

As we traced that well-worn path to the left across the slopes of Mt. Kilimanjaro, it was a trek among Goliaths on our constant, gradual ascent to Horombo Hut perched at over twelve thousand feet. Although the temperature was near-freezing when we started, the sun quickly heated that lava plain to a rolling simmer. All afternoon, a fierce wind whipped across the mountain's face and into ours, demanding full, undivided attention. The air grew thinner with every step, causing our breaths to become as carefully rationed as Prudence's pilchard fish. Occasionally, I'd run a finger up to my throat for a quick pulse check. There, at over eleven thousand feet, even a minor exertion would make our hearts race frantically. Whenever they'd beat too rapidly, we'd consciously slow our pace, allowing our blood flow to return to normal. Maintaining that sensible, steady stride, we tried not to let ourselves become overly intimidated by the few crazies who raced past.

Finally, after about five hours, we rounded one last hump in the trail. Horombo Hut greeted us on the horizon. Although its layout and cabin designs were nearly identical to those the night before, the cost of a soda at over twelve thousand feet had doubled, equal to several dollars. Still, it really didn't matter, since we preferred our high-energy glucose drinks and hard candies, anyway.

*We've made good time at this altitude, hiking eight and a half miles in just five hours. Physically we're still energetic, not winded or too exhausted. Although our breathing isn't forced, our hearts are suffering from months spent at sea level and lack of conditioning from riding around too much in that infernal truck.*

Again, we had a tidy A-framed cabin to ourselves. It was about ten by ten feet inside, just large enough to hold three miniature bunk beds. Although it might sleep six climbers in a pinch, a half-dozen would have made it 'tighter' than the Italians were the night before.

As night wore on, the wind whipped in off the mountains with a ferocious and growing intensity. Again, Patrick, Samuel and Galence rolled into camp about an hour after our arrival and then prepared a dinner even more disappointing than our 'feast' the night before. My famished partner and I split a scrawny chicken leg with meager potatoes and rice, while the climbers around us had more food than they could even finish. By the look of our paltry rations, I started to wonder if Patrick had simply pocketed the extra food money Winston had given him.

*Are seven of us surviving on rations meant for two?*

That evening, I had a long talk with our guide, who assured me, "Yes, dere ees enough food for the rest of de climb."

Still, I was far from convinced. "By the way, Patrick, where are our other two porters?" After two days together, I'd only seen Galence and Samuel.

*Did he keep the money for the third and fourth porters, too?*

"Oh, you will meet dem tomorrow," he sheepishly promised.

"Good, I look forward to it. We want to know them so we can share our candies with them on the trail." That was partly true.

*Who will materialize in the morning?*

Our third day was one of rest and acclimating at Horombo Hut. We hoped this investment would help ensure our success when it came time to push to the summit. I was surprised that we were the only ones who stayed that extra day, and with the other trekkers pressing on, I paced more anxiously than ever around camp.

Patrick had heard my concerns after all. Over an unusually huge breakfast, we met our missing porters, Peter and Breton. We'd noticed Peter scurrying around camp the day before. He was a slight man in his fifties who'd done much of our cooking, and we'd hiked behind young Breton, perhaps twelve, as he precariously balanced a full jerry can of water on his head.

It was a contemplative day. Staying close to the cabins, we mentally prepared ourselves for the difficult seven-hour climb to sixteen thousand-foot Kibo Hut in the morning. That afternoon, we wandered down to a bucolic stream, edged by giant bushes. We'd never seen plant life quite so unusual.

Those unique flowering trees ranged from two to a mutant eighteen feet in height. Large tobacco-like leaves hung from their trunks, while shoots of jade sprouted in blossoms from bushy tops. In that rarefied air and mystical high-alpine terrain, it was difficult to believe we were still in Africa.

We rose early the following morning, and after grabbing a light breakfast, immediately set off toward Kibo Hut. Again, the terrain was as diverse as the climbers. It changed dramatically within the first hour outside of camp, from rolling alpine meadows to a muted desert. Skirting along its surreal surface, we passed vast plains of dried flowers, thrashing in the steady wind. The tempest blew much colder, as it whipped across the face of Mt. Mawenzi. Still, the sun mercilessly beat down and seared our faces.

Several hours out, we suddenly spotted those climbers who hadn't spent the extra day at Horombo Hut, as they dragged across the desert trail toward us. They were clearly exhausted, yet had that triumphant glow of winners, because most had made it to Gillman's. Uhuru, they confirmed, was iced over and impossible to reach without crampons and ice picks. For one brief moment, we shared in their proud victory and secretly hoped we'd celebrate our own within twenty-four hours.

As the day progressed, the trail gradually soared higher. The earth became dustier, more bleak and desolate, as we laboriously traversed across the saddle, a barren stretch of cratered moonscape. Mt. Mawenzi towered defiantly to our right, egging us on, and Mt. Kilimanjaro loomed enticingly to our left. In the distance, on its face, we could now detect a narrow, winding chute of a path. At points, it seemed to rise straight up the side of the mountain. Yet examining it more closely, we could perceive minute switchbacks crisscrossing that giant mound of slag topped with ice and snow.

*Is that actually the trail we'll be climbing to the summit in the morning?*

For nearly six-and-a-half hours, we slowly advanced across the desert floor until we reached the desolate lodge known as Kibo Hut at around sixteen thousand feet. Patrick and weary, water-toting Samuel soon joined us there. All the other porters had remained below at Horombo awaiting our return. That primitive wooden hut with the corrugated tin roof had several rooms holding about ten bunk beds each. There was no running water. No heat. No dining hall. No soda shack. No singing Italians. Only the mountain. Her monumental challenge weighed on our backs, as it had all those who'd previously attempted to scale her slopes; equally heavy on both those who made it–and those who died trying.

Altogether, eight of us had come halfway around the world to dare an assault on Africa's highest peak. Our comrades included a flame-haired Finnish girl who'd attempted to climb the mountain in the past, had failed and bravely returned to try again. There was a pensive Australian who spent his evening throwing up due to altitude sickness, and an Irish couple in their late-thirties with two teenaged sons who'd test their mettle.

For a moment, I flashed on the daring Japanese climber who'd stayed at Kibo Hut just days before us. All night, we'd heard, he'd vomited from altitude sickness. However, in the morning, he insisted on continuing his quest to the summit. Eventually, he did reach Gillman's Point–and promptly fell into a serious coma. His guides, aware he had to receive treatment within twelve hours, rushed him back down to this hut, put him on a wheelbarrow stretcher and hustled him to the bottom. A few days later, when we began our trek, that unlucky climber still lay unconscious in a Moshi hospital. No one knew his fate.

By 6:00 that clouded night, the temperature outside plummeted far below freezing. The interior of our Spartan, unheated hut wasn't much warmer. By dim candlelight, we made one final check of all our gear. Dinner was just a cup of tea. For once, that was completely satisfying. We'd been warned not to eat too much, since it's hard digesting food at that lofty altitude.

In that rarefied mountain air, each gasp was labored; every breath was strained. Sleep was in short supply, too. We didn't suffer long, because before we knew it, it was already slightly past midnight and time to test our own resolve.

It was below freezing in the stillness of our room. My hands violently shook, as I tried to touch a bashful flame to the charred wick of candle stump stuck to the wooden tabletop. It flickered and reluctantly sputtered to life. We both shivered so hard that it was difficult to put on three layers of clothing. Still, we struggled to don a pair of thermals, pants, long sleeved t-shirt, sweatshirt, two pairs of cotton socks, heavy wool socks, wool mittens, nylon outer mittens, gaiters, cotton inner coat, nylon cap, bulky nylon outer coat with hood and a monstrous pair of mountaineering boots. The only things I actually carried were my camera (strapped inside my inner jacket), a canteen filled with a glucose drink, and a pocketful of hard candies.

By 1 a.m., after a quick snack of tea and biscuits, Cheryl and I embraced for what felt like it might be the last time, said a quick prayer, wished ourselves luck and set off. A black void greeted us outside. There was no light from the building. No moon cast its beam. There was only Patrick's small flashlight to illuminate our path up that treacherous slope. We kept a stony silence, each with our own personal challenge to face. Conversation would only break our concentration; only lessen our resolve.

The incline from Kibo Hut to the rim was three thousand feet of formidable, shifting, dusty slag. Every movement was measured; each step controlled. It was a long way to the bottom with nothing to grab onto, nothing to halt a plunge into a dark abyss.

As we slowly snaked our way forward through the darkness, our path never really became visible, since Patrick forged ahead with his solitary lamp, leaving us far in his wake. Occasionally, as we struggled straight upward, I paused and swore we'd lost the track completely. The air grew thinner with each step. Our climbing became more labored, stops more frequent. Together, we gasped short agonizing breaths, our lungs wheezing under the strain like leaking bellows. Then, for just a second, I shot a glance toward the canopy of stars overhead to verify that we were still alive, still heading upward.

As we approached the halfway mark, three hours above Kibo Hut, our pauses increased and we stopped every thirty or forty feet.

"Grab a candy, take a drink, breathe deeply," I silently coached myself, as a steady wind ripped down from the mountaintop, searing our faces, heightening our raw concentration, and strengthening our resolve.

Before long, midway to the summit, we caught our breath for a moment in the darkness of the Hans Meyer Cave, named for the first European to 'conquer' Kilimanjaro.

*How ridiculous to imagine anyone 'conquering' this mountain-or any for that matter. You can merely hope to survive, because either the mountain or God himself has willed it.*

No sooner had that sobering notion passed my mind than flickering lights and five figures appeared out of nowhere. It was the Irish family and their guide, rushing down the mountainside. They'd turned back due to altitude sickness, but at least they'd live to try another day.

We continued plodding our steady thirty paces–pause–thirty paces–pause rhythm, as Patrick, so totally oblivious to our condition, sped far ahead.

"Polepole, Patrick!" I shouted, again and again, in a strained voice with as much breath as I could muster.

Each time he'd grunt in response, then set-off again before we could even catch our breaths. His light grew dimmer and more faint, as he scurried forty feet and several switchbacks ahead.

Meanwhile, my courageous partner, at first close behind, fell farther and farther back. Suddenly, lost in the total darkness, she wailed a bone-chilling, "Waitttttt! Waitttttt!"

Frozen at the sound, I quickly slid back down to help her. We embraced for a moment. Hugging and panting together, heaped in fearful desperation, we struggled to catch our breaths. The last three-and-a-half hours had undoubtedly been the most physically demanding we'd ever experienced. We were mentally drained. Our bodies were racked with pain. Every breath was excruciating. Each step took super-human strength. Nothing was simple. Even opening canteens with numbed fingers became a chore.

At last, totally exhausted, Cheryl softly broke down in tears.

*It hurts to realize that she's holding on, at least partially, for my sake. We both know now that if one of us quits and returns with Patrick, the other will have to finish on their own in the dark–or turn back, as well.*

So I encouraged her, joked, consoled and held her. We even awkwardly tried walking hand-in-hand for awhile.

"Look," I promised, "we'll either make this together–or not at all."

Then without warning, just an hour from the crest, my own head started to swim. My once clear vision of the stars was blurred, as they ran together like tiny steel balls in a kid's plastic toy puzzle. My head was throbbing, about to explode.

*Oh, God, I'm blacking out!*

I stopped. Drawing Cheryl's head close to mine, I looked straight into her face. A gray, polished marble visage stared back. She looked dead to me, a ghost. For the first time, I seriously wondered if this was to be our last journey together. Shaking my head to clear the tears that welled up in my eyes, I said a silent prayer, then hunkered down with my last ounce of resolve to concentrate on the ragged crack of rocks looming above us.

"We can make it! We can make it!" I chanted, again and again, hoping that mantra might motivate me to do the impossible.

Out of nowhere, as if another cosmic test, huge boulders completely blocked our path. Scrambling on frozen hands and knees, we climbed up one side and slid down the other for an interminable hundred yards. Our awkward dance was slow and surreal, as if we were waltzing through a syrupy field.

Then, at just that moment, a brilliant silver sliver cracked through the darkness from the east. The sky was flooded in stunning violet. The stars dissolved. In their place appeared an even more magnificent sight–the top.

Pulling ourselves over that last ragged ridge, we reached down, and with hands shaking, feebly picked up a tiny battered wooden sign that read, "Gillman's Point–18,647 feet."

*We've made it!*

Dawn never rose so welcome. A sun never shone so brightly. We were so high above the clouds that we could trace the curvature of the earth. It was a celestial celebration. We hugged then beamed with smiles as wide as that crater. The color gradually returned to our pallid, weathered faces. I even dared to unzip my jacket long enough to whip out my camera for a few quick victory photos taken in the blood-freezing morning air.

Then remembering the others' admonitions, I realized there was no time to waste. We had to press on toward Uhuru, or 'Freedom' Point.

Continuing was tortuously slow. Not only because of that head-numbing altitude, but also because of the ice and snow that now completely obstructed our narrow path. We cautiously shuffled along the inside rim of that ancient, massive dome, aware that any misstep would send us plummeting into the white void below. Still, at that pace, it wasn't long before we met the Finn, Australian and their guide heading back toward us.

"It's impossible to continue," the redhead cried, choking back her tears.

The sun that we had all so eagerly yearned for all night had the last laugh, transforming the ice on that slender crest into a slippery sheet of glass.

The moment we heard those discouraging words, we stood about halfway to Uhuru on the summit of 'Stella' Point. It seemed a somewhat appropriate place to stop, because that day belonged to the stars.

It took us just ninety minutes to skid and slide our way back down to Kibo Hut. Surprisingly invigorated, we packed and immediately left for Horombo, where we spent that night.

Early the next morning, we pushed off for the trailhead, taking just four-and-a-half hours to descend what had taken us two days to climb.

Before leaving the park, we were happy to present each of our diligent porters with a small cadeau to show our gratitude for their assistance. One fellow gratefully received my down jacket, another my wool mittens, another wool socks. Our favorite, Samuel, had once sadly told us that Tanzanian children weren't named until their second birthday. Infant mortality was extremely high there, often because of dehydration from simple diarrhea. So we gave him something special for his 'nameless' sixteen-month old daughter–our extra rehydration powder packets. With any luck, they just might help her receive her long-awaited name.

# Chapter XIII
# Border Extortion

*"Rats don't dance in the cat's doorway."*
~ African proverb

HE TRAIN RIDE TO DAR ES SALAAM ('Dar') was comparatively cozy after we mastered the ticketing gyrations. Bribery was an important part of doing business in Tanzania. At first, the railway ticket agent sternly told us "no seats are available for weeks." However, after receiving a small 'gift' for his trouble, with a nicotine-stained grin, he magically discovered a choice first-class private couchette. But I wasn't grousing, because such small comforts were never more appreciated. After virtually sliding from nineteen thousand to sixteen thousand-feet, our bodies ached in places we never knew existed. That cabin was a godsend, allowing us to lick our wounds in private.

Actually, the only reason for our unexpected detour to Dar was to apply for Mozambique visas. At first, we planned to enter Zimbabwe through Zambia. Yet given their food riots and a needless six hundred mile detour, we decided to take our chances and travel instead across war-torn Mozambique to Harare, along a route affectionately known as the 'gun run'.

Early the next morning, as we leaned out of our grimy train cabin window, decrepit Dar came into view. It was a ghost town, an African *Twilight Zone*. In a city of over one and a half million souls, no one shuffled through the dusty streets. Not one animal was seen. Nothing was open, no stores, no restaurants and no banks for Tanzanian shillings. Even the embassy was closed for the weekend, postponing our visit another day. At least the absence of crowds made finding an inexpensive room that much easier.

We woke the following morning with the first roar and sputter of the herds of raucous cars and rushed off to the Mozambique Embassy. With its modern compound, it might have passed for an art gallery–if it wasn't for the high iron gates, barbed wire, surveillance cameras and machinegun-toting guards. We entered a palmed courtyard lobby. It was vacant except for an obese black woman seated behind an equally ample desk.

*Oh, no. Please don't tell me that this tired woman in rubber flip-flop holds sway over who enters her country. Tell me she's not the keeper of the keys.*

"Excuse me," I coughed. She glanced up, annoyed. "Where do we apply for transit visas?"

"Here. Take a number and seet over dere."

There was no one else in sight, so I figured we'd play along. We sat and waited, and waited some more. Finally, after twenty minutes I returned and asked, "Could we please have applications for visas."

"Tourist or transit?" she groaned, with a bothered frown.

"Transit."

"Here," she barked, handing me two applications. "Seet back down over dere. Dey take five working days to process."

"Five? We only want to cross Mozambique, not move there."

She nodded dourly, not appreciating my sarcasm. "Oh, den you want transit visas?"

*Yes. Isn't that what I said?*

"We'll only be in your country for maybe six hours."

"Take dis," she snapped, slamming it on her desk. "Feell it out. Leave me two photos each and twenty U.S. dollars. Eet will take tree working days."

The bureaucracy was in motion. The game was afoot.

Dar, dreary on its best days, had little improved from the day before. There were just more people shuffling like ants across a wedge of syrupy melon in the sun. Dar was fifty years and a lifetime behind the sophistication and productive bustle of its rival Nairobi. Traffic clogged and sputtered down dusty streets. Car mufflers were nonexistent. Vendors blocked every sidewalk. Rubbish shrouded every corner of that once great city. Plus, there was a feeling of fear in the air. Unfortunately we, two of the few travelers who mistakenly ventured into that city of neglect, felt the full brunt of strangers' suspicious glances.

*There must be something worthwhile to do while we're waiting.*

The Tanzanian National Museum was as empty as the street was crowded, with room after room of vacant cases. The Nutcracker Man exhibit, a world-famous anthropological discovery, was closed. Traditional music cases were empty. One entire building displayed only broken seashells.

The renowned Art Center, Dar's other 'must-see', featuring paintings, makonde carvings and batiks, was also closed.

So, after our fruitless search for art, we headed to sprawling Keriakoo Market, hoping to have better luck with Masai crafts. Dar's main trading area was located in a hodgepodge of grimy back streets swarming with ladies wrapped in colorful tangas, beggars, pickpockets and vocal vendors. We vainly searched every street corner for Masai folks offering beautifully beaded chokers and earrings, figuring prices might be better than in Nairobi. Finally, after roaming nearly an hour, we met four Masai women perched in front of a crumbling pharmacy.

"Jambo!" we cried, relieved to find people as out of place as we were.

"Jambo sana," the eldest woman smiled with a toothless grin.

"Your chokers are beautiful," Cheryl gushed, as she examined the delicate strands of orange, white and blue beads adorning their necks.

They beamed, surprised that a 'mzungu' appreciated their artistry, and anxious for a sale. Although dollars were always welcome, Masai commerce was still based on barter since hard currency and Western items were scarce. They were particularly fond of anything crimson. Maybe it set off their rainbow-hued beadwork or shocking ochre hair. In the Serengeti, we saw enough red plaid to clothe half the clans of Scotland. So, over the past six months, we'd saved our red t-shirts, kerchiefs and even Cheryl's prized red umbrella for just such an occasion.

"See what we have to trade with you," I started, proudly opening our daypack to display our goods.

Carefully inspecting our shirts, the ladies appeared less than impressed, although they fingered our red kerchief with distant admiration. Still, we'd left the best for last.

"And this, look at this!" my partner exclaimed, pulling out her umbrella and opening it right on the street.

The women tried to remain nonplussed, but their wide-eyed stares and subtle "ooohs" betrayed their keen interest.

"I'd like to trade this for a beaded bracelet like yours," she suggested, pointing to the woman's wrist. "Can you make one for me?"

One strikingly beautiful Masai seemed genuinely interested. Her eyes hardly left the scarlet sunshade. That is, until a self-appointed expert from the growing street crowd barged in.

"I've seen umbrellas like dose before. And eet's not worth a bracelet like yours!"

The group hummed a gentle, "Ah-haa."

That was it. Once the crowd gave its verdict, there was no way that lone Masai would disagree. We made one last offer–and they refused one last time.

"Well, that's that. We might as well try to find someone else who wants a beautiful, RED umbrella like this," I said, rubbing-in each word.

Turning, we set off, squeezing our way down the crowded street. Well, we hadn't walked more than fifty yards when I felt a tap-tap-tap on my shoulder. Wheeling around, half-expecting trouble, we came face-to-face with our Masai friend. She did want it after all.

"Would you please make me a bracelet for the umbrella?" Cheryl pleaded.

"No," the lady shook her bald, beaded head back and forth.

"Well, maybe you'll trade this for your choker?" my partner asked, pointing to umbrella and then to the brilliant beads encircling the woman's neck.

"Yes," she nodded enthusiastically. Radiant, she untied the rawhide strap of the blue, orange and white neck bracelet. Then motioning for Cheryl to lean down, she gingerly tied it around her neck. With that, my companion ceremoniously passed the Masai woman her umbrella, which she cradled as though it was the most treasured object in the world. Then, grinning the sweetest smile, the lady gave us a little wink and practically skipped back to her friends.

The following day at the Mozambique Embassy, we approached that same angry official still perched like a vulture behind her desk. With a bit of mock irritation, she pulled out our original transit visa forms and photos. They had never left her drawer. As we sat there, in a matter of three minutes, she applied all the right stamps, photos and signatures. We had our visas.

"Why the three-day wait?" I wondered aloud and shook my head in disgust.

Anxious and more than ready to leave Dar, we snatched our papers and rushed downtown. Knowing that the train ticketing system was a nightmare, we opted to catch the bus to Malawi. Plus, you couldn't beat the cost for the twenty-hour ride–just twelve dollars.

In retrospect, our bus to Lamu seemed crowded only because we hadn't ridden Tanzanian buses. Mothers and babies, sun-ripened men and chain-smoking teens filled every seat. The two of us, along with our backpacks, were shoehorned into the back seats (where else?) with four locals. Twenty last-minute stragglers overflowed into the narrow aisles, wedged among heaps of market baskets, burlap bags and cardboard suitcases.

Since it was jam-packed, cramming our bags between our knees was the only sane thing to do. Our only other option was to toss them onto the rooftop. With seeping vegetable sacks, rusted bicycles and clucking chickens constantly hoisted up and tossed down, who knew if our bags would ever arrive?

Our comedy of calamities started early. Why, even as we left the station, people already pointed to the side of our creaking, overladen, circa-1960 bus. Gasoline leaked from our punctured tank in a steady stream, but that didn't stop us. No, we were bound for Malawi, one way or another.

Right off, there was a little problem with our gears. That bus nearly came to a complete stop every time the driver rammed his gearshift from second to third. There was a gnashing of metal on metal, like gladiators in combat. Then, the babies wailed. Flies, awakened by the racket, buzzed from face to sweaty face. As if that weren't enough, not far from town, our radiator began to gush. So, every hour or so, we were forced to pull over while our driver toted a plastic bucket through fields to gather water from a nearby stream.

Yet everyone remained infinitely patient. It was amazing. No one complained. They'd seen it all before and were happy just to be moving.

As nighttime approached, people started curling up on the nearest bag for comfort and, if it was theirs, probably to make sure it was still there in the morning. Folks stretched out on sacks of food in the aisles. The flies finally settled down for the night, and the unsettling gnash of gears ground on.

Sometime during late afternoon of our journey's *second* day, after over twenty hours of our grind-and-coast trip down dusty roads, we pulled into Mbeya, still hours from the border. We paused just long enough for a group of local 'mechanics' to pull off that sieve-of-a-gas tank. It was hilarious to watch them siphoning, drinking and draining the beast a few liters at a time.

As the passengers clucked and chuckled to the unfolding drama, local boys surrounded our disabled coach, as they did throughout east Africa. They sold dry biscuits, tasty vegetable samosas, fresh eggs, cooked chickens, deep-fried vegetable strips, bunches of bananas, sodas and even bottled water. It was an instant African drive-thru. Wrapping your meal in a scrap of newspaper, they'd pass it through an open bus window, as you handed them a few cents.

After an amusing ninety-minute operation, as the sun set on Day Two of our 'twenty-four hour' journey, we sped at eighty miles an hour over unlit dirt roads, careened around hairpin turns and whisked down mountainsides–all with no headlights.

*I could swear that Henry's behind the wheel.*

Eventually, near midnight, we hobbled into the frontier town of Kyela. We were just slightly late, since we were due to arrive at 1:00 that afternoon. However, we counted our blessings to be there at all. It was still two, ten, fifteen or thirty miles to the border, depending on whom you asked. So we decided to continue with that same bus in the morning. At least, by that point, we knew what to expect.

*Besides, a night in a cozy hotel bed will be just the thing to get the circulation back into our blistered rumps.*

Stepping off the coach, we were immediately accosted by this cartoonish stork-like character dressed in a speckled business suit.

"Excuse me, please. My name ees Ibrahim," he began, squinting through thick, opaque, black-framed glasses.

*Oh no. Not someone else trying to sell us something. Now is not the time.*

"I want to warn you," he whispered. "Dees ees a dangerous town. Especially too-nite. De peoples dreenk too much!"

It was the end of a holiday and from the peals of laughter, yelling and bottles crashing, it sounded like they'd already been celebrating for days.

"Thanks," I replied, too weary to worry. "But where are we supposed to sleep, then?"

"You stay heere. On de boose. Weeth my family."

Cheryl and I shot each other a wary glance.

*Is this some new scam?*

"Well, quite a few passengers are staying on the bus," my exhausted partner noted. "If this is a holiday, we may not be able to find a room, anyway."

*She can be so practical at times.*

"All right. At least, if we sleep on the bus, they can't leave without us." Thanking our guardian, we reluctantly turned to climb back on board.

"By de way…" he hissed, gently grabbing my arm, "You have ainy Eenglish pounds to sell? I geeve you a very good price!"

"Maybe," I said, unwilling to play 'friendly banker' at that late hour. "We'll talk in the morning."

Exhausted, we crammed our bags between the seats, shoved our daypacks under our heads, sprawled out and began a fitful night's sleep. However, that didn't last long. About 4 a.m., we awoke with a start. People were already sleepily boarding, although we weren't scheduled to leave for another two hours. Quickly realizing that any more sleep was impossible, we wobbled out of the bus to stretch our cramped legs.

Suddenly, our Tanzanian friend, toting a large paper sack, popped out of the shadows. "How mooch can yoo change?" he demanded.

"Ten English pounds is all," I figured. That was plenty to get us into Malawi and we could change what was left to kwatchas on the other side.

Ibrahim looked crestfallen. Slowly, he opened his bag. Inside, he must have had three to four hundred thousand shillings–his life savings. Disappointed, he sadly doled out our ten pounds worth. Then he pleaded once again, "Can yoo change ainy more?"

"Sorry." I'd probably already changed too much, but a ten-pound note was the smallest we had. Quickly dividing the shillings, I tucked them deep into my two front pockets.

"I moost go den. It ees dangerous to carry thees much money here." Gratefully shaking my hand, he limped off into the shadows.

Six-thirty rolled around. Roosters rousted the village with tortured shrieks. Our bus still hadn't moved. Although people still climbed aboard, those with the choice seats hadn't budged for nearly forty-eight hours. They didn't dare, because they knew they'd be forced into riding in the back  mysterious seating chart, or not!

Oddly enough, when the driver and his assistant finally arrived, they ducked under the hood and started to tear the engine apart. It was evident from the greasy parts strewn across the front of the bus that we could be stranded for hours. I was worried. Each moment that slipped by brought us closer to missing our connection. We still needed to cross into Malawi, find the nearest bus station, then rendezvous with a ride to Chilumba where we'd catch a once-a-week lake boat to Monkey Bay. Although we'd quizzed tourism officials, travel agents and Tanzanian strangers, no one even knew what day that ship left port.

Figuring it was better to get to Malawi a little early than a little late, we wisely gave up on that bus and found another one loading just around the corner. Cautiously, we asked the driver, then a merchant, and then another passenger, "Does this bus go to the border?"

"Within about four-kilometers," we were told three times.

*That's a good sign. It meets another of our peculiar, yet dependable rules of the road. When it's important to get the correct answer, we always ask three different people the same question. Then take the majority answer. Otherwise, if you ask just one, they'll sometimes give you the answer they think you want just to please you.*

Within an hour or so, our new bus sputtered to a start and unceremoniously cruised out of that hung-over village, finally dropping us off "four kilometers from the border."

Hoisting up our packs, we began another sweaty trek down another endless dirt road, hoping the border wasn't another "over dere." Before long, we detected a drone, then the blur of a blue pickup speeding in from the horizon. Nearing us, it slowed, showering our faces and bags with a fine crimson powder.

"Hey mzungus, where you goin'?" the young black driver yelled, as he popped another cassette into his tape deck.

"Border," I wheezed, wiping the grime from my face.

"Hop in!" We jumped up onto the bed and were carried five or six kilometers until he swerved into a small roadside café, yelling, "End of de line!"

Thankful even for that short lift, we grabbed our bulky packs and continued our deliberate trek toward Malawi. There was still no border in sight. There was nothing and no one as far as the eye could see. Only a few scrawny acacia trees dotted the otherwise bleak landscape. And then again, there it was–that sweet, unmistakable buzz of an engine. Extreme exhaustion has a way of sharpening your sense of survival.

We stuck out our hand and were surprised when the semi skidded to a stop. With no more than a "hello," the kind Malawian gave us a lift up into his shiny new cab then carried us another five or six more kilometers out of his way. He dropped us on the front steps of an anonymous looking concrete-block building with a lone weathered flag drooping out front. It was the border.

It was a sleepy place—so quiet you could almost hear trouble simmering. To our left was the medical officer's concrete cubicle. The larger block building was evidently the customs office, and the last was a puny clapboard restaurant to our right, just off the road. Malawi lay just one hundred yards ahead across a simple wooden bridge.

"Let's go to the restaurant after we get stamped," I suggested, climbing the steps to the medical office. It had been almost two days since we'd eaten, not counting those 'window meals' of samosas and biscuits. We were ravenous.

We sailed through that medical office. Everything was properly stamped and noted in our yellow booklets. All that remained was customs. However, as soon as I opened the screen door, I felt a twinge of dread. In those boondocks, we were probably the only travelers they'd see the entire day. Unfortunately, when people get bored, they do inexplicable things.

"Come een," the beefy, black Customs Chief commanded. "You stand over dere. And you here," he barked, pointing to spots facing his beat-up desk.

Reluctantly, we took our positions, trying to guess what game this grand inquisitor and his grimy companion had cooked-up.

"Now, open your bags," he demanded.

"Both?" I innocently asked, hoping he'd settle for just one.

"Both. Hurry up. I don't have all day!"

*Actually, he probably has all week.*

His standard questions, "Where are you going," "Where have you been?" and "What do you do?" were just pleasant warm-up chitchat. Leaning back in his creaky metal chair, he shot us a diabolical little smile, then slowly asked like a child playing *Go Fish*, "Do you have any Tanzanian money?"

I'd forgotten that I had more than forty five hundred shillings in my pockets.

*The way this is going, they just might strip-search us.*

So, I reluctantly dug deeply into one pocket, dumping its contents onto his desktop. It was more than half the money I'd changed with Ibrahim.

"Ah, ha!" he exclaimed, eyes wide-open. "Dree thousand shillings! You know, eet ees illegal to export Tanzanian shillings!"

"No, we didn't," I truthfully replied.

*How were we supposed to know?*

"Empty your other pockets!" he impatiently ordered.

Nervously I fidgeted a little, stalling, handing him a comb, Swiss Army knife, some loose change. I was careful to conceal the remaining fifteen hundred shillings hidden in my smallest pocket, because we still would need it if we hoped to eat.

The bureaucrat and his comrade carefully scrutinized every item, then started ripping through our packs.

*What's next?*

I glanced over at my partner, who grew more anxious about the indignity of a strip-search.

Finding my camera, the chief's stooge turned it around and around in his hands. "What's dees worth?" he slobbered.

"Don't know," I shrugged nonchalantly, suggesting it wasn't worth his trouble. "It's very old."

Grabbing Cheryl's travel alarm from her pack, the official barked, "And dees? What weell you sell dees for?"

"Oh, it's just an old clock," my partner whispered. "You wouldn't, ah, be interested in it."

They continued rifling through our packs, our homes, for thirty minutes demanding, "How much you sell dees for?" again and again. We were feeling more than a little violated. Besides, we really didn't have that much with us.

Finally, bored with the treasure hunt, they turned to the matter of the excess shillings. "Now, you are allowed to export max-i-mum one thousand shillings each. Dat ees de law." The Chief shot a conniving glance to his partner. "So, you get one thousand shillings," he declared Solomon-like. "And you get one thousand," he said, pointing to Cheryl. "And we get one thousand shillings. Now, dat's fair eesn't it?"

"Ah, but sir," my hungry partner pleaded, "we haven't eaten in two days."

*Right now, we're hungry enough to devour three thousand shillings worth of almost anything.*

"Please, can we just go across to the restaurant for some food," I suggested. "Then, we'll come right back and split what's left."

Their eyes instantly lit up at my suggestion. "All right, but come right back," the official agreed, almost too easily.

Feeling a little like Brer' Rabbit had just struck a deal with ol' Brer' Fox, we limped across the road to the tiny café. The Fox had us after all. He knew there wasn't a scrap of food in the whole restaurant–except warm sodas and dry crackers. It was better than nothing. Still, after four sodas and two packs of crackers each, we were bouncing off the café walls from the caffeine and had only spent three hundred-fifty shillings.

In the end, that cunning customs official was content to extort nearly one thousand shillings from us. And we were more than happy to finally leave his company. Quickly re-stuffing our meager possessions into our ravaged bags, we trudged across the wobbly, wooden bridge and onto sweet Malawian soil.

# Chapter XIV
# Leave Your Pants at the Door

*"Lower your head modestly while
passing and you will harvest bananas."*
~ African proverb

HE BLOOD-RED DUST OF TANZANIA clung to our faces
and clothes. Washed by sweat, it ran in rivulets down our cheeks.
Thankfully, the Malawian checkpoint wasn't far from the bridge. Two-and-a-
half sleepless days on a crowded bus with little food and forced marches had
all taken their toll.

Although buoyant to escape Tanzania, I was worried about a book stashed
in my bag. Since an earlier edition of Lonely Planet's *Africa on a Shoestring*
contained a few unpopular comments about their government, our only source
of information for southern Africa was banned in Malawi. Still, it was foolish
to leave it behind and set off blind into those remaining four countries on our
itinerary. So, late one night in Dar, I pasted a photo of a soccer player and title
neatly along the book's edge. Presto, we had a sports book. We just hoped that
the customs fellows didn't have an interest in the game. As it turned out, they
were more concerned with my wife's fashion sense than with contraband.

"Women do not wear pants in Malawi!" the customs official dressed in
crisply starched khaki shorts impatiently clucked.

Now it wasn't as though my partner was dressed in anything remotely
revealing, although it was at least ninety-degrees in the shade. She was melting in baggy harem pants, since we'd just left a predominantly Muslim area.
Although we'd been warned about Malawi's 'pants law' back in Nairobi, during the events of the past few hours, she'd simply forgotten to change.

"You know," the bearded border official explained, "we refuse entry to
women wearing pants."

"All right," Cheryl sighed in a resigned, distant voice. "Where can I change?"

Pleased, he pointed to a windowless, thatched hut nearby. Grabbing her one and only skirt from inside her bag, my partner left to change.

When she reappeared on that border fashion runway, the officer practically fell over himself gushing, "Oh, you look much better, madam! Doesn't she look better?" he asked me with a wink.

"Ohhh, much," I agreed, nearly doubled over in pain from choking back my laughter. Cheryl still wore her faded black t-shirt. However, now she sported that bright red, tie-died skirt from West Africa–the one with the yellow and green bull's eye splayed across her fanny. The target still blinked when she walked, and her white high-top sneakers were the perfect finishing touch.

She said nothing, only shot me one of those 'If you laugh, I'm gonna kill you' glances especially reserved for husbands.

The official was pleased. That was all that mattered.

"Sir, is this the border?" I asked, hoping against hope, after our latest marathon.

"No, the border is over there," he replied, waving an unusually hairy hand down the road.

*Not another "over dere."*

"How far?"

"Twenty-five kilometers."

"Twenty-five?" I blurted, as if it would sound shorter if I said it quickly.

*If we're lucky that's only another fifteen miles across another desolate no-mans-land. And still, there's no traffic.*

Hoisting up our packs once more, resigned to our fate, we began trudging down the road.

"Enjoy Malawi!" the official cried in the distance.

The sun was high above the horizon. Heat waves sizzled off the endless expanse of lonely plains. Minute twisters sprung from the ground, clouding our eyes. We were insects toting leaves across a vast, bone-dry garden. However, we were far from alone for long.

Children, African urchins, flew out of their mud huts to greet us, screaming, "Hey, mzungu! Mzungu! Mzungu!" as we marched past. They'd obviously never seen travelers quite like us before.

We waved a papal greeting and returned "hellos," like some royal entourage accidentally stranded in the Malawian bush.

"Give me my pen," they shrieked.

Succumbing to the lunacy of the moment, I shouted back, "Give me my car!" as we desperately tried to shake off our fatigue.

Eventually, another cloud appeared on the horizon with its low, familiar rumble. We shot out our thumbs and a German road contractor slowed down, then motioned for us to jump in. It was a relief to be moving with some speed again, allowing the wind its cooling cure. We were momentarily saved. That Samaritan carried us twelve miles to another set of flapping flags that resembled a border post. Unfortunately, it wasn't. Yet by the time we realized that, he was gone. With gritty determination, we slowly trekked the remaining four miles to the final frontier.

As we wearily climbed creaking steps to a weathered border house, a sweaty, uniformed fellow with the suspicious demeanor of a small-town sheriff eyed us up and down.

"There a problem?" I asked, ready for another baggage search.

"No entry forms today," he grumbled. "Write down your names, address, passport numbers and number of days staying on this paper," he instructed, tearing a wrinkled slip of paper from an old theme tablet.

After he casually stamped those scraps, we were on our way. Simple as that—we thought. However, we waited and waited for the bus to take us to Karonga, where we'd catch another bus to Chilumba, where we'd board the once-a-week ship to Monkey Bay—if we hadn't missed it already. After thirty minutes and no sign of a matatu, we finally flagged down another pickup.

The Karonga bus platform writhed with throngs of people. Masses clambered for tickets. Flies swarmed over baskets of fruit that steamed to a pulpy mush in that stifling heat. A baby squatted and peed between two tired women. One young, already haggard mother resignedly grabbed a piece of cardboard and smeared hot urine across the cement, brushing away the last drops with her bare foot. Meanwhile, thirty men crowded in front of a barred ticket window, jostling and gently shoving, as they jockeyed toward the front of the line.

Due to my size, or their polite deference, I quickly maneuvered to the head of the pack. There were only two express seats left to Chilumba. Of course, they were in the rear of the bus, but we gratefully snatched them up.

Since we had at least a half-hour wait, we wandered over to a lone café, hoping to find more than crackers and soda. The dark, cool interior of the restaurant was inviting with its rustic wooden tables, three-legged stools and vintage cooler. As the ceiling fan 'swoosh, swoosh, swooshed' overhead, the mouthwatering aroma of roasting meat drifted along cobwebbed walls. There were no people, but voices and clanging rang from somewhere in back.

"Hello?" No answer. I poked my head around the corner toward the kitchen. An immense black woman, whose hair rose to sharp spikes like some antique sea mine, shuffled toward us.

"Hello. You want beer?" she asked, figuring that was all 'mzungus' ever wanted in her bar.

"Sure, two. Very cold, if you have 'em." I hoped her cooler still worked. "Say, what do you have to eat?"

"'Nsima' with beef."

"Give us two, please" I replied, ready for anything but more dry crackers. "By the way, what's 'nsima?'"

"Maize an' gravy!" she laughed, surprised we didn't know their national dish. "You'll like it," she promised.

At that point, anything would have been a gourmet treat. She ducked back into her kitchen and soon returned with two tin plates heaped with a generous portion of tasteless corn porridge, swimming in fatty beef soup. On the top, she'd spooned a fiery deep pool of hot pepper sauce.

"Well, it is the national dish," I reminded Cheryl.

Those icy beers were the perfect complement to the infamous Malawian chili sauce, hot enough to scorch the paint off your bowl. Our host watched us eat for awhile, half-expecting us to rush for water to relieve her incendiary sauce. Her husband even joined in the spectacle, waiting for some reaction.

*They have no way of knowing how much I enjoy hot sauce on everything but breakfast porridge. Now, even that possibility has been explored.*

Our bus eventually arrived, only an hour and a half late. Within another hour, we pulled into the quiet town of Chilumba. It was a lakefront village consisting of a bar, small grocery store, guesthouse, church and outdoor restaurant where grilled meat was served right from its front steps. Still harboring high hopes of catching a boat to Monkey Bay, we raced down the lake road until we stumbled upon the ticket office.

"Could you please tell us when the next ship leaves for Monkey Bay?" I asked, gasping for breath.

Thumbing through yellowed schedules, as if hundreds left each week, the crusty ticket agent mumbled, "Next Thursday."

"No, no, Jonah," his friend corrected him. "Next Friday."

That was nearly a week away. "How about the other ship?" I'd heard that two were plying that lake.

"Not running–hasn't for over a year. Been waiting for a spare part from Germany."

"For a year?" At that point, little surprised me. "Well, is there any other way to get to Monkey Bay and Cape McClear?"

"Well, there's a bus tomorrow afternoon at 3:30. It reaches Blantyre the next afternoon, then you switch to another for Monkey Bay."

Obviously a boat trip just wasn't in the cards for us. Any chance of cruising African waters had been stymied for months, beginning back in Mali. We thanked them and decided to wait for the bus. We were confident it couldn't be any worse than our latest forty-eight hour washboard ride.

Ready to collapse from lack of sleep, we eagerly checked into the town's one and only guesthouse: a monastic cell just barely large enough to accommodate a lone, battered bed. Nevertheless, it did boast a cold shower out back, drawing water directly from the crystalline lake. Although we looked forward to scraping that Tanzanian highway off our backs, we decided to wait till morning because there was no light in the primitive wash cell. In fact, after sunset, not a single light flickered in the entire village.

Early the next morning, my nymph-like partner finally seized her chance. Throwing open our door, Cheryl pranced with naked abandon to the waiting shower stall. Right before stepping inside though, she casually glanced over to the high rushes surrounding the shower–and did a double take. A pointed, scaly tail protruded from the weeds.

*Oh, a lizard. No big deal.*

Abruptly it swirled around, until she suddenly stood facing a five-foot caiman that glared with yellow eyes.

"AHHH!" she shrieked. Tossing her towel into the air, Cheryl raced back to our room. Neither she nor a shower was on the menu that morning.

Chilumba's 'rotating bank', a Japanese pick-up truck, was due for its weekly visit "under dat big tree" at 12:30. Since our Malawian kwatchas were nearly as exhausted as we were, we needed to exchange a few dollars for our bus trip to Blantyre. So, with no other choice, we waited in a line of three for two full hours in the shadow of that designated tree.

I was ready to promise that I'd never complain about waiting in a bank line ever again, when a small pick-up swerved off the dirt road and rolled into the shade. An army-green metal box, the 'safe', rested in its puny bed. A uni-formed soldier crouched beside it. He nervously fingered the trigger of an oversized machinegun mounted on a tripod. It was more suitable to shooting down jets than bank robbers, yet it certainly beat having FDIC insurance and a whole battalion of security cameras.

When I finally reached the truck and set my cash on their makeshift count-er, the muzzle of that young soldier's weapon rested just two feet from my chest.

*If he sneezes, I'll be shredded in seconds.*

"Ah, would you mind moving that over just a little?" I nervously laughed, motioning away his rifle.

Grinning ear-to-ear, he chuckled, inching his massive gun aside, while those bush bankers had a good guffaw.

Humor was always our best defense in Africa. If we made people see the absurdity of a situation, or if we poked fun at ourselves, they'd lower their guard. Comedy made us more than just 'mzungus'. Like Africans, we were all in this drama of life together, living, struggling and laughing against all odds.

Kwatchas finally in hand, we swept like vultures through that hamlet, searching for food, any food, for our upcoming journey. We were determined to never travel unprepared ever again. However, all we managed to scavenge were a few peanuts, beers and a single tin of corned beef. So grabbing those, we retreated to the town bar, the only place open, to wait for the 3:30 express.

Not too surprising, by 4:00 there was still no sign of the bus. We lugged our packs out onto the side of the road, so we couldn't possibly miss it. Otherwise, we'd be stranded for several more days. We waited and waited, sizzling pink in the sun. Five o'clock rolled by. At six, it grew dark in that village with no lights. Curious shadows approached us and sauntered past. Some screwed up the courage to mumble "hello." Others must have secretly chuckled at the two sun-crazed 'mzungus' who'd spent an entire afternoon sitting by the side of the road waiting for a bus–that everyone knew always ran four hours late.

It finally arrived at 7:15. A crowd of passengers materialized like ghosts out of the darkness, and after a little tussling we landed, as usual, in the back seats. It was an uneventful journey, except for the first time in a long while we met fellow travelers.

In the early morning, in a rural village far out in the bush, a couple about our age boarded. Dodging market baskets, they squeezed to the rear.

*They look too clean and rested to have been traveling long.*

The athletic man's eyes were shaded by reflective aviator glasses, even at that early hour. He wore a white t-shirt and khaki shorts, the traveler's standard uniform. A bronzed woman with large doe eyes and braided raven hair trailed behind him. Brass Zulu ankle bracelets jangled against her firm, tanned legs, and a scent of patchouli enveloped us, as she squeezed down the crowded aisle. Nodding "hello," they sat a few rows in front of us.

At first we didn't speak, because at that early hour I don't think it's too wise to talk someone's ear off. But later, after climbing off the bus to undergo yet another passport check and search, we joked and introduced ourselves. After a few relaxing minutes roadside, Noel and Joanna passed us a slip of paper with their address, inviting us to visit them in South Africa–if we made it that far. We were caught off-guard by their generous offer. Having never met any South Africans before, we didn't know quite what to expect, given their country's cruel reputation at the time for apartheid.

*But these are two witty, intelligent people, not so different from our friends at home. If we do visit South Africa, it'd certainly be more interesting to stay with them.*

Before long, we rolled into Blantyre, a university town and Malawi's busi ness hub. That tidy, modern city was decked out in multi-colored, flashing lights that blinked "Long Live Kamuzu" with all the festivity of a roller coaster ride. Malawi's President-for-Life, affectionately known as "Number One," was Dr. Kamuzu Banda. Blantyre was festive, gaudy and impressive, all at the same time, and we donned it as easily as a well-worn Hawaiian shirt. After a month of famine, here was a feast. Supermarkets swelled with well-stocked shelves, much of it from South Africa. There were wines, imported cheeses, meats of every description, famous Malawian gin and more searing chili, and a wide selection of juicy fruits and fresh vegetables. In return for accepting those South African imports, Malawi exported workers south to the R.S.A. where they could share in its hazardous work and higher wages.

We also discovered restaurants in abundance. There were libraries, a movie theater, and even an outdoor market selling well-made Malawian crafts: those famous high-back, carved wooden chairs, ivory pins, intricate malachite chess sets, wooden side tables with three intertwined legs carved from a single piece of wood, ironwood figurines, life-sized statues and Zairean malachite necklaces.

Blantyre, partially founded by David Livingstone and built around his stone church mission, provided us with a few days of needed respite before heading on to lakeside Cape McClear. We happily lodged at the Government Rest House, just down the road from his old mission. For fourteen kwatchas ($4.50 US), we rented a deluxe room with clean, comfy beds, a sink with hot water, ceiling fan, mosquito net, and a shower and toilet just down the hall. It might not have rated five Michelin stars, but with us it received five pineapples, our highest rating in months.

For four days we relaxed, ate like it was our last meal, and plotted our escape to Mozambique. We'd heard that the only way to travel via the 'corridor' across Mozambique was to buy a seat on a semi before it began its weekly run from Blantyre to Harare. Leaving each morning, they spent the night at the border, then continued into Zimbabwe the following day. However, when we spoke to three truck company managers, each denied carrying passengers anymore because of the danger of driving through the civil war.

We knew better. Free enterprise still allowed creative travel. We figured we'd stop a driver just as he left his parking lot and negotiate directly. Assuming we agreed on a price, we'd be aboard the treacherous "gun-run" before you could say, "Alexander Hamilton," (that wig-wearing colonial who graces our $10 bills).

The next morning, catching the 5:45 a.m. bus to Monkey Bay, we were the only Western travelers for much of the journey, until we stopped in the village of Zomba. There, another couple boarded, jostling and struggling with bags down the aisles. It was Noel and Joanna again. Coincidentally, we were all headed to Monkey Bay, then on to Steven's Place at Cape McClear.

Monkey Bay was another simple, rural village on the edge of Lake Malawi. Imagine our surprise when, pulling into town, we landed in the midst of an impressive warm-up welcome for a visiting Zimbabwean women's group. Ladies were decked out in their finest tangas, the ones featuring the president's portrait. As they danced, his face swung back and forth across their brightly swaying backsides. Drums pounded. Kids energetically clapped and hopped in time to the music, while a gaggle of turkeys strutted to its contagious beat.

Shortly, we caught a ride in a beat-up pickup through Lake Malawi National Park to Steven's Place. It was an institution with African travelers. What it lacked in frills, it made up for in charm. Our room, one of twelve, faced a motionless, pristine lake. Each hut was brightly whitewashed, clean and simply furnished with its own shower and kerosene lantern for only twelve kwatchas a double, about $4 U.S. a night. It was heaven.

Our front yard was a wide, sandy beach with a panoramic view of several tiny islands. Locals from a neighboring village were eager to take travelers in banana-shaped pirogues for a dive among a rainbow of fish, or a paddle to those offshore isles. Meanwhile, the nearby fish reserve's transparent waters were perfect for snorkeling, fish watching or just sunning on the rocks. It was the charming Malawian home of 'polepole'.

Paradise came with a unique set of operating instructions. The two crusty, gnome-like Steven brothers ran that exceptional resort on the honor system. After ordering a drink or meal, you simply placed a mark in the yellowed composition book next to your name. Then, the elder Mr. Steven, squinting through thick glasses, carefully deciphered and tallied the lines before you left.

His menu choices were equally simple: chicken or fish and rice or potatoes for the equivalent of $2 U.S. Each evening, about two hours before dinner, the chef took orders, and if twenty surf and ten cluck dinners were ordered, that's exactly what he'd fix—and not a single spud more. Still, Steven's was worth every cent.

As the sun cast another brilliant swath of luminescence across the lake, we ate dinner by candlelight, sang and strummed guitars, or swapped tales by firelight. Then we retreated to the privacy of our rooms. There was always tomorrow.

Time was irrelevant on the shores of that cape. The next several days were spent lounging at Otter Point, a tranquil cove in the National Park just down the road. There, travelers lay sprawled across tabletops of smoothed rocks, basking in the sun like their neighbors, the otters. Tropical fish pirouetted and spun through rifts along the lake bottom. Totally oblivious to our presence, they wove an iridescent mosaic of greens, cyan and yellows.

Our lazy hours of sun were tempered by thought-provoking political discussions with Noel and Joanna. Life in South Africa was certainly more complex than any thirty-second television news clip. It was a land in violent transition. Fissures between blacks and whites were just as wide as the growing chasm between blacks and blacks, and whites and whites. The one thing everyone shared in common was a personal bubble of fear.

"Blacks mostly divide along tribal lines," Noel explained in his uniquely clipped accent. "On one hand, Buthelezi leads the Inkatha Freedom Party consisting of mostly Zulus."

"The other, the African National Congress (ANC), is primarily made up of Xhosas led by Nelson Mandela," Joanna added with a smile.

"Of course, Inkatha mistrusts any exclusive coalition between the ANC and the white government that might erode their own influence."

"And, as you might expect, the ANC fears that the powerful Zulus, with government support, will subject the Xhosas to slaughter or oppression if they take power," Joanna said, shaking her head in disbelief. "Unfortunately, we whites are divided, too."

"Yes, white Dutch Afrikaaners still seem ready to die for apartheid and the old ways," Noel said, draining his gin and tonic. "Afrikaaners, well, they worry about blacks taking over the government and land, then driving whites into exile like happened in Rhodesia."

"Right. But personally, I think their anxieties are a bit unfounded, if you look at it more closely. And we're not alone. Many English South Africans like us are pressing for equality and a coalition government. That's the only way this country will ever work without bloodshed," Joanna concluded, with a worried look.

*No, it's not an issue simply solved by boycotting South Africa. We'll hear all sides of the story, see for ourselves, then make up our own minds.*

Leaving Cape McClear involved a little more ingenuity than most places. After a farewell party of Malawian cane rum and pineapple juice, we got up early–even if our brains remained under the covers. We'd seen the drill each day; the last minute scrambling as fifteen or twenty wild-eyed travelers with backpacks squeezed onto the tiny bed of Steven's rusted-out pickup.

So, while the others still relaxed over breakfast, the four of us settled our bill and assumed prime positions in the truck. Cheryl and Joanna sat in the front seats. Noel grabbed a wheel hump and I straddled across the back bars of the bed like some sumo. Then the rush began. Twelve others following our cue jockeyed for their position on that dilapidated three-dimensional puzzle. Some sat on the rim of the bed. Others balanced on its rear bumper. A few lay on top of packs. One even sprawled across the roof. All was fair, as long as one part of your body came into contact with the vehicle. For good measure, at the last moment, a few villagers even piled in with their woven baskets and giggling kids. With each added person that jitney creaked, groaned and sank closer to the ground.

Eventually, their driver appeared, merely shook his head and gunned the engine, bringing the Japanese low-rider wheezing to life.

The road back to Monkey Bay was rife with holes, some deep enough to swallow lesser trucks. With each hole we hit or dodged, there was a subtle shifting of human cargo until screams surfaced from underneath three layers of packs.

"You're standing on my hand!" someone shrieked, then another groaned, "Get off my head!" Everyone would readjust once more and hold on tight, to keep from diving headfirst onto the road, whizzing by just inches from the bed.

Finally arriving in front of the Monkey Bay store, we unlayered that truck just as systematically as we had loaded it, said goodbye to Noel and Joanna, and bused back to Blantyre. Eager to sew up our ride to Zimbabwe, we rushed to meet our contacts at the trucking company.

"We will get you a good driver to Harare, sir," the guards assured us. "It will cost no more than fifty kwatchas," they promised. "Don't worry. Come tomorrow afternoon at 1:30."

*There it is again, "Don't worry." What have we gotten ourselves into? After all, Mozambique has been in a civil war since the '70s. Will our truck be blown to smithereens by a land mine? Or, are we destined to become two more hostages held as bargaining chips by some third-world rebel leader?*

# Chapter XV
# Road of Pain, Legacy of Shame

*"Cross the river in a crowd and the crocodile won't eat you."*
~ African proverb

*A*T THE TRUCKING TERMINAL the next afternoon, those officious guards suddenly wouldn't allow us past their barbed wire gates. The best we could do was wait outside until the trucks were loaded, then approach individual drivers as they began to leave.

*So much for, "Don't worry."*

Two hours later, the drivers received their papers, revved their engines and began their slow exit. The first semi billowed smoke and lumbered up to the front gate. Its driver paused just long enough to hand over his papers, while I rushed over to propose my offer.

"Hey! Can we catch a lift with you to Harare? We'll pay."

"No, I don't take passengers," he huffed, glowering down at me.

*Well, there are plenty more.*

I flagged down the next truck.

"Excuse me, can we please catch a ride to Harare? We're willing to pay."

"Maybe, I could take you for fifty dollars," he laughed.

*That's nearly four times the going rate.*

"No, no thanks."

I cautiously approached the third, figuring I'd suggest a price up-front. "Say, can we ride with you to Harare? We'll pay you fifty kwatchas."

At first, that heavily muscled driver had a dubious glint in his eye, but his slight smile told us he might bite–if the price was right. Without skipping a beat, I sweetened our offer, adding, "And five U.S. dollars."

"Okay, hop in," he nodded, as he leaned over and popped open his passenger door.

Cheryl climbed five feet up into his cab. As I passed up our packs, she stacked them atop each other on a blanketed bed behind his front seat. Then, I hopped in, slamming the door behind. Easing off the clutch, the driver spun his heavy wheel sharply to the right, blasted his horn twice and spun out of the yard.

*Well, that wasn't too hard. Free enterprise and fate have an equal share in our journey.*

"Thanks for the lift," I said, as we introduced ourselves.

"I'm Geoff. Glad to help," the kind black man replied with a broad smile.

There was a pregnant pause. "Malawi's very beautiful. You live here?" I asked, attempting my best small talk.

*This is going to be a long ride.*

"No, in Harare. Much prettier," he bragged, his white teeth gleaming through his thick mustache.

"That's a long commute. Do you drive down here every couple of days?"

"No, just once a week. Or, whenever I can to spend time with my kids," he added with a proud grin.

"Do you have a big family?" my partner wondered.

"No. Only four boys an' three girls."

"Seven?" she laughed. "You must have your hands pretty full."

"You think so? Na, that is small," he added, in his musical Zimbabwean lilt. "My father had thirty-six children an' six wives."

*Thirty-six! That's enough to wear anyone out.*

"So, what do you haul?"

*I hope it isn't rifles, gold or spent plutonium.*

"Depends. Today I'm carryin' sugar. I used to go through Tanzania, but that became too dangerous. Too many hold-ups."

"So, is Malawian sugar sold in Harare?"

"No. It'll be shipped again, back up to the docks in Mozambique. Then on to Portugal in time for Christmas cakes."

*So, the old colonial ties still function when there's money to be made. Ironic, since I've heard that some Portuguese, out of spite, went so far as to dump concrete in the toilets when they returned the country to the locals.*

"Do you always drive to Harare?"

"No, sometimes I drive as far as Jo'Burg. Then I turn 'round and haul food or somethin' else back up here."

"That explains all the South African food in the Blantyre markets. In our country, people are boycotting South Africa because of apartheid," I said. "Funny, it seems like everyone in Malawi's trying to go to work down there. How come?"

"A man's wallet speaks louder than his politics," the big man sighed, with deep resignation. "Here, people run for office," he continued, popping a cassette in the tape deck, "and dey make big promises an' get elected. But nothin' changes. Dey soon forget the people and where dey came from."

*Some things are the same everywhere.*

Lively strains of soucous flooded his cab. The hours whipped by, while our eighteen-wheeler flew to the border. Those sweet Christmas cakes couldn't wait.

Suddenly, there was a loud "POP" and our truck violently shook and screamed to a stop.

"Flat!" Geoff spat, provoked at the bad timing. He threw open his door, climbed out, then carefully took off his short-sleeved shirt and meticulously folded it, placing it on his front seat. He was either seething mad, or eerily calm. Obviously not the kind of man to show his feelings, it was difficult to tell. We climbed down and stayed out of his way, squatting along the roadside. Before long, another big rig pulled in behind us. Then Geoff and the other driver spent the next thirty-minutes prying off that chewed-up tire, replacing it with his spare.

*At least it happened today. Tomorrow that convoy will never stop. There's too great a chance of attack–and we'll be left–stranded in rebel territory.*

We set off again, our headlights casting a swath of light across the murky, barren landscape. Before long, we swerved into a remote border village. It was a shell of a town. Nothing would keep you there, except possibly a cold beer or a little companionship. Men hollered in the bar. A dance hall droned reggae and a Biblical-era lodge promised a bed about as inviting as a night spent in any other mud hovel.

"What time do we leave tomorrow?" Cheryl asked.

"Meet me here at five. You two can sleep in the guesthouse."

We stumbled our way over to the lone hostelry. After banging and tripping our way around its shadowy courtyard looking for its owner, we were startled by a shrunken woman with opaque eyes. Although she only spoke a strange dialect, she instantly knew what we wanted. Grabbing my arm, she led us by candlelight's dim glow through a maze of red dirt huts topped by corrugated tin roofs to her 'special' room. Her bony, arthritic fingers fumbled with an ancient wooden latch until it was tediously lifted. Then shining her candlelight into the primitive chamber, we discerned the faint outline of a small bed.

"This'll be fine," I said, pulling some money from my pocket.

Flashing a toothless grin, she gratefully grabbed our equally wrinkled kwatchas, handed me the stub of candle and closed a lock-less door behind her.

"Well, Cheryl," I shrugged, "at least we're leaving at five."

Actually, we left earlier than that, met Geoff and joined an endless convoy of semis, inching their way the remaining mile or two to the border. As the trucks slowed to a halt, we pulled into position near the end of the line.

*The sooner we get out of here, the sooner we'll be through Mozambique.*

Snatching our passports, we slide down from the truck, trotted past the harsh glare of the headlights, and bounded after the other drivers toward a concrete-block house. Over its porch hung a weathered sign, dangling from the end of a loose, rusted chain. On it, a childlike hand had scrawled the single welcome word, 'CUSTOMS'. Creaking open the door, we cautiously edged inside.

The room was a study in chaos. Sixty drivers and thirty passengers from ten countries crammed and pushed against a central counter where two already-weary, sweating officials presided. They'd seen it all too often to get unnerved and were beyond the point of caring. Truckers slapped their passports onto the countertop like they were laying down winning poker hands. Some waved papers in the air like Wall Street traders, as others bullied their way through the throngs to pick up their completed documents.

Adding our passports to that growing pile on the counter, we waited, while guarding our pockets against pickpockets in the tense, smoky room.

Both plodding bureaucrats stamped documents from their private piles and the stacks gradually grew shorter. I was already handed my papers and anxious to leave, just waiting for Cheryl to grab hers. Then, as if someone pulled the plug, the room suddenly emptied. Lorry drivers and passengers returned to their rigs. Only seven of us remained while the number of passports on the countertop dwindled.

Looking at the remaining meager pile, we were struck by one stark realization. There were only green and burgundy booklets remaining—no blue American ones!

"Hey, where's your passport?" I whispered to my partner.

"I don't know?" she replied, as a look of terror shone in her eyes.

Frantically we searched boxes strewn across the floor, thinking it might have fallen off the counter. No luck. We checked alongside the warped wooden counter. Still, no luck. We even strained to peer over to the other side, until one of those belligerent 'functionaires' snapped, "What you looking at?"

"We've lost a passport!"

"Well, I don't have it," he barked, swabbing his sweaty forehead with a yellowed form.

Cheryl cried, "It was on the counter with the rest!"

"You accusing me of stealing it?"

"No, no," I diplomatically assured him, although there probably was a thriving market for American passports. "I just wondered if might have fallen off your counter."

"Well, it hasn't!"

If we didn't find her missing passport, we'd have big problems. She'd have to apply for a new one—and the nearest U.S. embassy was two days away—in Lilongwe. We had no kwatchas left, there were no buses to Lilongwe from the border and we couldn't enter Zimbabwe without one. We'd be stranded.

At that moment, the other official grabbed the final passport from his counter. Our hearts stopped. He flipped it open—and Cheryl's passport dropped out. It had been wedged between the covers of that larger green one.

Not surprisingly, the Mozambique border was reached by crossing the usual five or six miles of no-man's-land. For all the disorder at the Malawi border, theirs' was a model of efficiency. Once duly stamped, our convoy of sixty semis, flatbeds and gasoline tankers patiently waited for our escort, the crack Zimbabwean troops, to join us. It seemed odd that the army of one country was enlisted to protect trucks coming through a neighboring one. Apparently, in the past, the Mozambique forces tried to guard those valuable caravans but couldn't prevent guerillas from blowing them up or ambushing and looting them.

Our position at the rear of that convoy did little to ease our minds, since our precious, sweet cargo was just as valuable as rifles to starving rebels.

However, if shots were fired or grenades launched, our truck was a little safer than a gasoline tanker.

Eventually, our convoy set off across a harsh countryside toward the verdant hills of Zimbabwe. Mozambique's blood-red earth was parched and blistered from drought. Little vegetation grew. What did survive was seared away from both sides of the road for a hundred yards in either direction because the army had removed any groundcover that could harbor snipers. As we drove through that war-ravaged wasteland, a Zimbabwean troop carrier sped past our wary motorcade, sweeping what little remained of the shell-pocked road, as it searched for landmines and booby traps. Another guarded our rear. Soviet-made helicopters, like condors, circled overhead.

Years of bloody conflict had devastated that former Portuguese colony, creating a ghoulish horror. We hadn't seen such squalid conditions in all of Africa. Hundreds of children, many with bloated bellies and rickety legs, waved tiny, outstretched hands. We saw no men at all. Scores of what were probably once young women stared off in resignation. Their faces were furrowed with sorrow, as they feebly tried to nurse swollen babies from parched breasts. Mummified old women, their bodies shrunken from years of deprivation, leaned outside mud huts. On spotting our trucks, they begged for food, raising bony hands up and down to open, toothless mouths.

We, too, were helpless. Helpless to do anything but speed past.

Our truck finally paused in late morning, just before crossing the bridge at Tete. Because it was near collapse after its shelling by Soviet tanks, we cautiously crossed 'polepole', one truck at a time.

As we anxiously waited our turn, pitiful children approached us. They desperately tapped on the sides of our door, repeatedly bringing festered hands to ravenous lips. They didn't beg for sweets, or money, or ballpoint pens, as the rest of Africa, but simply for food. However, all we could offer them were a few oranges and bubble gum. That's all we had with us. Desperate, hollow eyes reflected the bitter fruits of war, more than any bloody battlefield. Poverty, ignorance and desperation were permanently etched in their prematurely aged, weary faces. The gripping agony and useless destruction of its own people had forever altered a nation's history.

After crossing that bridge, we kept our eyes glued to the sparse acacia trees lining the perimeter, half-expecting to spot some rebel movement, some rustle from a sniper in the treetops. Still, there was nothing.

Suddenly, in the late afternoon, our convoy slammed to a halt. Bursts of gunfire rose from the front. A troop carrier zoomed past with reinforcements. Meanwhile, those shiny steel semis with their valuable cargo of food and gasoline sat stock still on that pitted road, ducks on a pond. We couldn't have been easier targets. Then, it rang silent again. The trucks rolled once more.

For hours, we passed miles of squalid huts, useless land and thousands of begging children, whose pitiful plight touched our souls. Finally, in late afternoon, we arrived at the last frontier. Ahead lay promise for the future. Behind, only the forgotten refuse from the past.

As we pulled into that border post, we were shocked to see a canvas-covered Bedford truck with twenty overlanders cruise in just ahead. True to form, they did their best to slow what might have been a simple process. They disappeared in and out of lines and handed unfinished forms to frustrated Portuguese-speaking officials.

"At this rate, we'll be lucky to make it into Zimbabwe before the border closes at six," I warned Cheryl. "That means we'll have to spend the night here. Plus, we'll probably lose our ride, since Geoff's papers are always quickly cleared."

It took us an hour and a half to finally clear customs. Grabbing our bags, we literally ran toward the Zimbabwean border, knowing all too well what it took to move overlanders.

*Some things never change. They'll load everyone, fuss with passports then drive another fifty yards to the next hut. I hope that will give us ample time to beat them to that concrete hut on the other side.*

It did. We were lucky, too, considering how many others already waited in front of us. After a stringent customs check where we had to show 'sufficient funds' (a credit card or onward ticket would do), we were nearly the last travelers processed before their gate was locked for the night.

"So, where are you going to stay in Harare?" Geoff asked, as we sped down a shockingly modern, well-paved Zimbabwean highway.

"Oh, we have the names of a few places," I coyly answered, waiting for the other shoe to drop.

"You have reservations?"

"No, but if you'll drop us off downtown, we'll just make a few calls."

"Well, if you like, I know a lady who sometimes rents rooms in her house. She's my auntie. It's not fancy, but she does live downtown."

*That might be good. It'll save us hunting for a room at 9 p.m., plus we've heard that Harare's hotels are more expensive than Nairobi's.*

Reading my mind, Geoff added, "And, it might save you some money."

Before long, we reached the city and parked his rig in front of a tidy brick home. Hopping down, we walked over to its porch, swung open a creaky screen door, and stepped inside. There, an impish, gray-haired lady and her guest sipped tea, as they huddled around a coal space heater. Spotting us, she wrapped a faded Yankees baseball jacket tightly around her ample body, then asked us to join them. Her daughter was immediately sent off to the kitchen for more tea and toast.

"Auntie, I've brought you some guests," Geoff laughed. "Hope you have room."

"Always!" she beamed, warmly shaking our hands. "Welcome to Harare."

From the moment we met Auntie Mary, we knew we'd found a home. With her round, angelic face topped by tight, gray curls, she was every kid's favorite 'tutu', or Hawaiian aunt. I figured there were two sides to her. Obviously, she was the family's wheeler-dealer, confirmed by that knowing glint in her eyes. At the same time, she was the kind of lady who could affectionately call you "Honey" and you sensed she really meant it. We took an immediate liking to each other.

After marching us around her cozy home like some major-domo, she showed us a tiny room behind her house.

"It's fine, but," I reminded her, "we want to stay for a whole week."

"Oh!" she cooed. Flashing her ivory grin and nodding nappy curls, she swept us back inside. Her pink rubber sandals flip-flopped across the wooden floor, as she padded on swollen, brown feet to an inviting room filled by a massive chenille-covered bed. It was perfect. A hot bath waited down the hall. Plus, she'd even serve us tea and bread each morning. Best of all, at long last, if only for a week, we were part of a 'real' African family.

# Chapter XVI
# Zambezi, Sea of Torment

*"No one tests the depth of a river with both feet."*
~ African proverb

SINCE NAIROBI, we'd fantasized about the simple comforts Harare would offer: the chance to sleep in real beds, make phone calls, and most of all, let our guard down–if only for a day. On first glimpse, we were impressed. The city was a Mecca of shining office towers, pizza palaces, bustling walking malls, banks, movie complexes and deluxe high rises. By African standards, it had its lion's share of well-paved roads, electricity and water you actually could drink, right from the tap.

In reality, though, Harare was another harsh mirage. Our expectations far exceeded what she could deliver. For instance, the downtown mall, with all its well-stocked shops, was the haunt of scavengers who preyed on unwary travelers. Within twenty-four hours, Todd, a Brit, who'd already survived that 'gun run' aboard a gasoline tanker, had his bag, money and passport snatched while he made a phone call.

Harare also had its share of con men. One afternoon, as we sat listening to music in the park, two well-dressed men in their twenties walked past all the locals and suspiciously headed straight for us, the only Westerners in sight.

"We're collecting money for a charity walk-a-thon," the dark, slender one explained, flashing a sign-up sheet with sponsors' names, countries and their contributions.

I noticed that all the names were English.

*Who ever heard of an African walk-a-thon? Everyone walks in Africa. No African would ever pay someone to walk.*

"Will you donate?" his partner asked, with a fleeting glance.

237

By now, I'd learned to trust my instincts and something felt very wrong. "Not today, thanks."

"Please, we need sponsors for this very good cause," he pleaded. "Why won't you help us?"

"We can't," I calmly replied. "Now please, leave us alone."

"Come on. You're gonna give us some money, or else," the second guy threatened.

"Or else what?" I snarled, standing up, as I wrestled that wrinkled sheet from his hands. "Leave us alone, or I'm going to rip up this paper and call the police!"

Quickly snatching that torn paper, they fled.

Two days later, we read an article in the local newspaper about the con. Apparently, once you reached into your bag, purse or money belt to donate, they'd grab it and dash into the crowd.

Later, in that same park, we attended Harare's Crafts Fair, eager for an opportunity to bargain directly with the craftspeople. While perusing row after row of beautifully carved wood and soapstone, we suddenly ran into our old friends, Bear the mechanic and Clara, still sporting her cornrows. It was refreshing to see their grinning, familiar faces.

"You guys left at just the right time," our overland nurse confided, filling us in on all the latest gossip. "Henry's become even more obnoxious than ever, since there's no sand to keep him humble."

"Yeah," Bear laughed. "We finally had to fit him with a bullshit filter."

In those short minutes, we caught up on all the latest news: Slim, our Kiwi barman, found a tenty to call his own. Chester, now a mere shadow of his former self, even found a woman.

"She's so dense," Clara joked, "she thinks the 'kitty' person handles cats."

Still, our short hour together was more than mere gossip. It let us touch base with a similar reality and share our meager triumphs. Often, traveling was a lonely experience. Although surrounded by thousands of people, we seldom had lengthy companionship. As two of the few 'mzungus' wherever we went, it was an affirmation of our own identity to finally meet other travelers, especially ones we knew and trusted.

One reason for staying a week in Harare was to pick up South African visas, since we'd finally decided to visit that controversial country. However, even that wasn't as easy as it might seem. Outside the R.S.A. downtown embassy, a line of two hundred hopeful Zimbabweans patiently stood all day in the hot sun, as they awaited guest worker applications. It was a static queue without beginning or end.

"There's got to be a better way to do this," I figured, mopping a puddle of sweat from my forehead.

At just that moment, a young, black girl with plaited hair handed us a travel agency flyer, promising, "Get your South African visa in just three days. Guaranteed. Only $19 US."

Recognizing a solution when we see one, Cheryl and I rushed over to their office across the street. Grabbing my partner's hand, we flew up two flights of stairs, then furtively began moving from one door to the next. Some had numbers. Others only had shadows where numbers once had been. Finally, at the very end of the hall, we reached a beat-up door with no numbers or shadows.

"Must be the place," I guessed, creaking open the door. Gingerly, we stuck our heads inside. Dim light streamed through a grimy window, cascading an amber haze across aged travel posters hanging on the walls. There were two beat-up desks, looking like they'd been left in Rhodesia by fleeing colonials. One was empty. The other one might as well have been.

"Can I help you?" asked a young woman with spiked hair, as she dreamily gazed off into space.

"We saw your brochure and we'd like to get South African visas."

"We can do that. It'll be $19 U.S. an' it'll take three days."

"Are you positive you can have them by next Tuesday, because we have to leave early Wednesday?"

"No problem," she assured us, flipping through her calendar.

The thought of doing business with them seemed dicey from the start. As a rule, I hated leaving my passport with anyone. However, if we stood in that line, I suspected it could take us days to get applications, then weeks for our stamps. So, we quickly filled out the visa forms and handed them to her.

"Do we need to leave our passports?" I asked.

"No, they won't need them. Your visas will be issued on separate sheets of paper. Pay when you pick them up on Tuesday, okay?"

As we left, that small voice in the back of my mind told me that it had all been too easy. Still, I trusted in our luck–or in the Harare in which I desperately wanted to believe.

"Now that it's confirmed," I suggested to Cheryl, "we can buy tickets for Wednesday's flight to Vic Falls and reserve a chalet at the National Park."

Flying sounded like a simple enough answer to a complex problem. In Harare, it was difficult to travel to any major visitor attraction unless you took a group tour or flew. By road, you could either take a bus one day to Bulawayo and then head another day north to the Falls, or bus all the way across to Zambia then head south. Either could work, if you could get a ticket.

To save another two days of bad roads, we decided to splurge on our first African plane tickets and looked forward to the easy flight with relish.

Fortunately, on Monday we stopped by that same travel agency again just to verify we'd receive our visas on time.

"Oh, the embassy just called," the agent giggled, "and told us that they need to see your passports after all."

This all started to sound too suspicious. "All right," I sighed. "But when can we get them back? We still need them for banking." To change money, you always needed a passport.

"Pick them up here at 2:00."

*She neglected to say, "Don't worry."*

We gave her our passports, then returned at 2:00. No visas. We waited until 3:00. Still no sign.

*Our entire trip to South Africa is riding on this.*

Finally, by 3:30, we'd had enough. Storming out of their office, we ran across the street, back to the embassy. Knowing it closed at 4:00, we skipped their line, waved to the guards and traipsed on in like we belonged there. Their processing room was on the fourth floor. Under the harsh glare of fluorescent tubes, four white clerks sat behind thick plastic windows, screaming questions to befuddled black locals.

*Already, this looks like a disaster. We'll probably be turned away, since we don't have the 'proper' forms filled out in triplicate, or a number from the 'Next Serving' rod. But, hey, we're overlanders, damn it.*

Approaching the first free window and assuming my most 'Pardon me, but we must be lost' look, I started, "Excuse me. We applied for visas last week through a travel agency and just want to confirm they'll be ready tomorrow."

"The name of the agency?" the pert blonde asked. I told her and she replied, "Never heard of them," with a shake of her curly head.

"You're sure? They're right across the street." Our situation was sounding worse and worse. "They applied for our visas Friday and guaranteed we'd have them Tuesday."

"Why, they can't promise you that!" she huffed. "Visas take two weeks!"

"Well, you see, it's very important we get them because we're leaving town Wednesday," I explained. "Besides, we can't stay here two weeks, since our visas expire before then."

"Well, I don't have any applications here for you," she replied, thumbing through her thick manila file.

"Oh, no," I sighed, a bit dramatically. "No passports, either?" She shook her head. "Look, we've got a real problem," I started.

*It's going to take a major amount of groveling to save our situation.*

"Look, we've been traveling through Africa for seven months and we're exhausted, but we really want to see your beautiful country. We've always wanted to go there and need to make it to the Cape to fulfill our dream of crossing Africa. Well, you seem like a kind person, and I'm really sorry, I realize this is very unusual, and I know I'm asking a lot, but I'd be forever grateful if... I mean, is there any possible way, or something we could do to get our visas by tomorrow, pleeze?"

At just that moment, our travel agency's runner appeared at her office doorway.

"Oh, there's our agency's rep, now," I said, surprised by her perfect timing.

"Who do you think you are promising this man you could have his visa in three days?" the embassy clerk screamed, wagging her finger. "You know that's not possible! You know it takes at least two weeks. You have to stand in line like everyone else. How dare you take his money and promise him that. You have no right. Who are you? I don't even know your company. I never want to see you in here again!" she bellowed.

The visibly shaken woman slinked out the door.

*We're sunk. We'll never get our visas now.*

"Look, we don't normally do this," the woman sympathetically explained, "but if you fill out these applications and bring them with your passports and two photos in the morning, I'll see what we can do."

I was stunned. It was such an about-face from only a moment earlier.

We returned to that travel agency and someone easily located our missing passports and applications in the agent's desk drawer. They'd never left her office.

True to her word, that kindhearted embassy clerk pulled a few strings and we received our visas the following day. Without her uncommon help, although we'd traveled nearly 10,000 miles, we never would have made it to South Africa–or the Cape.

Early Wednesday morning, we caught an Air Zimbabwe shuttle bus to Harare Airport. Passing sleepy suburban streets, we finally congratulated ourselves on having the good sense to fly to Vic Falls. We'd be there in only two hours and could relax. However, any celebration was short-lived.

We arrived at the airport and the terminal was suspiciously still. Two hundred passengers milled around, but there were no ticket agents, no baggage handlers.

"D'ya hear?" a portly white businessman blurted. "Air Zim's on strike."

"That's impossible," I argued. "We just caught their shuttle from town."

"It's true. The banks, too!" someone else confirmed.

*Oh, great. Now we're stuck at an airport with no flights, in a country with no money.*

"So, what are we supposed to do?" I asked. "Are there any other flights?"

"No, Air Zim's our only domestic carrier," another woman explained. "A few years ago, they decided they didn't want any competition. So "gchriittt!"

She graphically drew a finger across her throat.

"Someone must have a solution," I figured. Eventually, I cornered an airport security guard hiding in the coffee shop. "Is it true?" I asked. "They really on strike?"

"Yep. Dey shut 'er down late last night."

"How can they do that?"

"Well, de government hasn't allowed strikes for twenty years. Last night de law finally ran out. So now, de airlines an' banks are both closed 'till who knows when," he pronounced, with a 'that's life' sort of shrug.

"Won't an airline official put us on another plane?" Again, I caught myself thinking like a Westerner. "Or reschedule us and move us back to town?" The city was thirty minutes away.

"Nope, you won't see dem here! They're all afraid," he whispered, with eyes wide as silver dollars. "Yea," he chuckled. "Afraid dey'll be hurt by all of you if dey show up."

We should have known better. Flying was just too simple for 'real' overlanders. Catching a tour bus back to town, we eventually connected with the next local bus bound for Bulawayo. Crowded with the usual overflowing baskets, clanging pots and clucking farm animals, true to its name, it stopped in each and every tiny village. Nevertheless it moved and 'polepole' was better than not at all.

Twelve hours and three hundred miles later, we rolled into Bulawayo, where we connected the next morning with the Wankie Express. The 'Wankie' stopped every few miles to pile more brightly garbed folks, like stacks of African Legos, higher and higher into those aisles. Spotting us in our usual back seats, each boarding villager looked shocked, because whites seldom rode public buses in Zimbabwe. However, after learning that we were Americans, not Afrikaaners, they welcomed us as part of their group, sharing food and millet beer, friendship and laughter along the way.

The village of Vic Falls was far different from what we'd imagined. With a two-block strip of English fast-food joints, tourist gewgaw shops, trip outfitters and overpriced hotels, it was a happy hunting ground where locals trapped tourist dollars–and lions openly prowled side streets.

Fortunately, our chalet was in a cease-fire zone. Decorated in rustic froufrou with laced curtains, dwarf-sized beds, an ancient refrigerator, a linoleum-topped aluminum dining table and thatched roof, it was unexpectedly friendly. Even our nearest neighbors, the voracious wart hogs, threw us a welcome by raiding our garbage cans.

The next day, refreshed from our journey, we anxiously hiked down the road for our first glimpse of Victoria Falls, the world's highest cascades, and one of Africa's most magnificent wonders. Even from a mile away, we could already hear the thunder of the mighty Zambezi as it plummeted to boulders below. As we entered the park, its fury increased in intensity and our excitement mounted.

243

A walkway edged that showery cliff amid tropical foliage. Carefully, we descended stairs through thick, overhanging trees, until finally majestic Devil's Cataract lay before us. Forty percolating cascades fringed that deep, primeval chasm, and there was a fresh scent of renewal. A Maxfield Parrish light celestially framed a verdant valley, complete with double rainbows. On the farthest ridge, the mighty Zambezi plunged several hundred feet to a churning cauldron, spraying our faces with a dewy mist as it wafted up from the swirling pool below. Another two hundred yards along her left bank, a bronze statue of David Livingstone, 'discoverer' of the falls, faced another impressive aquatic tableau. Ribbons of cascades streamed from the jungle then plunged in sheets to the bottom. From that heavenly perch, our vista spanned the length of the mystic canyon all the way to the Zambian border.

We stood in awed silence.

*Soon we'll be in that maelstrom.*

Her display of raw power gave us second thoughts about racing through those rapids in a tiny rubber raft, but just for an instant. We were fully committed to the lunacy and thrill of watching our lives flash before us.

*It's now–or never–since we've been told that a new dam is going to mean an end to these awesome rapids. What a travesty. According to the locals, it's bound to incur the gods' wrath–not to mention an end to the huge influx of traveler dollars.*

The following morning, after donning swimsuits, we met our fellow whitewater maniacs at the classic Victoria Falls Hotel. There we were introduced to Greg, a white Zimbabwean in his late twenties, who'd braved those waters maybe a hundred times before.

"There'll be seven inflatables goin' down the Zambezi today," he buoyantly explained in his clipped accent. "On each raft, there'll be seven of you an' one experienced oarsman."

Each of us hung on his every word, looking for some clue as to what we were up against.

"Now, I want to remind you of the dangers of raftin' the Zambezi," he continued. "These are class-five rapids, some of the toughest in the world. I want you to sign these release forms 'fore we go."

Cheryl and I shot each other wary glances.

"On the Zambezi, there's always the chance of being swept down river and drownin', smashin' your head on a rock, or capsizin' and bein' run over by your own raft. But no matter what, keep your lifejackets on, head for your boat and you'll be all right."

Although his words were dire, his confidence proved the perfect tonic.

"These rapids are numbered, not named as they are some places. Today we'll put in just above rapid ten and work our way down to nineteen."

As we sat listening, I couldn't help staring. Kayaks, with huge, bite-sized chunks missing, leaned against the hotel wall.

Noticing my curiosity, he explained, "And don't be too worried about those. The crocs and hippos usually stay upstream."

After my partner and I signed what could have been our lives away, we met our rafting partners: Anders, a stout Swedish social worker in his thirties and his Ingrid Bergman look-alike niece, Helene. Then, there was Jackie, a spunky Scot physiotherapist in her twenties, Remo and Pia, a Dutch diamond polisher and his wife, and our oarsman, Greg.

Quickly, we loaded into the van and set off up the road to meet the guides who'd already put-into the river.

"This is it!" Greg proclaimed, as we pulled in under a huge baobab. "Now, let's have some fun!" We planned on it, because we were the original gonzo rafters, weaned on Alaska's frigid whitewater.

It was an easy hike down to the river. Everyone was totally stoked, as we hoisted our rubber tubs into that brown Zambezi soup. Carefully climbing aboard, we assumed starting positions in the wobbly craft. Two of us sat both fore and aft, and three sat mid-ship. Later, we'd all switch positions.

As we floated just offshore in those sturdy yellow inflatables, Greg drilled us in maneuvers that might prevent us from capsizing. "High-side, front," he yelled, sending Helene and Jackie in the bow over the front, dipping the stern high out of the water. "High-side, back," sent Anders and me in the stern, flopping on our stomachs, face-to-face with the swirling water. Meanwhile, "High-side, left or right," sent Remo, Pia and Cheryl flying from the middle to that side, flat over the gunwale, as the opposite end rose from the water.

To someone watching from shore, it must have been a ridiculous sight, as seven rafts full of people, for no apparent reason, threw themselves back and forth across those rubber floats like fifty flopping flounders. Still, we practiced those synchronized movements, again and again, until they became second nature. In the midst of a whirlpool, there'd be no time to second guess.

Finally, we pushed off, not knowing quite what to expect–other than the challenge of a lifetime.

Zambezi Gorge was a world unto itself. As we glided through the deeply furrowed canyon, single branches sprouted from jagged umber ledges, providing a perch for keen-eyed fish hawks. Sunlight filtered through towering trees to cast shadows across the murky river. It was all deceivingly placid compared with the fury that lay ahead.

We saw the boiling spray and heard the locomotive roar of that first set of rapids for nearly half a mile. There was an uneasy look of fear or grim determination on everyone's face. We tightly grasped ropes encircling the top of our raft, while repeating that sequence of 'high-sides' repeatedly in our minds like some ancient mantra.

All of a sudden, we were in the midst of bubbling, murky soup. "High-side right!" Greg screamed, above the roar. As we flung ourselves over the port, face-to-face with the churning foam, water poured in from the side like we'd been split in two. As our tiny raft slipped into a five-foot chasm, Greg shouted, "High-side back!" Falling backward, we brought the bow high, up out of the water like a breaching whale.

We simmered in that stew for what seemed an eternity, but in actuality it was just moments before we shot out the other side. The raft behind us wasn't so lucky, though. Halfway through the set, one bewildered woman popped out of their raft like a watermelon seed. She disappeared for a frightening instant, but we spotted the bobbing orange glow of her lifejacket on the far side of the Zambezi.

"There she is! Over there!" I screamed.

Oaring over, Anders and I glanced down into her terrified childlike eyes. Quickly grabbing her lifejacket straps, we leaned back with all our weight and jerked her limp body aboard. For one silent moment, she huddled shaking on our floor, more from fear than cold. Then Greg neatly cruised over to her original raft, so she could continue with them.

Gradually, we began to read each unique set of rapids better. The awkward ballet of flinging our bodies became more controlled, although the addictive anticipation of each set grew. Nothing compared to that bone-chilling thrill of watching a ten-foot wall of water collapse onto your head, as you held on in white-knuckled terror. More shocking rapids came in succession like punches to a dazed boxer. We'd no sooner finish reeling from the first blow when the next collided with tons of power. Then another, still larger, nearly knocked us off the raft. Finally, spat out the other end, our raft, then a Zambezi wading pool, was half-filled with muddy water. Four of us frantically struggled to bale and drain it before the next and worst one struck.

Rapid eighteen even had Greg's respect. Its violent cascades suddenly drop ten feet into a seething whirlpool, capsizing thirty percent of everyone that attempts to pass.

There was no time for fear. Our tiny craft rode a sea of torment, as rapid eighteen loomed downstream. By then, I was cemented in the bow with Anders. My fingers and the rope became as one. We could hear the monster's roar echo throughout the canyon. Although Greg furiously back-paddled to slow us down, there was little time to catch our breaths. It was upon us before we knew it.

"Yaaahhhhhh!" We frantically flung ourselves "high-side right," then immediately turned to "high-side left." As we plunged into a churning brown pool, Anders and I threw ourselves forward, eye-to-eye with the bowels of Zambezi. A churning, funnel-shaped grotto pulsed just below us, reached up, grabbed our heads and swallowed our tensed bodies and half the boat in one gigantic gulp. There was a cannon's roar, a blinding flash of amber. Suddenly, it was dark. All we could do was hang on, until we burped out the other side.

"That was incredible," we sighed in unison, breathlessly shaking water from our ears.

At the end of the day, on the final rapid, Greg announced, "I'm gonna teach ya' the art of 'tubin'". All seven of ya' need to sit on the stern gunwale," he instructed. "Then, link arms and lean back. We'll ride through with the bow in the air. It's easy."

*Sounds like fun. Since we're through the worst part, what could possibly happen?*

Entering those rapids, we all innocently sat in the stern, wrapped arms and voluntarily threw ourselves backwards–a little too enthusiastically–somersaulting all seven of us together into the raging Zambezi.

*This water's freezing. I can't stop shivering. It's so murky. I can't see a thing! Tell top from bottom! Where am I? Look up. Damn, I'm under the raft! My pulse is racing. Quick. Rub my hands across the bottom of the boat. Look for the edge. Nothing. I have to find my way out. Can't panic. Have to get free before my lungs explode. My head is throbbing. The water's cold, so cold. My skin burns. It's so dark. Very dark. Wait...I feel...I feel an edge.*

At last, swinging myself out from under, I flung free and jettisoned downstream, as light as a leaf. Bobbing on the river's boiling surface, I gasped deep breaths of warm, sweet air, while our raft floated fifty yards upstream and the others climbed on board.

"Hey! Over here!"

They slowly headed toward me. As the muddy water rushed past my face, blurring my vision, I swam in long strokes upstream. It was slow going, struggling against the force of that deluge. Still, after a few breathless moments, I reached our rubber island and was hauled in—winded, yet never more alive.

The next morning, before leaving for Botswana, we'd planned a quick horseback safari It would give us the chance to spot game without the noise and distraction of a four-wheeler. We met Alice, our guide, at her ranch that sprawled among the bush and bronze hills at the far end of town.

A rugged, white-Zimbabwean frontier lady, Alice was as comfortable on a horse as other women are in SUVs. Life in the bush had etched itself into her lean, furrowed face, and her witty tales and gritty ways helped her cope with tenderfoots like us.

There were just six of us searching for wildlife that day: Alice, her friend Alex, a local big-game hunter, a young couple from Australia and us. Those others were experienced riders, and although I'd ridden quite a bit before, it had been far too long. My wary partner was even less experienced. But, hey, that was all part of our adventure.

As my partner mounted her sorrel mare and I saddled a young, black gelding, Alice warned us about the problems she'd recently had with lions. There'd been three unprovoked attacks over the past month, and my colt had gruesome, ten-inch claw marks to prove it.

"We had one fella here," Alice started in her clipped Zimbabwean cadence, "who said he rode all the time. Said he even belonged to some ridin' club. Well, we went out an' his horse caught the scent of a lion. Since it'd been attacked before, it spooked an' reared up an' threw the big guy off.

We stared in amazement.

"But instead of climbin' a tree or runnin' after his horse, he ran after his lady friend, grabbed her leg an' dragged her off her horse."

Cheryl and I suspiciously eyed each other.

"Then he rode off, leavin' her there!" she chuckled. "Can you imagine that? Well, good thing the lion lost interest."

"Don't worry," I whispered, winking at Cheryl.

*Oh, no. Now I've joined the "Don't worry" league.*

"Now, don't any of you men try that one," Alice warned, cinching up her palomino's saddle girth. "If you're charged by a lion, just head for the road."

*Good advice. But what road?*

After being handed a thin switch to keep our mounts moving, we followed Alice into the thick bush. It was an ideal day for spotting game. There was that toasty smell of grass, mingled with the sweet aroma of horse sweat and saddle soap.

*Here, on horseback, we're just two more animals out among the rest, just as likely to be the hunted–as the hunter.*

Trotting through the savanna, every few minutes we'd pause and spy gazelles bounding across the plain, watch waterbucks graze among spindly acacia, race cartoonish wart hogs, or spot the fluttering of guinea fowl. Still, the one animal we most hoped to find was the one we most feared–the lion.

We knew Alice's story was true. In town, people even warned us not to go walking off the main street at night because of those felines.

*Now, here we are riding through their dining room.*

All at once, Alice spotted something breaking through a clump of trees. From a distance, it was difficult to tell exactly what. She broke into a gallop, and we didn't plan to be left behind. So, following in single file, we joined her, racing through the trees and wild brush, dodging lethal three-inch acacia spikes, as we struggled to keep pace.

"Why is there no sad-dle ho-rn on th-is thing?" Cheryl screamed, as she bounced and jiggled from side-to-side in her military saddle. Suddenly, a massive baobab tree lay felled across her narrow path. "Stop!" my partner yelled, pulling hard on her reins. "I mean, WHOA!"

"What's the matter?" I asked, reining in my colt.

"I can't jump over that. I'm gonna kill myself."

I saw no other way around it. To both sides were thorny bushes, forming a barbed barrier. As we stood there debating, our partners gracefully leapt that tree like steeple-chasers and quickly raced out of sight.

"Let's put it this way," I explained, as I grew concerned about becoming separated from the others. "Your horse is going to jump. If you want to, too, you'd better hold on."

With that, I nudged my gelding on and neatly sailed over that fallen baobab.

Tightly gripping her reins, Cheryl ducked her head, switched her mare and bravely flew ahead, clearing the huge log and landing with a gentle thud. Soon, we caught up with Alice, but unfortunately whatever she'd seen had already disappeared.

After spending the better part of that morning out in the bush, Alice finally decided, "Well, we better take 'em back in." As we trotted back to her paddock, she wheeled around and confided, "Well, I guess I can tell you my other story now. There was 'nother Australian fella went ridin' here," she started. "Think he had your horse," she said, pointing to mine. "Well, this guy was ridin' along and everything was fine 'till he heard a lion growl close by."

We all stopped dead on the trail.

"That man an' his horse got so frightened that they rode smack into an acacia and his horse kept right on goin'. Well, with all those thorns, he thought he was bein' attacked by the lion, so he kept fightin' and squirmin' all 'round, climbin' higher up that tree. An' it kept rippin' his clothes and skin to shreds. There was blood all over the place."

Everyone started to chuckle.

"Well, just I burst out laughin'. There was no lion. It was just the tree. I finally had to calm him enough to try to git him down—which was a whole lot harder than gittin' him up there in the first place."

Later, back at our cabin, we quickly grabbed our packs and headed for the train. Arriving at the station, we were pleasantly surprised at the timeless elegance that awaited us. It was a tiny, six car, narrow-gauge steam locomotive. Each car was carefully preserved from the 1930s in the traditional comfort of that bygone era. Its walls were richly trimmed in polished wood. A mirror etched with the initials "R.R." for Rhodesian Railway even topped the silver, fold-down washbasin.

With great satisfaction, we stretched out on its plush seats in a suite built just for two. Meanwhile, that toy train chugged its way from Africa's past into the starry night.

# Chapter XVII
# Barking Dogs, Invisible Walls

*"Rain beats a leopard's skin, but it does not wash out the spots."*
~ African proverb

*T*HE NEXT MORNING, we chugged into Gaborone, Botswana, not far from the South African border. Curious to observe what it was like for a black to arrive in South Africa, we hopped one of their 'combis' into Johannesburg. These vans, often owned by black drivers, carried anywhere from eight to ten passengers plus baggage between Botswana and throughout South Africa.

All the same, very rarely did you ever see any whites aboard them due to some unspoken rule of segregation. On that particular day, we decided to break color barriers, rewrite the rules, and take that opportunity to talk directly with local blacks. Much to the driver's surprise and the initial anxiety of the other passengers, we joined their overland journey to Jo'Burg.

At first, we were met with hostile stares and a wall of silence, until we finally took the initiative to break the ice. Turning to the moonfaced lady sitting beside us, I honestly admitted (in my best all-American accent), "We're very eager to see your country, especially after all that's been happening."

"You're not Afrikaaners?" she choked, with an undisguised look of amazement,

"Do I look like an Afrikaaner?" I laughed. On second thought, since I do look the part with my blond hair and blue eyes, I replied, "No, we're just Americans who want to see South Africa for ourselves."

Funny, that simple truth dramatically changed everything. All at once, soucous played. There were warm smiles from the ladies, handshakes from the men, and general outpouring of emotion. The story of our journey was met with wide-eyed amazement. Then, we were anxious to hear their tale.

"We heard your government is dismantling apartheid," I began, "and we're wondering what difference it's made in your lives so far?"

*Will they be honest with me? Or, will they be afraid to talk openly with a stranger.*

A tall, bearded student in the front seat finally broke their silence, whispering, "None at all."

"How can that be? Now, you have the right to use the same facilities, the same buses, even the same toilets as the whites."

"That's true. But why do I want to use a white man's toilet?" he laughed. "Those freedoms really don't mean anything."

"Well, aren't the neighborhoods becoming integrated now?" Cheryl asked.

"They can change laws," he explained bitterly, stroking his beard. "Still, that doesn't mean I could ever live in a white neighborhood. Or, that I'd want to."

"Why not?"

"Because you gotta have money," he patiently explained, jabbing his bony finger into the seat. "And how you gonna buy a nice house–if you can't get a good job?"

"Besides," the teacher sitting next to us continued, "there have already been blacks and whites living in the same neighborhoods for years in 'gray' areas."

We'd never heard of those. "Well, what about the Afrikaaners? How are they reacting to the changes?"

"Oh, they threaten civil war. But hey, I don't mind them," the student admitted. "At least, I know where I stand. It's all black and white to them. It's those liberals I can't stand," he confided, bringing a finger to his lips, as though revealing a deep secret. "They act like they're your friend. Then one day, their house gets robbed, or somebody they know has problems with a black man. Suddenly, they're worse than the Afrikaaners. You just can't trust them," he fumed, spitting out those words. "But you know what it all comes down to? Money." He glanced around, seeking agreement from the group.

The ladies all nodded and "Uh-ha'd" in unison.

"All I want, all we want, is a fair chance to earn good money–and a good education."

"Yes, there's a very long way to go," the teacher agreed.

"I don't wanna live next door to whites," the student argued. "I don't wanna use their toilets. I just want the chance to make the same money."

At that, the crowd erupted into a chorus of, "That's right" and "You said it" like some Southern Baptist church service.

"Till then, nothin's really changed," he concluded, as he tossed his hat with tired resignation onto the dashboard of the van.

Within a few hours, the modern skyline of Jo'Burg loomed on the horizon. As the bush melded into suburban tracts with neatly hedged houses, our highway grew into a multi-laned freeway. Trees were soon replaced by a forest of fast-food joint neon icons.

Noel and Joanna, our cane juice drinking buddies from Cape McClear, had graciously extended an invitation for us to stay with their friend Paul in Jo'Burg. So, as soon as we reached the train station, we immediately phoned his girlfriend to let them know we'd arrived.

*Oh, how I dread making this sort of traveler's cold-call.*

"Hello, Nancy? We met Noel and Joanna in Malawi and we're on our way south to visit them. They gave us Paul's number, thinking he might be able to show us around Jo'Burg a few days before we head down to Cape. Is he there?"

"Oh, we've split up," the woman sighed.

In retrospect, she must have wondered who we were, since we later learned that Paul had never told her we were coming, and she hardly knew Noel and Joanna.

"Ah, sorry to hear that."

*She doesn't know how sorry. Now, we'll have to figure out this big city on our own.*

"Well, I can't speak for him, but since you're a friend of Noel and Joanna's, if you don't mind," Nancy hesitated, "you two could stay with me."

*Mind?*

Nancy adopted us and over the next few days did her best to make us feel at home. We didn't do much touring of Jo'Burg, at least none of the usual museums or historic sights. Instead, she made sure we saw another side of the republic's business hub: the local Zulu and Xhosa craft markets, shopping malls and jazz clubs. She and her friends even held a traditional barbecue, a 'braaivleis', in our honor. This feast of grilled 'borewors', the local kielbasa-style sausage, was topped off with subtle South African white wines.

255

However, as much as she and her friends made us welcome, Jo'Burg remained an enigma. Visually, it reminded us of a large American city. The rolling hills of its countryside were pastoral. Its food was similar, the language was close enough, the films were identical and the shopping malls could have been borrowed from our Midwest. Still, there were walls everywhere, both real and perceived. Downtown was black turf. Whites stayed sequestered in their suburbs, physically not far away, but in an entirely different world. Breathing in an air of prosperity, they exhaled fear. Locked in brick houses with manicured lawns and swimming pools, whites nervously hid behind barricades of tall iron fences, elaborate security systems and trained attack dogs. No matter what their politics, right or left, they worried what would happen if, or when, the majority blacks moved to take over the country. Mass riots, looting, civil war? Who knew?

Many whites, somehow recognizing us as outsiders, glared with suspicion, wondering why we were there. Worse still, blacks generally assumed we were Afrikaaners. Never before in Africa had we faced such glares of resentment from both groups. Hatred had aged in the casks of prejudice over the past century. Nevertheless, we knew we needed to see the black townships for ourselves, firsthand, before heading south.

So, en route to Kimberley, we visited the ramshackle squalor of Soweto, Jo'Burg's notorious township. There, in little more than concentration camps, Afrikaaners housed hundreds of thousands of black workers to save their neighborhoods from integration. We stared in shocked sadness, as we gazed across mile after mile of scrap board or concrete block shanties. Throngs of blacks lived desperate lives in a land of plenty. To make matters worse, longstanding Xhosa and Zulu rivalries turned violent in that township during our visit. Over three hundred were speared or hacked to death.

Later that afternoon, just outside Soweto my partner and I were dropped with our packs along the N-1 Highway. It was a bone-chilling, drizzling spring day, which perfectly matched our sullen mood. Hitching was impossible. Cars whizzed by on the wide freeway, rushing to reach the Cape. After an hour, no one even slowed down, no matter how much we smiled or tried to act non-threatening.

*Traveling at this speed, they'll never stop. Besides, it's just too darned cold to hitch.*

Then, all of a sudden, as we turned to head defeated back into town, a blue pickup skidded to a stop a hundred yards ahead.

"We can take you as far as Bloemfontein," the driver yelled through his small rear window.

"Great! That's over halfway."

Running with our packs, we hopped into the back and they sped off. Together, my partner and I huddled on that exposed pickup bed while the frigid wind slashed across our faces. Feeling naked and vulnerable, we tried to make some sense from all the senseless images of those past few days.

It was a starless night and bitter cold by the time we pulled into sleepy Bloemfontein. Its reputation preceded it, as one of the most conservative towns in the heart of the Orange Free State. So, we wasted no time in walking to their brick train station and boarded a waiting bus. It was designed like an eighteen-wheeler except with windows on either side. Its white driver sat in a separate compartment, apart from his black cargo. Cautiously stepping inside, we spotted forty or fifty shrouded shadows huddled in the darkness. Old men rolled cigarettes by the dim light of the street lamps. Patient mothers rocked their babies, pulling nappy heads to their ample laps. Sleepy boys sprawled across the seats with their thin legs blocking the aisle. Eventually, we found vacant seats in the back (where else?) and settled in. Then our moving pen chugged out of the station, carting us like livestock to the slaughter.

During our refrigerated two-hour journey to Kimberley, once home to the world's largest diamond mines, the coach's doors kept flying open and letting in the freezing night air. Shivering, we matched the bus shake for deafening shake.

Finally, that tired old cattle-coach dropped us off on the outskirts of town at the youth hostel. It was a 1950s motel-style complex, ringed with barbed wire and a high chain link fence—not quite the picture of hospitality. Still, it was too late to shop around and we were exhausted.

These days, Kimberley's 'Big Hole' only mines visitors. During its hundred-year history, it yielded millions of carats of diamonds. However, in the process, it had turned a pastoral hillside into a colossal pockmark—and blacks into low-paid human-gophers. Now, capitalizing on its notoriety, the town has recreated an entire village around that ugly blemish. So, for a morning, we wandered through an Afrikaaner 'Frontier Land' and panned for gems at a recreated diamond sluice.

Eager to reach Cape Town, South Africa's "Oz," we caught another black combi south at nightfall. It was interesting to hear the way that South Africans reverently referred to Cape Town. There was a certain awe in their voice, a wonder, as we were told time and again that people only lived in Jo'Burg long enough to earn money—then escaped to the Cape.

With high expectations, we neared South Africa's city of dreams, only to have that fantasy dashed when we swerved into another seedy township, right off the white-bricked road to Oz. As our combi wove its way through row after row of bee-hived hovels, dropping passengers at their doors, we saw how the other 80% lived. It was just another cracked-mirror image of Soweto.

Eventually, we hopped off at the Cape Town train station, catching a bus to the youth hostel at Camps Bay on the other side of Table Mountain. Our guidebook had recommended it, and the hostel certainly lived up to its reputation.

Dramatically perched on the edge of the promontory, that inn was nearly two thousand feet above the craggy shore. Our room boasted a million-dollar view of the glistening ocean and verdant forest that cascaded down the steep hillside to the beach community below. Better still, the jolly woman who ran the simple lodge was eager to supply us with information, fix breakfast and even do our laundry.

Cape Town is cradled in an unsurpassed setting. Using the local bus system and more black combis, we explored an area reminiscent of northern California. With its magical combination of rugged mountains, lapis sea, lush vegetation and unpredictable weather, the Cape evoked memories of San Francisco in the summertime. Beach communities such as Sea Point, with its fine art galleries, restaurants and nightclubs, fringed Table Mountain. Hout Bay, once a pirate cove, had been transformed into a wharfside marina. And at Table Bay, one of the oldest pubs on the Cape still brewed its own creamy ale.

Still, the same air of suspicion shrouded even that seaside kingdom.

After five days of tasting both the bitter and the sweet of Cape Town, Cheryl and I rented a car and headed for the Cape Point, on the southernmost tip of the African continent. Driving those last twenty miles was the most practical way of completing our goal of traveling from the top to the tip of Africa.

Our only other options were to bicycle through gusty winds or catch an organized tour–and you could imagine how we felt about that.

Parking our car at the road's end, with growing excitement, we hiked a short trail to Africa's tip. Our bodies strained against the surging winds, those same gusts that have thrown fear into the hearts of sailors from the beginning of time. Thoughts of those ancient mariners sailed through my mind, as we climbed the final few steps up that narrow ledge. There, where the Atlantic and Indian Oceans exchange lapping peaks, boiled some of the world's most treacherous waters. Along its desolate crag of scraggy rock, winds could change in seconds and snap masts like matchsticks with unbridled power.

Rounding the crest of the cliff, suddenly, we were at the trail's end. Only waves remained, thundering below.

"This is it!" I shouted like a madman. "Cheryl, we made it!"

"I can't believe it," she cried, as tears welled up in her eyes.

After all those months of struggle, doubts of sanity and infinite challenges, we'd fulfilled our dream. We'd crossed the length of Africa from Ceuta to the Cape. Hugging, our voices mute and humbled by the crashing waves, memories flooded our minds.

Following a brief pilgrimage to the Cape of Good Hope, not far from Cape Point, we continued driving up that rocky shoreline, across suspension bridges, and through grassy 'veld' to the tiny harbor town of Knysna. That night, snuggled in a cabin on the edge of a sublime lagoon, we lay transfixed by the sound of the ocean, the earth's blood, colliding against rocky cliffs below.

For five hours the following morning, we traversed that same shoreline, then crossed an informal border into the Ciskei. There was no customs, no border officials. Yet again, we slid through an invisible wall and into an area designated as a 'homeland' for black South Africans. We left the familiar box-shaped Western houses and cluttering conveniences behind. There were no taxi stands or fast-food restaurants, no galleries or noisy bistros–only pastoral hillsides where folks tended goats and cattle. Traditional, round, mud huts in 'kraals' dotted a timeless landscape. Serenity reigned again.

Over the next several days, at Noel and Joanna's bucolic country farm, my tanned partner and I relaxed on a peaceful white sand beach, collected fresh oysters and shopped for traditional Zulu handicrafts. Cradled in those rolling pastures, we felt insulated from the daily reports of violence broadcast from Jo'Burg and the Natal. However, those winds of change would soon upset everyone's life in South Africa. The only question was, "How much–and how soon?"

Our new friends had recently experienced a tragic preview of their own. One night, under darkness, their prize bull was grabbed by blacks and slaughtered on the roadside in front of their farm–not for food, but for some unknown retribution, a senseless bloody sacrifice. Still, during our stay, perhaps to portend the nation's own future, a new calf was born, the bull's progeny. Wobbly at first, within hours it stood sturdily on its own.

After a few days enjoying their good company, we caught the bus east to Durban. Waving goodbye, I couldn't help but wonder how the next few years would change their liberal idealism, or temper their trust in the future?

Our bus made good time, as it wended east. At 9 p.m., just before our arrival, a young, quirky fellow with bug eyes bounded up the aisle, stopping between us and the two Canadians sitting just in front.

"Hello. I'm Danny. I was just wondering if you guys need a place to stay in "The Durbs" tonight?" he asked, with more enthusiasm than I could certainly muster at that hour.

"Why?" asked the Canadian, peering over his wire rims.

"Well, if the four of you need a room, my wife and I'd be happy to let you sleep at our place. You can find a hotel in the morning when it's light."

"Sounds like a great idea," his sleepy friend replied.

It was already late and I sure didn't relish looking for a room.

"Yea, that's really nice of you," I added.

Honestly, I couldn't imagine that generosity happening at home. We were constantly surprised in South Africa. For all the hatred exuded by some, others were exceedingly hospitable, as if to compensate for their countrymen. It was an odd duality.

"Great! Get your bags when we pull into the station," Danny said. "I'll be just a minute. I need to call my parents. They'll give us a lift to my apartment."

Danny's folks eventually drove up to the station in their tiny Japanese compact and poked their heads out. With his button-down cardigan and her blue bouffant hair, they looked like a typical television sitcom family. Staring in disbelief at the four of us, they sized-up our four large bags and backpacks, then shot a quizzical glance at their son. Finally, his father shrugged and asked, "Is this everything?"

*Isn't it enough?*

Seeing the seven of us pile into their Toyota was like watching clowns cramming into their miniature circus car. Four of us scrunched into a tiny backseat. Cheryl was packed on my lap, my face plastered against the rear door window. The Canadians were wedged in with backpacks blocking their faces, and Danny and his parents were shoehorned into two tight front bucket seats. Curiously, at that particular moment, with a tinge of ill-timed civic pride, Danny's father decided to give us a city tour–in the dark–when none of us could see past our bags. It was hilarious. There we were, unable to see anything, with his father narrating.

"And here on your right is the 'coloreds' beach. On your left are the 'blacks' houses," and "Down there's the 'whites' beach."

It was hard not to laugh. Still, every once in a while, we took turns offering just the right amount of, "Oohs! Aahs!" and "Yes, isn't that great!"

Durban is best known as a major surfing and resort region. After moving to a downtown hotel the next day, we looked forward to warm, relaxing days spent on the beach. Instead, we found a different face to surfer's paradise, as unwelcome as its pounding rain. In contrast to Cape Town, "the Durbs'" sophisticated glitter faded long ago. Sure, there were large hotels and beachside pools with waterslides, malls and theaters. There were terraces where pianists tinkled keys and geriatric diners choked down plates of 'bunny chow', that East Indian favorite of curried meat stuffed into a hollow loaf of bread. All the same, even Durban wasn't immune to the virus that followed us across that vast, otherwise beautiful nation. We felt its fever most poignantly on our last day there.

Frigid, torrential rains started early in the morning. We spent the day downtown, ducking in and out of shops, searching for last minute handicrafts. Finally, as it grew late, we decided to head back to our hotel. Making a quick run to the bus stop, Cheryl and I nearly got drenched in the downpour. As we waited under the meager shelter of a willowy tree, a bus appeared at the traffic light on the next corner. Quickly leaping out, I frantically waved both arms to have him stop for us. However, the driver drove right past, leaving a tidal wave in his wake.

"What's his problem?" my partner fumed, shivering under that scrawny tree.

Then, we saw another bus. Rushing out into the spring storm, I tried a second time. It passed us, too. Then, a third sped by without stopping.

"That's it!" I screamed.

Finally, as a taxi headed down that main thoroughfare, I jumped out and flagged him down. Running toward its door, I suddenly hit an oil slick on the rain-drenched streets. Before I knew it, I went sailing into the air, and landed, grinding my nose across four lanes of 'the Durbs'" finest blacktop. With traffic momentarily stopped at the light, we dragged our waterlogged bodies into that taxi and slammed the door behind us.

"I can't believe it," I complained to our East Indian (or as they're known in South Africa, 'colored') driver. "What's the secret of catching a bus here? We were out in the rain at a stop, but three passed us by without even slowing down."

"Dat's because you are white and de drivers are black."

"You're kidding!"

*I can't believe it! After all the buses we've ridden in, all over Africa, now this?*

"I weesh I was," he said, staring at us through his rearview mirror. "De blacks hate de coloreds and hate de whites. Last week, I stopped for three black men. Dey heet me over de head in broad daylight and stole six hundred rand! Now, I don't stop for blacks anymore. I hate dem right back."

Our decision to leave South Africa was easily made. If the mood were less tense, we'd have enjoyed viewing their well-stocked game parks or camping in the Transkei. However, hatred was the national sport, violence the national pastime.

Early the next morning, we caught one last black combi from Durban back to Jo'Burg, where we'd overnight and connect to Harare. That ride was different from all the rest. There was no laughter, no storytelling, no sharing of food. People were sullen and silent as we sped down that road, rattling back and forth in the tense and utter stillness.

We overnighted with Nancy on our way back to Harare. Hugging as we left, we wished that we could help her gain the freedom to travel, as much as she had helped us find respite from the freedom of the road. Unfortunately, even then, their government's strict currency controls and visa restrictions prevented most South Africans from ever traveling very far abroad.

Our express bus to Harare took another twenty-two hours, but we were relieved to arrive. That metropolis, with all its foibles and Auntie Mary's kindness, never looked better. Still, our visit was to be short, as we were flying out of Africa the next evening.

*Then again, it's Zimbabwe. Anything can happen.*

BRANDON WILSON

# Chapter XVIII
# Assembling the Mosaic

*"When there is no enemy within, the enemies outside cannot hurt you."*
~ African proverb

*W*E FELT AN INTENSE SADNESS, as we realized our journey across Africa was completed. Somberly stuffing our well-traveled packs one final time, we hugged Auntie Mary, then caught a shuttle to the airport, hoping this flight would be more successful than our last try. Although not scheduled to leave until 8:15 p.m., we arrived hours earlier, uncertain how long customs might take. Not surprisingly, our flight was on 'African time'. So it came as no shock when 9:00 p.m. rolled around before we even started loading for our flight to the island of Cyprus in the Mediterranean for a little well deserved ouzo, fried haloumi cheese and beach lounging. It was a direct flight, so we weren't too worried.

However, all that would soon change. Shortly after our seventies-era jet taxied down the ribbon of dark runway and took flight, it happened. Only forty minutes outside of Harare, we heard those words that doused our celebration with a bucket of anxiety.

"La-dies and Gen-tle-men, dis is your pilot spea-king. I have an im-por-tant an-nounce-ment. We have had a fire in engine num-ber four. Don't wor-ry."

*There are those words again.*

"Our fuel has been dumped and we are returning to Harare. Sorry for de delay."

Landing on three engines, we unloaded and waited in the passenger lounge with three hundred testy, chain-smoking Greeks. It was still early, so everyone remained optimistic we'd reload in ninety minutes, as Air Zim had promised.

*After all, if it can't be repaired, how long could it take to switch us to another plane?*

265

As if in answer, a porcine little man wandered over. Nervously tapping his foot, he forecast, "We'll never leave tonight. Don't even think about it." Stuffing his face with a cheese Danish, he mumbled, "I take this route all the time and every third flight never takes off."

That was the last news we needed to hear.

"Air Zim plans it that way, so they can fill all their seats."

As it grew late, our chance of departing grew less probable. It felt all too familiar. We hadn't seen any airline staff for an hour. Finally, another two hours later, the airport's public address system squawked, "Sorry, but all passengers on de Air Zim-bab-we flight to Larnacca, your flight will be de-layed 'til morning. You are all asked to report to customs immeeediately."

At that announcement, the stunned, irritable mob, grabbing their carry-ons, reluctantly stormed into the cramped customs zone.

"You weell all need to fill out de entry forms!" screamed the lone exhausted official.

"Why do we have to fill these out again?" yelled a bedraggled Athenian, wearing ten pounds of gold on each hand. "We haven't been lucky enough to leave yet!"

The official barked back, "Reg-u-lations," obviously upset that he'd have to process all of us by himself.

So, at midnight, we pecked through tedious multiple-entry forms and currency declarations. Then we stood in single file for passport checks, and whispered mutinous curses in several languages at a system that kept us from relaxing on our island oasis, as well as in our own warm beds.

As that plodding official processed each booklet, our crowd, collectively sighing like some ancient chorus, watched two clumsy baggage handlers unload the plane. Everyone's bags circled piggly-wiggly on a shaky, rotating belt, each begging to fall off and erupt across the floor. Each weary traveler shuffled forward to reclaim his or her bags, then trudged to the waiting courtesy shuttle. Slowly, that hodgepodge of suitcases dwindled, until none were left. Unfortunately, ten of us still waited, as patiently as could be expected, with baggage claims in hand.

"My suitcases! Where are my suitcases?" demanded one matriarch.

"Dat's it," the baggage handler mumbled with a shrug.

*Do I detect a grin on his face?*

"What do you mean?" I fumed. "How can you lose all these bags from a plane that's hardly left the airport?"

The two handlers just stood there openly smirking.

"What-are-you-laughing-at?" my frustrated wife growled.

"You think it's so funny to lose someone's bags?" another Greek cried.

The more upset each of us became, the more those baggage handlers grinned. Their smiles soon grew to full-blown guffaws. This was all too frustrating for 1:00 a.m. in the morning.

"Come on, let's find someone who's in charge," I suggested, and our mob stormed upstairs. Eventually, we found the airport duty station, well hidden behind an unmarked door.

*At least, we can file reports. Maybe they'll find them by morning.*

"Oh, you can't file reports here," insisted the diffident clerk at Air Zim. "You have to wait 'til you land een Cyprus."

"Ridiculous!" one man shouted, pounding the counter. "Those bags were loaded here and were already missing when we landed."

"So they're either here in the airport, stolen by your crew, or sent on the wrong plane," I added.

With that, our chorus joined in on cue, shaking fists and shouting at the top of their lungs.

Reluctantly, that poor fellow's chubby manager finally interceded, tired of our racket. "Maybe de bags were sent on de wrong flight, because dey are not in de terminal or on de plane."

That made sense.

"Dere were flights to Frankfurt and London tonight, so I weell telex dem with instructions to find de twenty bags and forward dem to Cyprus," he suggested. "All right?"

"Great. We'll drop by tomorrow morning before we leave," I promised, satisfied we'd done all we could. "Hopefully, by then, you'll know where they are. Right?"

Of course, having an airline lose your bag is always trying. However, it's especially difficult when you're halfway around the world and your journal and photos are inside (my bad planning). It's worse still when you're certain, if nothing is done, that your bags will be on sale in Harare Market within twenty-four hours.

The next morning, little had changed. There was still no reply to our flurry of telexes. Air Zim had raised buck-passing to a fine art. We re-cleared customs, then waited. Eventually, after three long hours, we boarded and were soon soaring over vast umber plains that had recently taken us days to cross. As we dove into the clouds, our struggles were left far below.

My mind filled with images from the past seven months; pictures that lay scattered like colored tiles, a mosaic of Africa. As your perspective of the earth changes when viewed from a plane, perceptions change when you travel and live in a country and discover an affinity with the land and its people. We had discovered many 'Africas', as many as the countries in Asia and Europe combined. They were people who were brought together and split apart by tribalism, language, customs, communication and education.

During our time on the vast continent, we'd heard about many of those changes. Some were learned as we huddled in our tent, scouring the air with our short-wave radio. Locals shared others with us in hushed tones. Often, in remote villages and even larger towns, Africans would approach us, anxious for news. As outsiders, we were envied as people who had the key, since their newspapers were censored, radios were scarce and television was nearly nonexistent. Censorship and flagrant propaganda had long been used to quell dissent, as is seen in many countries today.

In spite of, or maybe because of those barriers to freedom, significant events rocked Africa to its foundation during what we called our 'freedom tour'. Algeria had elected a fundamentalist Muslim government. There was an attempted coup in Nigeria. Riots and demonstrations for multi-party systems raged in Kenya, Cameroon, Togo and Zaire. America's aid to Zaire ended amid talks of corruption. Mozambique entered peace talks, as Liberia began its own civil war. Malawians whispered of governmental repression. Zambia suffered food riots. ANC and Inkatha members hacked each other to death in South African townships, while white extremists threatened civil war. The Zimbabwean government began confiscating farms from white landowners. Soon after, their president Mugabe bluntly told Western leaders to "Go to hell!" when they suggested he adopt a multi-party system.

Other upheavals hit Africans on an even more personal level. Donated aid was confiscated and funneled to private coffers or civil wars, as the other more deadly AIDs spread like wildfire, decimating families and raining death along

Africa's trucking routes. Rainforests were vanquished to grow cash crops for export, forcing millions to starve on nutrient-rich lands. Donated Western clothing and food became a status symbol, replacing traditional diets and material with expensive imports. Even the sanctity of the village eroded, as men hung up hoes and left families to become laborers, or joined the teeming legions of unemployed in cities.

However, after witnessing the struggles of a few of those hundreds of millions of Africans, our perceptions were altered. Africa got under our skin. It became part of our consciousness. Admittedly, before our journey, we could avoid facing their problems, as easily as changing a television channel. Unfortunately, for many around the world today, Africa's horror stories are still too inconceivable, too easily dismissed, too far removed from their daily reality. Some might even believe that Africa is just too far away to affect us.

Yet in today's global village, how long can we turn our backs before Africa's problems arrive on our own doorsteps?

Won't widespread social action taken now benefit every citizen of our fragile planet more than any unilateral military action taken in the near future?

Remarkably, despite all the violent transitions we encountered, we seldom felt personally threatened. In fact, we'd never met people as genuinely kind and open. No matter how remote or impoverished the village, whatever they had was shared, even if it was just a smile.

Perhaps for some, we were meant to carry a message to the world. If there was one, it was a missive of hope and desire. Africans want to communicate with the world. They want to be educated, as we'd witnessed by those throngs of children constantly begging us for books, pens and paper. They want good healthcare and economic security. They want multi-party systems. Africans want an equal chance and are willing to do almost anything to better their lives. They want economic justice and deserve debt relief. They even hold an optimistic hope for the future, since governments and despots pass like the rainy seasons. Through it all, the underlying power in Africa, the family, survives.

Other tiles of that African mosaic were natural. Nothing could prepare us for the cosmic brilliance of a starlit Saharan night, the primeval splendor of the mountainous jungles, the crimson sunsets across the Serengeti or lapis waves breaking on the Cape.

269

The final tiles completing that many-faceted image of the continent were our uniquely African adventures. We'd zoomed down the Zambezi and survived the Sahara. Climbed Kilimanjaro and crossed the Equator. Vaulted up volcanoes and marveled at gorillas. We'd hunted with Pygmies, traded with Masai, celebrated with voodoo villagers, and out-scammed the scammers. We'd run the 'gun-run', crossed Africa top-to-tip, and in the process learned more about ourselves (and overlanders) than we ever thought possible. Still, truthfully, we knew that we'd only scratched its surface.

We came to believe that travel is like a mirror held up against the world. It gives us a different perspective on life. And if we hold it just right, we might catch a glimmer of our own soul.

Today, that bit of ourselves that we left behind keeps haunting us, flooding our minds with memories, and calling us back to that remarkable 'Land of Endless Sky'.

By the way, ten days later after a score of telexes and phone calls to London, Frankfurt and Harare, Air Zim finally located our bags in Lusaka, Zambia. In a land of 'polepole', it's reassuring to know that some things never change.

# About the Author

Brandon Wilson is an award-winning author and photographer, explorer, internationally published adventure-travel writer and expert light trekker.

A voracious explorer of over ninety countries, he's particularly passionate about inspiring others with the possibility of discovery through long-distance trekking.

Hours spent walking in those African jungles first opened his eyes to the deep satisfaction of traveling 'one-step-at-a-time'. By slowing down, he believes, we absorb the hidden magic in the world. We travel outside–while traveling within.

After Africa, he and Cheryl went on to become the first Western couple to trek 1000-kilometers (650-miles) over the Himalayan plateau from Lhasa, Tibet to Kathmandu. Their story is told in the award-winning, true adventure tale, *Yak Butter Blues: A Tibetan Trek of Faith.*

Besides crossing Tibet, the author has twice hiked the famed Camino de Santiago across Spain, the St. Olav's Way across Norway, and he was the first American to complete the 9th century, 1150-mile Via Francigena trail from England to Rome. He also enjoys wandering long-distance GR trails across Austria, the Czech Republic, France, Tuscany, the Pyrenees, Dolomites and Alps. These physical, mental and spiritual journeys help fuel his irrepressible wanderlust.

His photographs have won awards from *National Geographic Traveler* and *Islands* magazines. He is a member of The Explorers Club and Artists Without Frontiers.

For expedition photos, exciting links,
ordering information, and a free preview
of his critically acclaimed book
*Yak Butter Blues: A Tibetan Trek of Faith,*
please visit: www. PilgrimsTales.com

# Other Books by the Author

**Yak Butter Blues: A Tibetan Trek of Faith...**is an inspiring book of Tibetan adventure. It exposes the raw challenge of traveling deliberately, one-step-at-a-time on an incredible 1000-kilometer (650-mile) trek across the unforgiving Himalayan plains.

Join Brandon and Cheryl, along with Sadhu their Tibetan horse, as they set off to become probably the first Western couple to trek this ancient trail across the earth's most remote corner.

What begins as an adventure quickly turns into so much more. Discovering that Tibetans cannot trek this same pilgrim's trail of faith from Lhasa to Kathmandu, they decide to walk it in their place and prove to the Chinese authorities that it can be done without repercussions.

Their true story is a riveting tale of human endurance. It also provides a candid firsthand look at the lives of the Tibetan families who secreted them into their homes–and at a culture teetering on the edge of extinction.

Nothing could prepare the couple for what would become the ultimate test of their resolve, love, faith...and very survival.

2005 Independent Publisher "IPPY" Award-Winner

*"A wonderful and wild read...The writing is charged, alive, and a little threatening. Yak Butter Blues flickers insistently like a flashbulb afterimage in the mind long after the book is tucked away."* ~ Richard Bangs, author of *The Lost River* and *Mystery of the Nile*/ adventurer/executive producer Yahoo Media Group

*"Recommended for adventure travel and Tibetan culture collections."* ~ *Library Journal*

*"A soaring travel diary. It places the reader in the thick of the action every bit as well as Marco Polo transported Italians to China and, as it seems to me, better than Lowell Thomas led readers in the dust of Lawrence of Arabia..."* ~ Joseph W. Bean, *Maui Weekly*

*"A moving and emotional testimony, and a travelogue that is the next most vivid experience to hiking upon the trail oneself."* ~ *Midwest Book Review*

*"I came under the spell of Brandon Wilson's lively and vivid prose. He is a fine writer– perceptive, funny, a great way with words–making the book a whopping good read."* ~ Royal Robbins, legendary mountaineer/adventure kayaker

*"Told with humour and insight, you experience life at true Tibetan pace: so close, you almost smell the yak butter."* ~ Michael Buckley, author of *TIBET: the Bradt Travel Guide*

## Give the Gift of Adventure Travel
## to Your Friends, Schools,
## Libraries and Colleagues.

### ~ Order Here Today ~

❐ Yes, I want ___ paperback copies of **Dead Men Don't Leave Tips: Adventures X Africa** signed by the author for only $16.95 each.

❐ Yes, I want ___ paperback copies of **Yak Butter Blues: A Tibetan Trek of Faith** signed by the author for only $16.95 each.

❐ Yes, I want ___ paperback sets of **Dead Men Don't Leave Tips: Adventures X Africa** *and* **Yak Butter Blues: A Tibetan Trek of Faith** signed by the author at the discounted price of only $30.00 per set.

Include $3.95 shipping and handling for one book and $1.95 for each additional book. Hawaii residents must include applicable sales tax. International orders must include payment in US funds. Payment must accompany orders. Allow 3 weeks for delivery.

My check or money order for $ _____ is enclosed.

Name_____

Address_____

City/State/Zip_____

E-Mail (in case there's a problem with your order)

_____

Special signing instructions_____

Make your check payable and mail to:
Pilgrim's Tales, Inc.
P.O. Box 791613
Paia, Hawaii 96779 USA

Or order a signed copy via our web site at:
**www.PilgrimsTales.com**

273

Printed in the United States
135769LV00002B/130/A